Congratulations to

Brian Conn

Winner of the
2013 Bard Fiction Prize

Brian Conn, author of *The Fixed Stars*,
joins previous winners
Nathan Englander, Emily Barton, Monique Truong,
Paul La Farge, Edie Meidav, Peter Orner,
Salvador Plascencia, Fiona Maazel, Samantha Hunt,
Karen Russell, and Benjamin Hale.

The Bard Fiction Prize is awarded annually to a
promising emerging writer who is an American citizen
aged thirty-nine years or younger at the time
of application. In addition to a monetary award
of $30,000, the winner receives an appointment
as writer in residence at Bard College for one semester
without the expectation that he or she will teach
traditional courses. The recipient will give at least one
public lecture and meet informally with students.

For more information, please contact:

Bard Fiction Prize
Bard College
PO Box 5000
Annandale-on-Hudson, NY 12504-5000

COMING UP IN THE SPRING

Conjunctions:60
IN ABSENTIA

Edited by Bradford Morrow

Missing persons. Phantom limbs. Sensory deprivation. Amnesia. Lost masterpieces. Artifacts in shards. Overheard conversations and half-heard whispers. Unretraceable routes. Islands that sink under the skin of the sea.

In Absentia explores the presence of absence, the losses that gain on us, the black holes in our everyday lives: the darkness as well as the light that blinds. The concept of the partial, of the unwhole (and unwholesome) is elucidated in stories, poems, and memoirs that take vanishing and vacancy as both their subjects and their forms, creating fractional characters and void-riddled landscapes. This landmark 60th issue of Conjunctions continues its tradition of bringing together contemporary masters with visionary new voices, featuring the work of Joyce Carol Oates, Stephen O'Connor, Karen Hays, Julia Elliott, Miranda Mellis, Samuel R. Delany, and many others.

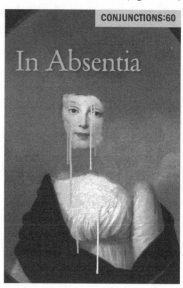

One-year subscriptions to Conjunctions are only $18 (two years for $32) for more than seven hundred pages per year of contemporary literature and art. Subscribe or renew online at conjunctions.com, or mail your check to Conjunctions, Bard College, Annandale-on-Hudson, NY 12504. For questions or to request an invoice, e-mail conjunctions@bard.edu or call (845) 758-7054.

CONJUNCTIONS

Bi-Annual Volumes of New Writing

Edited by
Bradford Morrow

published by Bard College

EDITOR: Bradford Morrow
MANAGING EDITOR: Micaela Morrissette
SENIOR EDITORS: Robert Antoni, Peter Constantine, J. W. McCormack,
    Edie Meidav, Pat Sims, Alan Tinkler
COPY EDITOR: Pat Sims
ASSOCIATE EDITORS: Jedediah Berry, Andrew Durbin, Nicole Nyhan, Eric Olson
PUBLICITY: Mark R. Primoff, Darren O'Sullivan
EDITORIAL ASSISTANTS: Michael Blum, Emma Horwitz, Wendy Lotterman,
    Amy Pedulla, Lily Schroedel, Cassandra Seltman, Soli Shin, Emma Smith-
    Stevens, Shawn Wen

CONJUNCTIONS is published in the Spring and Fall of each year by Bard College, Annandale-on-Hudson, NY 12504. This issue is made possible in part with the generous funding of the National Endowment for the Arts, and with public funds from the New York State Council on the Arts, a State Agency.

SUBSCRIPTIONS: Use our secure online ordering system at www.conjunctions.com, or send subscription orders to CONJUNCTIONS, Bard College, Annandale-on-Hudson, NY 12504. Single year (two volumes): $18.00 for individuals; $40.00 for institutions and overseas. Two years (four volumes): $32.00 for individuals; $80.00 for institutions and overseas. For information about subscriptions, back issues, and advertising, contact us at (845) 758-7054 or conjunctions@bard.edu.

Editorial communications should be sent to Bradford Morrow, *Conjunctions*, 21 East 10th Street, 3E, New York, NY 10003. Unsolicited manuscripts cannot be returned unless accompanied by a stamped, self-addressed envelope. Electronic and simultaneous submissions will not be considered. If you are submitting from outside the United States, contact conjunctions@bard.edu for instructions (please do not send International Response Coupons as postage).

Conjunctions is listed and indexed in Humanities International Complete and included in EBSCO*host*.

Visit the *Conjunctions* website at www.conjunctions.com and follow us on Facebook and Twitter.

Cover design by Jerry Kelly, New York. Front and back covers feature details from *Jesus in the Olive Grove*, by the Master Vyšší Brod (the Master of Hohenfurth), c. 1350. 85 x 95 cm. Narodni Galerie, Prague, Czech Republic. © Erich Lessing.

Available through D.A.P./Distributed Art Publishers, Inc., 155 Sixth Avenue, New York, NY 10013. Telephone: (212) 627-1999. Fax: (212) 627-9484.

Printers: Edwards Brothers Malloy

Typesetter: Bill White, Typeworks

ISSN 0278-2324

ISBN 978-0-941964-75-3

Manufactured in the United States of America.

TABLE OF CONTENTS

COLLOQUY

Edited by Bradford Morrow

* * *

ON THE MONSTROUS: A PORTFOLIO
Edited by Peter Straub

THE ALPHABET AND ITS PRETENSES: A PORTFOLIO
Edited by Robert Coover and Bradford Morrow

EDITOR'S NOTE

EVERY ISSUE OF *CONJUNCTIONS* could, I suppose, be construed as a colloquy. The idea for this issue was to assemble works that were not bound, even loosely, to any specific theme. It was a concept thwarted from the start, as the reader will see. These fictions, poems, essays, letters, and pieces that defy genre definition—works by some of my favorite contemporary writers—draw on quite different linguistic approaches to quite different thematic visions, giving the issue an almost symphonic quality with unexpected harmonies abounding from page to page. Once it was understood that despite ourselves we *did* have a theme, however subtle, the portfolios on the Word (co-edited by Robert Coover and me) and the Monstrous (edited by Peter Straub) came into being, adding new depth and dimension to our colloquy.

We are particularly honored to publish a generous selection of William Gaddis letters excerpted from the forthcoming Dalkey Archive volume of collected letters. Renowned for the towering achievement of his novels, Gaddis was a very private man. His correspondence, printed here for the first time, spans the arc of his life, from the earliest days when he was beginning to research and write *The Recognitions*—that touchstone masterpiece that infamously drew critical disdain when originally issued in 1955 and is now required reading for anyone interested in American fiction—to his fourth major novel, *A Frolic of His Own*, an indictment of the jurisprudence game, just as the 1975 *J R* examined the lust for money in its myriad forms. In his letters we witness Gaddis as son, father, friend, colleague—at all times intellectually engaged and curious, hilariously self-deprecatory (consider his self-portrait reproduced here as a frontispiece!), critical of fools, deeply empathetic and precise, and finally as complex and insightful as the novels he wrote. Many thanks to Sarah Gaddis, Martin Riker, John O'Brien, Steven Moore, and the Andrew Wylie Agency for their help in making it possible for us to publish this important correspondence. Thanks, too, as always to my remarkable staff editors—Micaela Morrissette, Pat Sims, J.W. McCormack, Nicole Nyhan, Andrew Durbin, and Soli Shin—with whom I have the privilege of working. True colloquists all.

—Bradford Morrow
October 2012
New York City

Selected Letters
William Gaddis

To Barney Emmart

Mexico City
April, 1947

dear Barney,

Just a note of greeting. And to say that I earnestly wish you were here, because I am working like every other half-baked Harvard boy who never learned a trade—on a novel. Dear heaven, I need your inventive store of knowledge. Because of course it is rather a moral book, and concerns itself with good and evil, or rather, as Mr. Forster taught us, good-and-evil. You see, I call out your name, because other bits of life proving too burdensome, I have taken to the philosophers—having been pleasantly involved with Epictetus for about a year, and now taking him more slowly and seriously. And of course I come upon Pyrrho, and see much that you hold dear, and why. Also David Hume, whose style I find quite delightful.

Shall I describe Mexico City to you? It is very pleasant, and warm, and colourful of course—and we are here, and cannot get jobs because we are tourists, and live on about 30¢ worth of native food a day. And I'm sure you would like it. Also, we grow hair on our faces. And plan, as soon as we can manage to sell the Cord—beautiful auto—to purchase two horses, and the requisite impedimenta, and go off and live in the woods, or desert, or whatever they have down here. There I shall finish *Blague*—that is the novel. And have George Grosz illustrate it—he has the same preoccupation with nates that I do—grounds enough to ask him.

Well old man, this is just to let you know dum spiro spero—I haven't learned Spanish yet—a noodle language if I ever heard one. Please give John Snow my very best greeting, tell him I shall write, would give anything for a drink and talk with you all. But must work. A dumb letter, but I am very tired.

Anyhow, my best
Bill

William Gaddis

[*Barney Emmart was a lifelong Harvard friend who worked in marketing in the 1950s, taught English for a year at the University of Massachusetts in 1967, and died in 1989.*]

* * *

To Edith Gaddis

Pedro Miguel, Canal Zone
[9 January 1948]

dear Mother.

Wouldn't it be nice if I could write a good novel? Well, that is what I have been trying to do all morning. Now it is near time for lunch, and then my presence and talents are required at the Miraflores lock until 11 pm, to take up with my crane. And coming in near midnight after that leaves me not wanting very much to jump out of bed in the morning for the great prose epic that is daily escaping from under my hand.

This is to thank you for the attaché case attempt—and to say that it's hardly a necessity. Because for the writing, I don't think I have anything really worth-while carrying in one yet. I think the attaché case will just always be one of those distant beautiful images that lure us through this life and keep us believing that our intelligence is worthy. Meanwhile don't trouble about it. Perhaps, if in the summer I can get up there with something worth showing a publisher, one of the objects of (instant) beauty will be mine, and I shall have something worth carrying in it. As you may gather, I am not in very high nor triumphal spirits.

I enquired at the post office. There is no duty on anything sent for the recipient's personal use. If you get in touch with Bernie (PL81299) I'd like to know if he's in NY. Or what. Also he has a small alarm clock, a little green one—and I need an alarm. Could you find where he got it? And if you could get and send me one like it?

Also badly need a haircut. I borrowed 10$ from Juan Diaz, my kind friend, so am seeing through quite well. Sorry about the trouble over the 'phone call. I don't understand about the 30th of Dec. call—I was at the 'phone station from 850 until 930. They're all insane down here anyhow. But I'll call in a few weeks, after I get paid, just for the fun of it.

Love, Bill

[*Poet, critic, and artist Bernard Winebaum (1922–1989) was a Harvard and Greenwich Village friend of Gaddis.*]

* * *

To Katherine Anne Porter

Pedro Miguel, Canal Zone
21 january, 48

My dear Miss Porter.

A friend at *Harper's* was kind enough to send me your address—I hope you don't mind—when I wrote him asking for it, in order that I might be able to tell you how much your piece on Gertrude Stein provoked and cleared up and articulated for me.

To get this out of the way, I am one of the thousands of Harvard boys who never learned a trade, and are writing novels furiously with both hands. In order to avoid the mental waste (conversation &c.) that staying in New York imposes, I am here working on a crane on the canal and writing the inevitable novel at night.

I have never written such a letter as this—never felt impelled to (but once, in college, an outburst which I fortunately did not mail to Markova, after seeing her 'Giselle')—But your piece on Gertrude Stein—and your letter that accompanied it—kept me occupied for three days. And since I have no one here to talk with about it—thank heavens—I presume to write you. Having read very little of your work—remember being greatly impressed by 'Pale Horse'—so none of that comes in.

How you have put the finger on Miss Stein. Because she has worried me—not for as long nor as intelligently as she has you certainly, but since I have come on so many acclamations of her work, read and been excited and cons[t]ernated, and not realised that emptiness until you told me about it. I read your piece just nodding ignorantly throughout, agreeing, failing to understand the failure in her which you were accounting. Expecting it to be simply another laudatory article like so many that explain and analyse an artist away, into senseless admiration (the kind Mr. Maugham is managing now in *Atlantic*). Toward the end of your piece I was seriously troubled— how far can a writers' writer go? (V. "She and Alice B. Toklas enjoyed both the wars—") —until I found your letter in the front of the magazine. Then I began to understand, and started the investigation with you again. Thank God someone has found her defeat, and accused her of it. And it was a great thing because it should teach us afterward places where the answer is not.

Certainly she did it with a monumental thoroughness. Now

"Everything being equal, unimportant in itself, important because it happened to her and she was writing about it"—was a great trick. And: "her judgements were neither moral nor intellectual, and least of all aesthetic, indeed they were not even judgements—" which in this time of people judging people is in a way admirable. But that her nihilism was, eventually, culpable—and that her rewards did finally reach her, "struggling to unfold" as she did, all wrong somehow and almost knowing it. Her absolute denial of responsibility—and this is what always troubled me most—made so much possible. And how your clearly-accounted accusation shows the result.

It must have been a fantastically big talent—and I feel that we are fortunate that she used it as she did, teaching by that example (when understood, as your piece helped me to do)—for in our time if we do not understand and recognise the responsibility of freedom we are lost.

I should look forward to a piece on Waugh; though mine is the accepted blithe opinion of "a very clever one who knew he was writing for a very sick time."

Thank you again, for writing what you did, and for allowing this letter.

Sincerely,
William Gaddis

[*Porter's essay "Gertrude Stein: A Self-Portrait" was published in the December 1947 issue of* Harper's.]

* * *

To Charles Socarides

Pedro Miguel, Canal Zone
[February or March 1948]

Dear Charles.

First—please don't be alarmed by the weight of a correspondence which I may seem to be thrusting on you. But when you write a letter like this that I have just received, honestly I go quite off my head with excitement. Am fearfully nervous now.

All because I have been away for 3 days, on a neighboring island, working frantically on this novel. Which looks so *bad*. But here: you see, what you say in these letters—most specifically this last—upset me because the pictures you draw, the facts you offer, are just as this novel is growing. It is a good novel, terrific, the whole thread of the story, the happenings, the franticness. The man who (metaphorically) sells himself to the devil, the young man hunting so for father figure, chasing the older to his (younger's) death. And the "girl"—who finally compleatly loses her identity, she who has tried to make an original myth is lost because her last witness (a fellow who takes heroin) is sent to jail—the young man ('hero') the informer. Here's the frantic point: that it all *happened*. Not really, maybe, but with the facts in recent life and my running, it *happened*. All the time, every minute the thing grows in me, I "think of" (or remember) new facts of the novel—the Truth About the Past (alternate title). (The title is *Ducdame, called 'some people who were naked.'*) But this growing fiction fits so insanely well with facts of life that sometimes I can not stand it, must burst (as I am doing here). And *then* I *ruin* it by *bad writing*. Like trying to be clever—this perhaps because I am afraid to be sincere? But I watch myself ruin it. And then—because when I was writing in college I went so over board, now it must be reserved, understated, intimated. Or bad bits of writing just run on. Look: "There are few instances when we are not trying to control time; either frantically urging it on, or fearfully watching its winged chariot ragging by, spattering us with the mud that we call memory." Isn't that *awful*. You see, it just *happened*, was out of my control until the sentence reached the period. To be facile can kill what *must* be alive.

That's why I hated Wolfe—that he cried out so. Because my point is, no crying out, no pity. We are alone, naked—and nakedness must choose between vulgarity and reason. Every one of us, *responsible*. Still those lines you quote (Wolfe) excite me horribly. Not to have Forster's understatement. No room for Lawrence's lust. Perhaps Flaubert, or Gide. But I am not good enough as they. It is sickening this killing the best-loved—work.

Now I should like to see you, if you could look at this thing, flatly condense (parts of) it—the writing, exposition. God I know all this fear, but have *no* sympathy with it. Fools. I can not afford to be one.

As though your letter anticipated what I am just putting down as fiction.

I can't come home before June. Because of *money*. Always that. After June I can live on Long Island, not before summer though, you see? Must work on this goddamned canal until April, hope to save around 600$, enough to live on until June and get home. I hate it, paid 12$ a day—or night—to *waste*. Now it is 10:15pm—and I must be at the canal at 11, "work" until 7am. But I have to because of money. Perhaps good I don't have money, crazy in love with the daughter of this local island's governor—not Mex, Panamanian, but Spanish. Splendid nose. Good Werther love, doesn't trouble her. It is hell not to have either the time nor the money to *live*.

Then there is a man here with a sail boat going to Sweden. And if the novel suddenly looks too *bad* I may go, he needs someone to work, a very small boat, sail boat.

God the running, running. You *understand* it, don't you? I almost do. But if I can't make a *good* novel then I must keep running, until I know all through me—not just as a philosophical fact, as *truth* which I "believe" and am trying to sell—but can sit down and know without having to try to sell it (writing) to *everybody*.

Thanks. I shall *write* you.
W.

[*Socarides was a Harvard friend. This is the earliest letter to explain the essential idea and plot of* The Recognitions.]

* * *

To Katherine Anne Porter

Panama, R.P.
7 April, 1948.

My dear Miss Porter.

Perhaps you can understand how well your letter was received, how many times read; and how much I want to repay your kindness by trying very hard to write you an honest letter. I find it difficult always (or rather of course make it difficult for myself) to write an honest letter because I am not clear yet about writing a letter, and especially as now when this writing I do is not going well then to write a letter is more strange still because it becomes an outlet which it should not be but the writing should be. Not that the writing is an outlet, but as though the outlet is the purpose. Well when the writing is consistently unsatisfactory then the purpose is all confused, and one may run to letter-writing saying, —Here is what I have to say, you will see how important it is, and what a worthy one I am . . . no, I haven't quite finished the story, the novel, the play, but meanwhile you must appreciate . . . Well you understand, that it can be like that morass of conversation. And so now often in the middle of a letter I must stop and say, —What filthy little vanity is this, Willie, that you are relishing so. And stop, furious with myself and also the person who does not get the letter. Still it is all wrong, absolutely, to then turn and revel in the idea of not being able to write a letter. You know, I have so many letters from NY that start out, —I started to write you a letter last week, but it turned out to be . . . , and —I have written you twice, and the letters are here unmailed. Well those people are writing to themselves, and would do better to not bother using someone else's name at the head of the sheet as an excuse. But the vanity of letter-writing, of shouting out for witnesses. I have thought a great deal about this whole insistence on a witness that we all make, that is certainly one reason why so many bad novels are so bad. Much of it seems to be a very American thing too, I see the American with the camera everywhere, that filthy silent witness; and to jump off of the aeroplane when it lands in one country after another: no time to look at the volcano or feel the air except to say to another how hot it is, but (because the 'plane will only be in Guatemala, in Nicaragua, in Costa Rica, for fifteen minutes) that one must get to the counter and send off postal cards with a picture of the volcano he did not see, to witnesses. I have recently finished reading the New Testament, which makes much of witnesses. Now what did Jesus mean, (this is Matthew 9:30, 31, after he has healed a blind man). And their eyes were opened; and Jesus straitly charged them, saying, See that no man know it. But they, when they were departed, spread abroad his fame in all that country. Now certainly the largest reason he carried on these miracles was simply for witnesses, later he charges the apostles *as* witnesses. No; but getting back, everyone running about insisting on having them. (And that often splendid comedian Jimmy Durante's —Everybody wants to get into the act. Well.) Certainly a prophet needs witnesses, otherwise the whole thing is to little avail. But the instant a piece of writing takes on the note of, —See what I have done, where I have been, what I have read; but do not forget that these things cannot happen to you but through me . . . well then the whole thing is vile, will not do. And the other side of that dirty coin is all of the snivelling confessionals, they are the most infuriating and it seems to be the way the coin is falling now. Oh, these soft-handed little boys who suffer so with themselves and their boys and 'men', I am intolerant. Or of the loneliness of our lot, without a poet of stature that sensibility snivels. But Goethe's (I do not read German, I have learned some by rote—I am trying to be honest) Nur wer die Sehnsucht kennt weiss was Ich leide, Allein und

abgetrennt von alle Freude—that that stands up in suffering; or
Rilke's Who if I cried would hear me in the angelic orders. This distinction between loneliness and alone-ness. But to start this bad
argument at its beginning: Did you have trouble with people anticipating you? that an idea which you had discovered and formulated
for yourself and then were working to deliver it, find it was not yours
(in the mean sense) but (if you thought further, with courage and (if
you were not mean) gratitude) eventually yours most because given
to all, because perhaps one may have the brass to say it is a truth?
Well, and so when you said in your letter of distinguishing loneliness
and solitude, I was immediately troubled, even (witness this meanness) offended. Do you understand? As though, what business had
you, to offer in some fifteen words, what I discovered finally some
six or eight months ago, discovered with such triumph! And really
what meaner more unchristian thing than one who would try to
covet a truth. And these months past I have been running around
pounding the board for recognition of aloneness and (this above all)
the incumbent responsibility. Discovery indeed! And then to read
Sartre's *Les Mouches*. This, if ever was, a time to find joy and triumph when truth is shared, and to tear out meanness where it
grows, to be Christian. (The only poetry I have been reading here—
after the tiresome disappointment of Auden's *The Age of Anxiety*—
is Eliot; and I say this because a line suddenly comes up, —I am no
prophet, but here's no great matter; I have seen my head (grown
slightly bald) brought in upon a platter &c.)

This business of owning an idea, a line, an image. For instance, I
remember finding the notion that some people are 'not big enough
for tragedy,' and believe me I have worked it out in a wonderful number of useless words: and then found it in Forster, in one sentence.
(That was four or five years ago, I was in college.) But even now it has
happened again, this time not a notion but a line, the title I had settled on for this work I am at now is Some people who were naked,
that is what I want, it is the whole idea. And then I have just had recommended to read, and finally had the courage to read, a play by
Pirandello, the title of course is *Vestire gli ignudi*, Clothing the
Naked. That was a start. Then, his heroine, Ersilia, says (with infinite sadness, but with a smile nevertheless), In that case, I shall not
be the woman I was, nor the woman I am, but still another! (My
Esme (even the name, you see) was one who was uncertain as to her
identity, finally could not stand to be alone (knowing though that
aloneness is essential) because without a witness she could not

know if she had really done things, and finally loses all concept of being anyone at all) (Ersilia finishes the P —play with, —that I am dead . . . yes, and that I died naked!). My elder protagonist to be one who (exactly in the same manner of Faust, paraphrasus of the circumstances, dog and all) sells himself to the devil (a publisher, entrepreneur) to forge paintings. And to find P—'s protagonist sending the letter to Ersilia signed Faust. Well.

But you will see the whole thing clearly enough to understand that it cannot be simply this disconcerting discovery and relinquishing of ideas. Because there they are anyhow, and not new. And so one is forced to say 'style'? That word! And what ridiculous arguments, wasteful discussions it brings forth. I remember one, in which I had commented on what a fine style in David Hume; my antagonist started immediately with saying that Hume did not try to write in a style, but the style came about as he wrote writing to say what he had to say. You see where this argument is going. Two people without style arguing on the same side against each other; still I would try to say that, now that Hume is through, one reads him and sees an excellent style, after the fact. Glenway Wescott a fine stylist; and Rebecca West extraordinary: (so extraordinary, that once during the most recent war I was working on the *New Yorker*, and one of her pieces, a report on a trial for treason, described with such wondrous style a room in Lords, &c &c, that we could not eventually make out which room she meant: she did not once say, the fact simply wasn't there in all of that style). And a preoccupation with style for itself is admittedly ruinous.

Penned in, in your letter (of writing): but it is fun, isn't it . . . well that was compleatly disconcerting, effacing, happy, infuriating. I don't know, when it begins to be fun then I know myself badly enough to immediately hold it suspect. You know, the temptations? Well, to be clever, for one. That is one of the worst, and how it kills. Then to preach and prophesy (Remember, it was I who told you this . . .); the tangent of going off and having fun for its own sake, no matter that it contributes nothing (though some do it infuriatingly well); and then the absolute necessity of making a character's experience *his* and not one's own, and that is certainly one of the most difficult requisites. To discriminate, perhaps that is the most important. Here is a line of Katherine Mansfield's, you may recognise it, from a book review of about 25 years back: —These are moments that set the soul yearning to be taken suddenly, snatched out of the very heart of some fearful joy, and set before its Maker, hatless, dishevelled and gay, with its spirit unbroken. (Now allow this presumption, simply for the sake of the hypothesis) That if I had written that I can imagine being very doubtful about it; but here I found it (the collection of reviews called *Novels and Novelists*) with fantastic pleasure, could not put it down, was troubled that it should be buried in an old book review. Or if I had been sure of it, should have wanted it published prominently, as mine, perhaps a little edition by itself. You see how 'lamentable' this is, will not do.

It is *enthusiasm* that I mistrust.

Presumption may not be the worst of sins (though it is when I think of it) but it is pretty bad. So there is the worry of pretentious and presumptuous work. But I could no more sit down and write *When the mountain fell* (Ramuz) than . . . well, the usual things people say, 'fly' for instance. Do you know the trouble I am in, right now, that any part of this letter may sound pretentious? I started a novel in Mexico last winter, it was an allegory, and Good and Evil were two apparently always drunk fellows who gave driving lessons in a dual-control car. Well, writing that was fun, so damn' much fun that it took me five months to realise how pretentious it was, and there is a kind fellow at an agency in NY (Harold Matson's) who wanted me to finish it, he wanted to sell it. Thank God a couple of publishers said no thanks &c and I came to Panama, to write an honest novel. Right now that is what he thinks I am doing. Oh dear.

In the Canal Zone I have done a great deal of 'thinking' (I want it to be) about our country, which depresses me but must not to the point of simply saying oh dear. (And then I came on this, in James, 1:23,24[,] For if any be a hearer of the word and not a doer, he is like a man beholding his natural face in a glass: For he beholdeth himself, and goeth his way, and straightway forgetteth what manner of man he was. And Paul to the Corinthians, 8:11 Now therefore perform the doing of it; that as there was a readiness to will, so there may be a performance also out of that which ye have.) At any rate, this Zone is all wrong, a transgression because of its *sterility*. Now (for a while) I am free of the concrete-buster and the air-hammers shaking me to pieces, and the crane, though all of that was good, to do work, it was the enforced idleness that was bad, being paid to be idle was horrible. It is terrifying that people can live here and for years, they bring up their children here and the children are empty boxes too, they usually stay, and so many of them are pale and I cannot love pale people in a sun country. Bloodless somehow, the Panamanians have blood, and the west indians who are niggers and are held off with disapproval and low wages but the Americans have radios, you can walk up a street past the house after house the same colour (that is the regulation, they are grey) and hear every radio playing the same programme, the mechanical-laugh programme from the States, the movies do well also new cars running around like crazy with the wives who are also some of them the young pretty ones pretty slick articles, but not when they stay and stay, then they are dumpy and sad and all the same colour but no one has told them they are sad so they do not know they are but talk to each other instead. And no one goes into Panama except he is a man and then for the reasons that any sailor is glad to make a port, and as wearily ready to leave it.

To get to the war. Two years ago I wrote (badly) a story of a man who is devastated by a dream of Armageddon—with *no* idea that H. G. Wells had written a (bad) story called "A Dream of Armageddon"—and I have been worrying it since. Reading the prophesies in the Great Pyramid, or Nostradamus, and in Ezekial and Revelation. And have been obsessed with the idea of Armageddon coming in 1949. That we will live to see Good & Evil defined in battle? And then to have followed (with the lazy layman's eye, I confess) the developments in political geography since, and now. This thing (it is still just a thing) that I am trying to work on now ends with that; and so I have put myself under this insane press of time, that it must be done before, just before, this final violence comes. That we must *choose*, there is the trouble. And how are we equipped? All of the thesis of despair in "That is not what I meant at all" (and the Kaiser, after the other war—as Lawrence quotes him in *Women in Love*—This is not what I meant, this is not how I meant it to come out at all . . .). That intentions are most wasteful of the energies we spend, I believe. Except perhaps bitterness, somehow bitterness is the worst, the least pardonable, the most culpably wasteful.

When there was a civil war in Spain, the young Americans who wanted to fight the Good Fight went to fight Fascism, beside the Communists. And now see us. What is it? that in these countries without a middle class there is material only for the extremes, and that only the extremes war? Here is Costa Rica. Where does one fight? Or is it two evils, which will not abide one another? These are not precious thoughts, and the precious will have to think them and choose. And after there will not be one small voice saying, That is not what I meant.

There is such an accumulation. Did you have the feeling, early

19

when you were writing, a novel, say, that you must get everything in? Everything. And where will this fit? . . . and this? Idea, and incident, and image. It is as though (I thought last night, thinking how should I say to you what it is like) one were in deep water, and this accumulation bobbing all around, as far as can be seen but all within reach; and that one may grab at any of them to present, to say Look, does this not prove me worthy? and another to swim firmly past them, through the water, while another still (and this somehow a woman) not for a moment recognising the water, but at intelligent leisure take this, and that, perfectly chosen, while further on one may float among it all on his back and the eyes closed, while his considerate (civilised) neighbor drowns with silent dignity. And as though I were in the middle of mine, beating the water into a foam but not waves, shouting Whoopee, Look! Look! at all these things of mine, they are mine, take any that you want. (They are mine.) And then, with Mr Eliot, the moment of silence, I have heard the mermaids singing each to each. [xxxxxxx] I do not think that they will sing for me.

I have tried to write you honestly. And have justified the lengthiness by believing that you will read it all, if you were good enough to spend the time for me that you did in the letter you sent to me. Of course, there are other things, of vulgarity and reason, and Salvation wearing a political face (mostly stolen from Mann). And if it has seemed upset, I have quit the Canal Zone and if I can get papers and this money together am going to fly to Costa Rica in the morning. I have not put down an address (and even that has come to seem presumptuous, to put a return on a letter, presuming an answer) because I intend to have none for a while. Because I do not wish to say here why I am going to San Jose, because anything I should say would be intentions, and those I will not trust.

With it all, if things go as I 'intend,' I hope to be back in New York June or July, and if I could meet you, and talk, not chatter, perhaps you would talk.

Cordially, and sincerely,
William Gaddis

* * *

To John and Pauline Napper

a/c Consulado de los EE. UU.
Junqueras, 18, Barcelona, Spain
7 September 1950

dear John and Pauline,

—menaced by monsters, fancy lights, Risking enchantment . . . We had some balloons over Palamos, causing great excitement among the natives—and I by now unkempt enough to be a member of the local unwashed—we all ran out into the streets, dogs and children, to the point about the lighthouse, where these balloons, three of them, rose higher over the hot evening air above land, then came down in the sea, two did, the other carried a little light in its basket, it just went right on up. And that blazing sky, useless to try to describe it. Do you know that point of land? its view covers the whole harbour and then around to east (to the left). I suppose they were meteorological balloons, but we here prefer any pagan to scientific explanation.

Aside from that, nothing has happened. Nothing.

Except newspapers you know get in, and with them the idiotic haruspicating and scrying going on in My country, warwards. How can grown-up men make such fools of themselves? But on *every* level. It seems that nothing else draws nearer. Margaret, heaven knows, does not. Perhaps it's better, a bonnie over the ocean than one under-foot, wanting to dinner at Fouquets, a drink at the Crillon, tea at Claridges? I don't know. All I know right now is that things reached such a pass this morning, in the way of trying to straighten out characters, incidents, situations, interviews, and one suicide (but she a very old woman), that I wrote every one a bit of paper, and have spent the afternoon sitting like a simple child making a village of confetti, trying to arrange them in order that will satisfy Aristotle's theory of dramatic unity, William James's of pragmatism, the Boston Watch & Ward Society, for Morals, the Catholic Index, the publisher's for Something New, the reader's prolepsis and my analepsis. Some must suffer. Boston and the index first. Then Aristotle. I sometimes even imagine cutting it down to myself and the reader. At any rate, it goes on, between balloons.

I hope you both found the rest here to send you back heavily to work there. But how long does that lust last? I feel like I was born here, by this time; it seems as though I've spent my life at this machine, at this window, and staring across at the old man they put out on a balcony in the afternoon with a piece of bread, and take him

21

in at night. Some times the hand shakes, and the words (slipping, sliding, perishing) will not stay in place, and I mightily wish you were here for a coffee, or a glass at Boodles'. You did leave quite a vacuum on your departure, and I find myself again talking with myself, getting the same vacant variety of answers. Lord, to be a real, legitimate member of a myth, a screaming Catholic, an Albigensian, a Stuart or Hanover or John D Rockefeller, instead of sitting in one damn hall bedroom after another trying to manufacture one. Though I suppose the rewards are greater when you do finish. Do you finish? I just go on accumulating. (I like a title of a book I've never read by Tomlinson, *Old Junk*).

But now I find I'm owed 30,000francs in Paris, and temptation rises to go there and cut a figure of mean disaster for a few days, then return, be tattooed, and enter the Franciscan orders. Your mill pond looks like it would be rousing cold in winter, and my blood is as thin as sewing-machine oil by now. But how I look forward to stopping there to see you. I've so many reasons for wanting to come to London, all good, all self-indulgent, Edwardian enough, they include books and tailors. But I must wait for the Trollope reason (and *no* pun intended here), the summons to the church, the walk hand-in-hand in the heather . . . tea at Claridges. I don't like Paris, but may have to go up briefly in October, then return here if there's no summons to Southampton, and just go right on hoping for the wrong things and praying for the wrong things until the Balloon goes up. Meanwhile I'll write of any change of scene; thanks again for your patient listening and words here, I need them so much more than I realised, and I'm excited about seeing you again and enlarging on them, asking the questions which have grown from those answers.

All my best wishes to you both,
W. Gaddis

[*John Napper (1916–2001) married his second wife, Pauline Davidson, in 1945. He was a popular society portrait painter before expanding his palette to expressionistic oils, vivid watercolors, and book illustrations. The Nappers met Gaddis in the summer of 1950 on the beach at Palamós. As Pauline Napper later told Crystal Alberts, the beach was almost deserted except for "a solitary figure, a man sitting surrounded by sheets of writing paper which kept shifting in the slight wind and which he was desperately trying to hold down." When John walked over to help, he "asked him if he was English and Willie replied rather abruptly, 'No, I am American and I am working!'" Later Gaddis came over to "apologize for his abruptness and suggested [they] meet for a drink later at a café by the harbor." They became lifelong friends.*]

* * *

To Edith Gaddis

Paris

28 November 1950

dear Mother,

Lava from Mt Etna, I understand, is flowing at the rate of 120 feet a minute; the United States Atlantic seaboard under 26 feet of water; and the Belgian coast under the heaviest fog in its history. Aside from these prodigies of nature—including a wind of 120 miles an hour on top of Mt Washington in New Hampshire (though what anyone is doing up there I haven't figured out)—we have such ingenuous contributions of human origin as the Long Island Railroad, and the little girl with the sunflower growing in her lungs. Fortunately the Pope has proclaimed the dogma of the Assumption, so I suppose there's really nothing to worry about. (They say that the bubonic plague has re-appeared in north-Africa.)

In times like these, a small person returns to his own pitifully limited means of accomplishing disaster; and the best one can accomplish is lampshades of human skin, or soap made of human bones. Recalling the crucifix at Burgos (in the north of Spain), where for many centuries it was believed that the Figure was made of human skin, though eventually someone proved it to be buffalo hide. There was also, somewhere in the annals of the entertainment world, a mermaid presented at sideshows fashioned from the upper half of a monkey and the lower end of a codfish. Bringing us back to the world of Freddie's Football Dogs, and the play *The Deserter* (presented in London in the late 19th century) entirely acted by animals.

Material, one might say, for a novel.

Speaking of novels, I've the author of something called *Love Me Sailor* settled here in the back room. He is an Australian, and if you know any Australians that's enough said. Very nice fellow. It seems his book is going to be a real Best Seller.

Thanksgiving was very pleasant. Not turkey, but rabbit with a mustard sauce. Mathilde was ill, and husband Clements trying to go to a dinner party in a cream-coloured sports shirt; so I was asked over to keep her company, which I did, enjoyably, in just such a frame as people think a young man's life in Paris should be—the lovely lady with red hair cascading to her waist, and the small table set for two in the bedroom before a fireplace and a fire. And so I made a number of grogs, buttered rum, and the evening went on for some time, when Clements returned with a red carnation because it was his name day, St Clement. The tooth gave little bother, though its old niche is still sore.

I think the notion of sending the player to William B Hart (of the Hopalong Cassidy Harts?) (or red-Heart dogfood?) is excellent, if *Atlantic* can't use it. Of course I'm still here hoping.

HG Wells said, somewhere,—We seem to go through life waiting for something to happen, and then . . . it doesn't happen. I am waiting for something to happen; though as might be said quite justly, isn't Mt Etna, the LIRR, and 26 feet of snow enough for you? No.

Yes, I did get a pleasant enough note from Congdon. I'm going to write him now, telling him that if I sell the player piano anywhere he is not going to get any %. $. %"_#&$(%*@@@@¾¾!) He doesn't know why he hasn't had a letter from me. What would I write him about? I've nothing finished to sell. I've two ideas that I want to ask him about. If he thinks they are good or worth($)while, maybe we can recover our lost intimacy. Otherwise I shall continue to play Greensleeves on the recorder, in the Gardens of Spain.

In spite of my pretentiously erudite references, Burgos and Freddie's Football Dogs, this isn't a very intelligent letter. Is it.

I'm glad you found Ormonde entertaining and reassuring. It's some days since I've heard from Margaret. I don't know what she's up to? Perhaps on the High Seas, cast perilously adrift on a raft of her own fashioning between Woodmere and Greenpoint. Or forging ahead, Scott of the Antarctic. (I read recently that an Exquimo was eaten by his sledge dogs—news from Copenhagen.)

You were extremely kind to send me make-up money for the dentist, and the news that my bank balance is undisturbed. Unfortunately I can never present you with a Toothpaste Smile, because my teeth just won't be pearly, they haven't got it in them. But they are clean, and serve to ruminate what crusts come my way.

And so, recently, I study about old Flemish painters, having reached a snag in my work, which, since it concerns a man who is forging paintings (it is his father who is counterfeiting a religion, that's why I needed *Forerunners and Rivals of Christianity*), I must know more of than I do. And so, in my mind this wet Paris morning, I have only pictures of St Bartholomew being skinned alive, proof, perhaps, that the mediaeval imagination was as equal to conceiving outdoor sports commensurate with its capabilities as our own.

Be to her Persephone, All the things I might not be;
Take her head upon your knee,
My dear, my dear, It's not so dreadful here
One wonders where to fit Leda and the Swan into all this.

Unless the lava flows northward, or Margaret eastward, I hope to be in London by mid-December. More of that, though, in December. Meanwhile I also stand and wait.

> love from your son,
> W.

* * *

To John Napper

> (this winter:) 210 East 26th Street
> New York City
> 15 December 1954

dear John

Of course, I am not on board anything bound in that direction, and heaven knows when I ever shall. These I am afraid are the moments one suspects that youth is gone indeed, & it is time at last to settle down to something with an income attached. But you may imagine the suspense, with this book due for publication in March here, and copies of it already spread out among "critics" &c, so that I am constantly hearing fragmentary reports & remarks kind & otherwise of course, but even the kindest ones haven't a penny attached, and that, certainly, is one of the oldest problems of the artist.

But I must tell you, that in spite of my insignificance with my publishers now the thing is done (though they insured my life when I was working on it!), I did prevail upon them to send you an advance reading copy (paper-bound), and I hope you will——what? not, I'm afraid, "enjoy" it, for in spite of my own feelings about its entertainment value, I gather it is not a book people will "like." And there are mistakes, I mean aside from grammar, or historical accuracy: aesthetic mistakes. The bulk could have been cut down greatly, and some of the tiresome sophomorics which betray it as a first novel removed (& some of [them] were in fact written 4 or 5 years ago). But I knew that if I settled down to do that, it might well end up the MS in the bottom bureau drawer. And so best to get rid of it, with all its mistakes, and set forth with the Iron Duke's admonition, Publish and be damned, ringing in one's ears from the outset——And what sense would there be here in writing an apology for a book which took 7 years trying to explain itself to *me*? So at last I suppose not fare well but fare forward——[. . .]

W.

* * *

To J. Robert Oppenheimer

New York City
4 January 1955

Dear Doctor Oppenheimer.

I have already taken a greater liberty than this, asking your attention to my letter, in having called Harcourt, Brace & Co., who are publishing a long novel I have written, to ask that they send you a copy. You must receive mail of all sorts, crank notes and fan letters of every description, but few I should think of half a million words. And since I can also well imagine that you seldom if ever read novels, if only for not having the time, it is an added imposition to have sent you such a bulky one.

But for having read your recent address at Columbia's anniversary, I should never have presumed to do so. But I was so *stricken* by the succinctness, and the use of the language, with which you stated the problems which it has taken me seven years to assemble and almost a thousand pages to present, that my first thought was to send you a copy. And I do submit this book to you with deepest respect. Because I believe that *The Recognitions* was written about "the massive character of the dissolution and corruption of authority, in belief, in ritual and in temporal order . . ." about our histories and traditions as "both bonds and barriers among us," and our art which "brings us together and sets us apart." And if I may go on presuming to use your words, it is a novel in which I tried my prolonged best to show "the integrity of the intimate, the detailed, the true art, the integrity of craftsmanship and preservation of the familiar, of the humorous and the beautiful" standing in "massive contrast to the vastness of life, the greatness of the globe, the otherness of people, the otherness of ways, and the all-encompassing dark."

The book is a novel about forgery. I know that if you do get into it, you will find boring passages, offensive incidents, and some pretty painful sophomorics, all these in my attempts to present "the evils of superficiality and the terrors of fatigue" as I have seen them: I tried to present the shadowy struggle of a man surrounded by those who have "dissolved in a universal confusion," those who "know nothing and love nothing."

However you feel about the book, please allow my most humble congratulations on your address which provoked my taking the liberty of sending it to you, and in expression of my deepest admiration for men like yourself in the world you described.

[*The American physicist J. Robert Oppenheimer (1904–67) was known for his work on the atomic bomb. On December 26, 1954, he gave a lecture entitled "Prospects in the Arts and Sciences" at Columbia University's bicentennial anniversary celebration, reprinted in his book* The Open Mind *(1955). The above letter is a corrected draft.*]

* * *

To William Gaddis

Massapequa, L. Isld. N.Y.
27 August 1956

Though my first memory of bringing into conversation, with Donn A Pennebaker & others, the central idea to the book on which I am now working was during this past winter, in February 1956 I believe, the idea itself was older with me than that, though I should have no evidence of how much older. I started to develop this idea into a short novel no later than March 1956; and so far as I know it is one entirely original with myself, in substance and treatment.

In very brief it is this: a young boy, ten or eleven or so years of age, 'goes into business' and makes a business fortune, by developing and following through the basically very simple procedures needed to assemble extensive financial interests, to build a 'big business' in a system of comparative free enterprise employing the numerous (again basically simple) encouragements (as tax benefits &c) which are so prominent in the business world of America today. By taking straightforward advantage of the possibilities which I believe might well be obvious to the eye and judgment of a child this age, brought up on the sets of values and the criteria of success which prevail here in our country today, he becomes a business tycoon, handling and manipulating controlling interests in such diverse fields of enterprise as oil, cattle-raising, insurance, drugs, textiles, &c., transportation, twine and batting, greeting cards &c.

This boy (named here 'J.R.') employs, as a 'front man' to handle matters, the press &c, a young man innocent in matters of money and business, whose name (which I got in a dream) is Bast. Other characters include Bast's two aunts, the heads of companies which JR takes over, his board of directors, figures in a syndicate which fights his company for control in a stockholders' battle, charity heads to whom his company gives money, &c.

This book is projected as essentially a satire on business and money matters as they occur and are handled here in America today; and on the people who handle them; it is also a morality study of a straightforward boy reared in our culture, of a young man with an artist's conscience, and of the figures who surround them in such a competitive and material economy as ours.

The book just now is provisionally entitled both *Sensation* and *J.R.*

William Gaddis

[*Gaddis sent this registered letter to himself to protect his idea for* J R *from any future copyright infringement. Oscar does likewise in* A Frolic of His Own: *"I sent a copy to myself registered mail in a sealed envelope against just such a piece of dirty work as this one." Donn A. Pennebaker is an American documentary filmmaker (1925–), perhaps best known for the Bob Dylan tour film* Don't Look Back. *See his memoir "Remembering Gaddis,"* Conjunctions:33, Crossing Over *(Fall 1999).*]

* * *

To Tom Jenkins

New York City
30 December 1960

dear Mr. Jenkins.

I appreciate your writing me about *The Recognitions*. I had got your earlier letter (forwarded by Harcourt) but simply had not managed to answer it.

Ch. Rolo was one reviewer I felt at the time who had seriously tried to behave in a responsible way: first, he read the book (which proved more rare among reviewers than I had anticipated). And the summary statement of his which you quote is probably quite accurate as far as it goes; however it does stop short of Wyatt's lines on page 898–9—and the revelation "love and do what you will." This however does inevitably bring up the problem of *grace*, which I felt uncertain about then and I believe my uncertainty shows. (I am more uncertain about it now, more dubious.) What might be appended to Rolo's statement too is the fact of the inescapableness of forgery as a part of the finite condition—if you will allow forgery to include necessarily imperfect representations of eventually inexpressible absolutes (in Plato's sense of the 'ideals'), but that this is the best we have, the best we can do: what is vital is the faith that the absolute— the 'perfect,' etc.—*does* exist (thus Wyatt's "Thank God there was the gold to forge"—top of page 689), gold=perfection=absolute=love, in an alchemical scheme where Brown=matter (to be redeemed), Valentine=mind, Wyatt=creative spirit without love, Esme=love. That is a fragment of one undercurrent of interpretation, at any rate.

You might be interested in the project of someone here in New York who has spent the past year or so on the book (without any assist from me) and who is currently doing some pieces on it in a publication which he writes, duplicates & mails out himself. He is: Jack Green / newspaper / box 114 / New York 12 / NY. And I think he will send you the 4 issues as they come out if you send him $1.

As for time spent writing the book, it went on over 7 years, 1 or 2 of which were entirely fallow, 2 of which were on the other hand dawn-till-night periods of quite isolated, I might even say obsessed intensity. I can't say how much research I did for the book; most of it was specific or started out being so and then of course led on to other possibilities and insights. Certainly I did not sit down, envision, and write the book simply drawing on (what reviewers insisted upon calling) "vast erudition," though what pained me most about the reviewers was their refusal—their fear—to relax somewhat with the book and be entertained.

Yours,
William Gaddis

ps. My only work recently has been on a play which in present draft is too long & complicated.

[*Jenkins was a journalist who wrote about detective novels; his friend David Markson recommended that he read* The Recognitions. *Ch. Rolo refers to Charles J. Rolo (1916–82), who reviewed* The Recognitions *in* The Atlantic Monthly, *April 1955.*]

* * *

William Gaddis

To David Markson

New York City
28 February 1961

Dear David Markson.

After lo these many (six) years—or these many low (sick) years—if I can presume to answer yours dated 11 June '55: I could evade embarrassment by saying that it had indeed been misdirected to Dr Weisgall and reached me only now, but I'm afraid you know us both too well. In fact I was in low enough state for a good while after the book came out that I could not find it in me to answer letters that said anything, only those (to quote yours again) that offered 'I just loved your gorgeous book and I think Mithra is so charming. . . .' Partly appalled at what I counted then the book's apparent failure, partly wearied at the prospect of contention, advice and criticism, and partly just drained of any more supporting arguments, as honestly embarrassed at high praise as resentful of patronising censure. And I must say, things (people) don't change, just get more so; and I think there is still the mixture, waiting to greet such continuing interest as yours, of vain gratification and fear of being found out, still ridden with the notion of the people as a fatuous jury (counting reviewers as people), publishers the police station house (where if as I trust you must have some experience of being brought in, you know what I mean by their dulled but flattering indifference to your precious crime: they see them every day), and finally the perfect book as, inevitably, the perfect crime (the point of this last phrase being, for some reason which insists further development of this rambling metaphor, that the criminal is never caught). So, as you may see by the letterhead on the backside here, I am hung up with an operation of international piracy that deals in drugs, writing speeches on the balance of payments deficit but mostly staring out the window, serving the goal that Basil Valentine damned in 'the people, whose idea of necessity is paying the gas bill' . . . (A little frightening how easily it all comes back.) But sustained by the secret awareness that the secret police, Jack Green and yourself and some others, may expose it all yet.

This intervention by Tom Jenkins was indeed a happy accident (though, to exhaust the above, there are no accidents in Interpol), and I was highly entertained by the page-in-the-typewriter in your *Epitaph for a Tramp*. I of course had to go back and find the context (properly left-handed), then back to the beginning to find the context of the context, and finally through to the end and your fine cool dialogue (monologue) which I envied and realised how far all that had come since '51 & 2, how refined from such crudities as 'Daddy-o, up in thy way-out pad . . .' And it being the only 'cop story' (phrase via Tom Jenkins) or maybe 2nd or 3rd that I've read, had a fine time with it. (And not that you'd entered it as a Great Book; but great God! have you seen the writing in such things as *Exodus* and *Anatomy of a Murder*? Can one ever cease to be appalled at how little is asked?)

I should add I am somewhat stirred at the moment regarding the possibility of being exhumed in paperback, one of the 'better' houses (Meridian) has apparently made an offer to Harcourt Brace, who since they brought it out surreptitiously in '55 have seemed quite content to leave it lay where Jesus flung it, but now I gather begin to suspect that they have something of value and are going to be quite as brave as the dog in the manger about protecting it. Though they may surprise me by doing the decent and I should not anticipate their depravity so high-handedly I suppose. Very little money involved but publication (in the real sense of the word) which might be welcome novelty.

And to really wring the throat of absurdity—having found publishers a razor's edge tribe between phoniness and dishonesty—I have been working on a play, a presently overlong and overcomplicated and really quite straight figment of the Civil War: publishers almost shine in comparison to the show-business staples, as 'I never read anything over 100 pages' or, hefting the script, (without opening it), 'Too long.' The consummate annoyance though being that gap between reading the press (publicity) interview-profile of a currently successful Broadway director whose lament over the difficulty of getting hold of 'plays of ideas' simply rings in one's head as one's agent, having struggled through it, shakes his head in baleful awe and delivers the hopeless compliment, '. . . but it's a play of ideas'—a real escape hatch for everybody in the 'game' (a felicitous word) whose one idea coming and going is $. And I'm behaving as though all this is news to me.

Incidentally—or rather not incidentally at all, quite hungrily—Jenkins mentioned from a letter of yours a most provocative phrase from a comment by Malcolm Lowry on *The Recognitions* which whetted my paranoid appetite, I am most curious to know what he might have said about it (or rather what he did say about it, with any thorns left on). I cannot say I read his book which came out when I was in Mexico, 1947 as I remember, and I started it, found it coming both too close to home and too far from what I thought I was trying to do, and lost or had it lifted from me before I ever resolved things.

31

(Yes, in my case one of the books that the book-club ads blackmail the vacuum with 'Have you caught yourself saying Yes, I've been meaning to read it. . . .' (they mean *Exodus*).) But I am picking up a copy for a new look. Good luck on your current obsession.

with best regards,
W. Gaddis

[*David Markson (1927–2010), later to become an esteemed novelist, had written a master's thesis on novelist Malcolm Lowry, author of* Under the Volcano, *in 1951. He read* The Recognitions *twice when it first came out and wrote to Gaddis in June 1955 to express his admiration. The two novelists would continue to correspond, and occasionally see each other, until Gaddis's death. Dr. Weisgall is a dentist in* The Recognitions *who receives several unwanted letters from Agnes Deigh after she mistakenly reports him to the police.*]

* * *

To Judith Thompson

Tues. pm [April? 1967]

My Whole World:

how you've saturated my life, there's not a corner anywhere inside or out where I don't find you waiting, and not there, from that yawning half of Altnaveigh's bed to the hot-dog cart on 9A where I pass hungry & daren't stop, I know I'd choke, to Storrs's theatre showing last night *Blowup*, without you ergo w/out me, I couldn't pull a Jablow on you, instead accepted dinner from the people who had me last week named Davis in part I think because she felt her last week Tetrazzini (sp?) was dry & lacking & didn't want me to carry that impression around when she could & did serve a fine Bourgognionne (damned French) & I left at a decent hour, back to Altnaveigh where the old dog came right into the room & went to sleep under the bed. Cold comfort but I thought it was terribly thoughtful of him to know how much I missed you & try in his own way to help.

The [camping] trip? Oh Lord, the trip. [. . .] But, we did cook over a fire, cut wood, sleep 3" off the floor, toss marshmallows to raccoons at night, light kerosene lanterns, & I guess pretty generally do all the things we'd have done if we had really been penniless, illiterate, & never amounted to anything back in the hills. I love you. Though it began with our arriving in Washington early enough to go to the Lincoln Memorial & walk around, then out to visit a friend of mine named MacDonald who is with the Office of the Chief of Military

History & will probably be in charge of the official history of Vietnam, all that strained because of under-current battle between him & his wife, charming British exballet dancer but Lord you cannot know other people's marriages and Lord! I thought of us & I thought never! never! we can never let that happen. [. . .]

Too possibly what follows will sound like I'm doing everything to evade work, but it's really trying to get things long postponed done, a note from Arabelle Porter asking how things were going so I will face her Friday lunch [. . .]. And if manageable expect to go into town tomorrow night or so to talk with this fellow Moore about the most denigrating ways a composer can make a living, to get Edward Bast back on the tracks.

And you, you . . . can't bear this letter writing business because mine are so marvelous! they're not, no, and I almost think it would be terrible if we became adept, exchanged sparkling & accomplished correspondence, things mustn't get to that point! No, our letters have to stay awkward & just blundering around I love you and I miss you to extinction & don't dare destroy another word you write me, if you knew how since we talked Sun I've waited to get back & get your letter, & how I love your letters, especially this with its enclosure, in today's mail and what a packet: a letter regarding father's estate; Pfizer's Annual Report; Special Money-Saving Certificate for 27 Capital Gain Stocks; solicitation to buy a book "like nothing else that has ever appeared in North America, the secrets of African Sex revealed to you for the first time!" and another containing (also For the First Time) "Over 210 photographs of coital positions!" (this one a product of "Renowned Oriental doctors"); and eighteen fragmentary manuscripts totaling 79 pages ("I'd like you to read the few stories that I enclosed and to give me your opinion of them . . .") from Adrian Grunberg of West 189th st, of whom I had heretofore been unaware ("He was walking on a hot desert road. There was no one around for miles and the sun was burning fiercely. Suddenly, like a merciful sign from heaven, two huge female breasts appeared in the sky . . .") Well Judith, dearest, darling, do you wonder how I fight through such offerings for a glimpse of your writing? how when I find it I put it aside to keep for last, pour tea, sit, can't wait, don't, . . . you come first. [. . .]

And your antiquing, how I thought of you, and your mother, and of you, those 80 miles out into Virginia where it seemed everyone who'd found an old bottle in the cellar and could spell the word had out a sign 'Antiques' & I'm sure the practiced eye could have found those seamless lipless bottles we learned bring $50 & heaven knows what else. We'll do that. And we'll ransack that place up beyond Storrs. And we'll . . . oh the things, the things we'll do! And, having taken Robt Graves up to Storrs last night, Be bird, be blossom, comet, star, Be paradisal gates ajar, But still, as woman, cleave you must To who alone endures your trust (me).

> with you know what & you know why
> W

[*Judith (1940–   ) would become Gaddis's second wife in June 1968.*]

* * *

To David Markson

> Piermont, N.Y.
> 5 March 1970

Dear David.

Your letter touches on a difficult area, one I have never entirely resolved in anything but practice which is why it has taken me so long to respond.

At the outset though to try to keep up minute-by-minute with the reception of a book that has cost one as much as this one has cost you, let alone to try to take part in it, is plain Chinese water torture, drop by drop, when you are in the most vulnerable position conceivable, quoting the *Library Journal* of all things, 'suspenseful plot, superb dialogue,' you know it ends up like the psychiatrist being greeted with "Good morning . . ." muttering "What do you think he meant by that?" And hell you know all this, you have neither the body of Jacqueline Susann nor the prim crust of a non-adventurer like Capote, and 'If I were you . . .' as advice never tires of phrasing it I would lay hands on every available penny take wife and children and pack up, let the book go out and do what it's going to do anyhow.

My feeling essentially is that a book really goes out on its own, for the human remains that wrote it to run along after it is suicidal since there's clearly no separating them until the mortal partner drops. I don't think 'one decent blurb or two' is going to alter Asher's promotion at all, I don't think lack of them is going to deter it; and the whole God damned area is to me like trying to make magic that will shape a course already implicit and then, if the course takes the feared-for direction, blaming the ex post facto magic, or the lack of it. I've never had my name on anybody else's book jack or ad that I know of, I honestly do not think it would help sell a copy, it reeks a bit of self-advertisement though perhaps, out of a deep mistrust for human motives or rather of them and the abyss between them and their expression this is merely an extreme inverted vanity on my part. Because on the other hand I do admire the generosity of people of stature like, say, Robert Graves, Norman Mailer, TS Eliot writing jacket blurbs for Faber, all of these people quite open-handed. I don't know. I think of a boy I had at Univ of Connecticut working on a novel which I greatly encouraged, think publishable & have tried to help him place, he's someone who's never published and I hope to see have a chance, when/if his book is published, what. I don't know.

I do marvel at the way in your book you have managed to sustain the tension of atmosphere to a point of shutting out a reader's day-to-day reality that is eventually any writer's (real writer's) objective. By the same token I don't believe that phrased for a blurb would sell or not sell. Ask Aaron Asher about my reaction to the string of blurbs on the back of Meridian's *The Recognitions*; but he was publishing it, a fact for which I am of course eternally grateful, as I was to you for helping to stimulate his interest in it, & as its publisher how he handled things was his business, I told him my feelings & stepped out, & he did a fine job of it.

Are reviewers influenced/cowed by blurbs? and does it matter one simple God damn anyhow? Recall the now quite forgotten 'critical acclaim' of the most widely unread best seller of the time, *By Love Possessed*—and reread Dwight MacDonald's destruction of that review chorus. I as much as any & perhaps more than many am vividly aware of the exaggerated pain of every reviewer's stab or even patronizing applause; but Jesus Christ looking at it all what's become of the Hicks Geismars Sterling Norths, nothing left but a whine in the air somewhere. I remain or rather, *The Recognitions* does. So does Lowry's *Volcano*, so does yours unless you confuse yourself with them is my feeling, if you play their game not your own.

best regards
W. Gaddis

[*Markson had asked Gaddis for a blurb for his novel* Going Down *(1970).*]

* * *

35

William Gaddis

To Thomas J. J. Altizer

Piermont, NY
10 February 1973

Dear Dr. Altizer.

I am sorry to be late answering your letter and, next, to send you the unsatisfactory response this will probably prove to be. Of course I was and remain most impressed and gratified by your response to *The Recognitions* especially upon looking at the list of your own publications, all of which may be why I found your letter a difficult one to rise to and may also partly explain the time I have taken preoccupied by why this should be so.

First certainly the aspect of Christianity itself and the distant thing it has become to me in these 20 years since the book was written. I am not being facetious when I say it is a long time since I have read it; but certainly it betrays my suspicions even then just inhowfar I was sincere and serious in its preoccupation with Christian redemption as opposed to the attraction of versions of Christianity as vehicles for writing about redemption. Regarding Roman Catholicism for instance it obviously had its attractions and I was pleased at the time the literate Catholics who saw the derogatory & ridiculous 'anti' Church material as all there to strengthen rather than weaken the idea of the Church that could survive it. But in the years since I've come finally to regard Roman Catholicism as the most thoroughly irritating and irrelevant anachronism in sight and the incongruity of the Papacy simply appalling, really surprised at the vehemence of my own feelings.

Basically I suppose what seems to have drained away is any but the faintest nostalgia for absolutes, finite imperfectability without Wyatt's grateful revelation that 'there was the gold to forge.' What's remained seems to be preoccupation with the Faust legend as pivotal posing the question: what is worth doing? (Wyatt was meant to be not the depth of genius, which knows, but just short of it & therewith the dilemma, the very height of talent, which doesn't.)

At any rate it is this question what is worth doing? that has dogged me all my life, both in terms of my own life and work where I am trying now again in another book to fight off its destructive element and paralyzing effects; and in terms of America which has been in such desperate haste to succeed in finding all the wrong answers. In this present book satire comic or what have you on money and business I get the feeling sometimes I'm writing a secular version of its predecessor.

Returning to *The Recognitions* I had pretty much from the first a feeling of sending it out on its own, of being (top of p. 96) simply 'the human shambles that follows it around'; and both time and its original meager reception have I suppose only gone to strengthen that feeling, again not being flippant I wonder how much use I would be in discussing it, still surprised (of course greatly pleased) at letters from college age students who find it relevant.

Surely none of this lessens my appreciation of your estimate of it and I would be most intrigued to see any use you made of it in your own work (I'm not that clear remembering *Under the Volcano* and never read *Ulysses*), right now about 30 miles up the Hudson here panic stricken in terms of time work money this book but would look forward to meeting and talking with you at some point if the above isn't entirely self defeating.

Thank you again for all in your letter and its tacit encouragement at a welcome time.

Yours,
William Gaddis

[*Altizer is a radical theologian and author (1927–), then teaching at SUNY Stony Brook.*]

* * *

To Judith Gaddis

REPORTREPORTREPORTREPORTREPORTREPORTREPORT

EYES ONLY EYES ONLY EYES ONLY EYES ONLY EYES ONLY

<u>AM</u> 26FEB74 OFFICIAL CLASSIFIED 26FEB74 OFFICIAL CLASSIFIED

08:25   waved
08:26   watched down hill to make sure car turned corner safely; waved
08:28   walked dog to Aufieri garbage can and returned
08:31   poured coffee
08:45   decided to move car back to house so I would not keep looking out and thinking Judith had gone on errand and would return

08:46   saw bag with grapefruit, put it by door to remember to give to Jack

08:47   let cat in

08:48   poured coffee

08:49   saw MIL's letter

08:59   went in to look for stamp for MIL's letter

09:00   saw work laid out on table, decided to have drink

09:01   let cat out; decided not to have drink

09:02   decided to move car back to house so I would not keep looking out and thinking Judith had gone on errand and would return

09:04   burned toast

09:09   called John, reached hoarse lady who said he would call back

09:11   let cat in

09:12   poured coffee, looked at work laid out on table

09:14   decided to clear kitchen table and bring typewriter there to be near 'phone

09:16   tied up newspapers

09:23   emptied ashtray

09:25   decided to make list of things I must do

09:29   could not think of anything so decided not to make list

09:31   cleared kitchen table

09:34   John called; read him note from his Mrs emphasizing all underlined words but did not know Pat's 'phone number. Haha.

09:44   let cat out

09:45   decided to move car back to house so I would not keep looking out and thinking I had gone on errand and would not return

09:46   moved car back to house

09:58   looked at work laid out on table, decided to have cereal

09:59   made cereal

10:02   ate cereal reading Swarthmore alumni bulletin; noted one alumnus who claimed 3 billion dependents for federal taxes and given 9 months in prison for filing fraudulent W-4 form, decided must remember to warn MIL who might consider something similar

10:40   looked at work spread out on table

10:41   twinge at noticing coffee cups &c, put them in dishwasher to not be reminded of departure

10:48	examined contents of refrigerator, discovered spaghetti sauce with Message and put it in freezer
10:50	discovered corned beef and potatoes
10:55	thought I should probably go down and get butter; checked first, found 4 sticks of butter
10:57	let cat in
10:58	hung up coat
10:59	put trash out
10:00 [*sic*]	listened to news on radio
10:04	went upstairs and looked around
10:08	came downstairs and looked around
10:13	sat down and studied design in kitchen floor linoleum
10:20	looked outside for car to make sure I had not gone on errand and might not return
10:22	decided I should probably go down and get cigarettes; checked first, found 5 packs
10:24	brought typewriter in to kitchen table to be near 'phone
10:28	decided to have nap till suppertime when I could have corned beef
10:29	sat down in livingroom chair
10:33	woke startled by ghastly liquid snoring, decided I had horrible cold and should have drink
10:34	discovered snoring was being done by dog, very relieved
10:37	decided not to have drink, went to typewriter in kitchen to work
10:41	decided I should get some letters out of the way before settling down to work, got paper
10:50	could think of no one to write to
10:51	stacked wood more neatly on porch, checked newspapers to make sure they were well tied
10:57	returned to kitchen and listened to refrigerator hum
11:01	examined contents of refrigerator
11:04	thought I should probably go down and get milk; checked first, found a full quart
11:06	looked to see if mail had come but flag was still down
11:09	discovered memorandum WILLIAM THINGS TO REMEMBER and read carefully
11:29	put cat out
11:31	examined clam chowder from refrigerator
11:33	decided clam chowder looked thin, decided to add potatoes
11:34	peeled and diced 3 small potatoes and put on boil

11:51   heard mailbox, got mail

11:55   opened mail, one item from American Express with new card and literature which said read enclosed agreement carefully

11:56   read agreement carefully

PM

12:18   diced potatoes somewhat soft, added them to chowder; decided chowder looked somewhat thick, got spoon

12:22   served bowl of hot chowder, got spoon

12:23   'phone rang: talked with Hy Cohen at agency who said check should arrive this week; who also said Aaron Asher is leaving Holt and was concerned that Asher's departure would not or might upset me; I told him I was not unless Holt wanted their money back; he said that would be fine, certainly sell it elsewhere; I told him I was working hard on it right this minute; he said Asher might go to Dutton which would be logical following on Hal Sharlatt's death; I said Dutton had no money; he said we will think about it, it could all work out extremely well especially if I finish the book soon; I said I would finish the book soon, was working on it right this minute; he did not answer; I told him my only real dismay at this moment was confidence and faith Asher has shown in me and my work over many years and would be a shame to part with him at this point; he said we will talk about it, that the Dutton possibility is only a possibility; I said I will not tell a soul; he said we'll be in touch with you I said boy you better.

12:55   poured chowder back into pan to reheat

12:56   listened to news on radio

01:00   ate chowder, reading interesting article on Alaska in Swarthmore bulletin

01:21   checked upstairs, nothing changed

01:23   checked downstairs, emptied ashtray

01:26   looked at work spread out on table, noticed stamp for MIL's letter

01:29   walked out with dog to mail MIL's letter

01:42   returning from walk waved cheerful friendly wave to neighbor standing on corner

01:43   realised neighbor standing on corner was really Jack's garbage can, hurried inside hoping no one had noticed

01:52   sat down at typewriter to work

01:58	phone rang, talked with Mr Cody a real estate agent who wished to be helpful if we wished to rent or sell our Saltaire house this summer; wrote reminder to call Savages
02:11	got notes for present sequence in book beside typewriter
02:13	suddenly realized I had better get cat food before stores closed; checked and found 2 full cans of cat food
02:19	decided to call Hy Coen back with some ideas
02:35	could not think of any ideas so declined to call Hy Coen back
02:36	reread notes for present sequence in book
02:39	reread notes for present sequence in book
02:41	decided to reread whole book through up to this point
02:42	looked at MS, decided not to reread whole book up to this point
02:44	reread notes for present sequence in book
02:47	began to type rough version of present sequence in book
03:05	dog passed through going east to west
03:07	dog passed through going west to east
04:01	began to type second page of rough draft
04:26	dog passed through west to east
04:27	dog passed through east to west
04:44	read two pages of rough version of present sequence in book
04:48	began to type third page of rough version
05:26	decided to have drink as Adrienne rang doorbell, told her to come back in the spring
05:26	fixed drink
05:28	sat down to read pages of rough version just written
05:31	laughed heartily
06:31	decided might be a good idea to start checking motels in Virginia, North and South Carolina
06:35	could not find Mobil guide to motels in Virginia, North and South Carolina; wondered where they were
06:44	wondered where they were
06:55	turned on oven to heat corned beef, dog passed through west to east; let cat in
06:57	reread pages of rough version just written
07:02	did not chuckle; wondered where they were
07:09	put in corned beef to warm; wondered where they were
07:16	fed dog; wondered where they were
07:18	fed cat; wondered where they were
07:41	served corned beef

William Gaddis

07:42 ate corned beef

08:01 watched *Benny Goodman Story* did not know he was such
   a sap and wondered where on earth they were

[*Written after Judith left for a trip, formatted to look like a classified report. "MIL"
means mother-in-law. "Jack" is Jack Hoffmeister, a neighbor.*]

* * *

To John Napper

Piermont

13 October 1977

Dear John,

 I know how much time & thought & feeling went into your letter
& to say I appreciate it is thin stuff —in fact if there is one real revelation & awfully good thing that's got to me in this entire mess it's
been the marvelous importance of friends, in which I'm terribly fortunate —I don't mean simply as people to deluge with one's troubles,
but some closer look at what friendship's all about & which may, in
the last analysis (which one thinks about these autumn days), be the
only thing in this turbulent world worth the having. In fact Judith's
been away for so damned long by this time (since the end of
February) that she's rapidly becoming rather an idea than a person.
Still a terribly quiet house & somehow a chilly one, wash out one's
shirts, cook for 1, nobody to share the small great things of life with
like the turning of the leaves, nobody but the fool cat stamping about
& shouting for his supper while the porch steps collapse & I add that
project to my list of things undone, invitations to stylish openings
unattended in favour of sitting here with a glass of whisky & wishing I could write a maudlin popular song (viz. one current: 'The windows of the world are covered with rain . . .'), you see what I mean.
But frankly there is also a modicum of comfort in the sense of one
less person to disappoint, a personal extension of the collapse of the
Protestant Ethic which I suppose is my eventual obsession.

 And so nothing at all in your letter looking sympathetically at
these girls' & women's plight annoys me or upsets me, I understand
it & know it's all true, that one 'can't stand still & protected behind
someone else,' that 'love must be free from dependence' &c &c, &
that in essence it's as difficult if not more so for them (Judith) as for
us (me) to be participants in this historic watershed between the

42

madness of the Judeo-Christian oppression & what's ever ahead, where surely the Buddhist approach you note must have a place if we are to survive at all.

And yet. And yet. All the interlaced guilt in the P.E. notwithstanding these concepts of *personal* responsibility that come down with it, mangled as they have become, are a central fact I cannot escape (unless of course, op. cit., some one else's action gives me 'one less person to disappoint'). There's Matthew for instance, he's come up with some bad numbers but got through them & right now is working a 9 hour day in a Boston restaurant & taking 2 evening classes at Harvard, & even though I think it will prove too much for him to handle a great deal of what he's trying to do emerges from almost 20 years of me as his father & I can't see, or even seek, any alternative to another 3 or 4 years of tuitions though I cannot presently imagine how I can meet them. Sarah got into & did well at the excellent school & the excellent college I herded her toward over years of deplorable circumstances, now is working in a furniture store & planning a marriage in March as no nickel-&-dime affair; again I cannot imagine how I shall pay for it but the point is that it is all an extension & an entirely logical one of her concept of my concept of her as a person. Of course it's different children & wives; but once one grants that inhowfar different is it?

Inflamed at the moment perhaps by 2 friends of 30 years, each in his 50s in a second marriage to younger women (2 small children in one case & 3 in the other) who are pulling out to 'find themselves' & honestly, both these men are attractive, generous, just so essentially hard working & decent & going through what I did 12 years ago over Sarah & Matthew but don't think I could handle it a second time at this age as they are faced with doing. I mean God damn it John did the word 'fairness' disappear from the language when John Kennedy aptly observed that 'life isn't fair': isn't it one's place here then to try to redress that unfairness insofar as one can rather than join it? join the forces of Chaos in other words?

I know it is absurd even insulting to be writing such things to you whose capacities for generosity decency &c I've known all these years beyond most, know it isn't their (Judith's) fault, know that it is a part of a major historical readjustment for which no single victim or knife-wielder can be blamed, 'blame' itself having gone out the window with the bath water. But with it I've got to say sympathy too. Notice of course that my 'responsibility' references to Sarah & Matthew above both take the shape of money; but I know & you know, perhaps more forcefully here than in England but really throughout the West, that this in these situations & those that follow is the prevailing, recurring, constant reality; that at our ages it means weariness, debt & starting again, & being plainly expected on all hands to start again, to follow through on the responsibilities one has in all good faith taken upon one's self. So frankly John I'm a bit sick & tired of people stepping out to 'find themselves' coming up at last with too often, in Cyril Connolly's exquisitely harsh phrase, 'a cheap sentimental humanism at someone else's expense.'

Extreme cases, extreme judgments (another hand-me-down from the Judeo-Christian mess), I still feel strongly about it all though most of the agony of my situation with Judith is exhausted, she writes that she feels she can't come back till she can 'be very sure she can return my love & give me all the things I want & need & deserve &c &c,' each of us fearful of letting the other down which is finally pretty ridiculous & the last roe of shad, as my mother used to say, regarding the Protestant Ethic. At this point I can see it going either way right to the grave, the real problems here—& those which brought all the foregoing to a head I think—being my anxiety-ridden outlook for any income whatever after this teaching stint ends at Christmas approximately; & really worse that I have no work of my own & haven't for a year so the 4th or 5th whisky doesn't get that down since it's not there, simply not one damned idea after the terminal obsession of *J R* that holds enough interest, enough passion, for me to sit down to it with any sense of sustaining these things for long enough to complete it, to resolve it. Though perhaps looking back up the lines of words I've dumped upon you here there may be something, a latter-day American version of Waugh's *Handful of Dust* perhaps which I've always admired & may now be mean enough to try to write.

Thanks for your letter, and again for your efforts on Matthew's behalf. As Graham Greene said, It's a battlefield. But not Conrad's 'The horror. The horror . . .' Not yet,

> with love to you both,
> Willie

* * *

To Steven Weisenburger

Wainscott, N.Y. 11975
18 September 1981

Dear Steven Weisenburger.

I ordered (prompted by A Broyard's most grudging mention in his *NY Times* review), finally received & have just read your piece on *J R* in *Money Talks*. Generally I have resisted responding to reviews or critical pieces with notes either of thanks or indignation, but in this case feel obliged to let you know that I read yours with pleasure and appreciation. Self serving as this must inevitably sound, given your bias for the book, I did find your approach, your informed analysis & exploration of the themes, & your conclusions, (& a most coherent style), to be extremely gratifying, & confirming that what I thought I had put there is really there.

This last I suppose provoked by this cursed word inaccessible which has haunted both these Big Books & far worse in the case of *The Recognitions* 25 years ago. Oddly enough things seemed to be reversed with *J R*, where what one might have feared as 'provincial' reviewers—from the *Cleveland Plain Dealer* to the *Hibernian*—sailed right through & had a marvelous time whereas a 'serious critic' such as Steiner seemed to take the whole thing as a personal affront &, finding it unreadable from the outset, went right on to review it anyhow to prove it was unreadable: some sort of contradiction, or non seq, or oxymoron there somewhere. The only piece that really annoyed me was John Gardner's thoroughly dishonest job in the *NY Review*: jauntily challenging Steiner's charge & finding the book immensely readable in order to set it up for his own sloppily contorted conclusion (a common stunt of his) as totally negative, Art (pure) the victim of (dirty) Commerce &c &c. (Ah Bartleby! Ah moral fiction!)

I only mention Gardner here because his egregious pose in seizing the wrong end of the stick is too typical of the simplistic stupidity that has found my work entirely negative (incidentally, as you may have noticed the titles on p. 515 of *J R* are anagrams of *The Recognitions* & all of the blurbs (except for delicately evocative & yummy read) are from reviews it received); whereas your grasp of the Art/Commerce relationship, & of seeing Bast shaped as triumph, are of course what the whole damned book is about. Just as (your p. 95) everything outside Art diminishing in worth, the counterpoint of Bast's diminishing vision of his talents from grand opera to cantata to suite to finally the lonely piece for cello is refinement rather than the defeat that carelessness reads in, & the fact that this is all the triumph needed. In this whole area I find your insight immensely heartening.

Now what follows may be simply carping but I hope, in the light of my appreciation of what is of real importance in your piece, that you'll see these items supplied simply should you ever want to reprint or expand it. Clearly they also reflect my own constant concern that it is my fault when such details are mistaken when I'd thought them clear to a serious reader.

Ergo: foot of p. 95, a Long Island (not a Brooklyn) school; 96, 97 Amy Joubert is the daughter of Moncrief [*sic*]; Cates is her great uncle; 97 he buys picnic forks from the Navy (*J R* 169) not Air Force, sells to Army; 98 (& I've always regretted that I didn't make this more clear) last lines J R on the phone, I don't understand where you got J R anticipating a tour of college campuses; what he's really got in mind is some undefined career 'in public life,' ie politics in which Bast again presumably will 'help him out,' though how he could manage such a thing is purposely left unclear: point is J R has 'learned' in terms of shifting his view of where the power lies in this junk world which is to say he's learned nothing, and will persist.

One item I apparently made clear to no one unfortunately since, while a prank like *The Recognitions* anagrammed, contained more than that but I don't believe anyone saw it there so clearly my fault, & damn. It's this: the lettering over the school entrance, proposed by Schepperman, was Marx's FROM EACH ACCORDING TO HIS ABILITY &c; when the school learned this 'communist' they were alarmed & Gibbs stepped in to the rescue by simply having the letters altered to 'look' Greek, as here:

ΕΒΦΜ ΣΑΟΗ ΑΘΘΦΒΡ—&c

Also, p. 99 (*J R* p. 142) while Bast is echoing the Ring motif on the piano the lines he's declaiming (Rift the hills . . . Rain or hail! &c) are from Tennyson's Locksley Hall.

Also liked your rescuing the passage (your 103) regarding the unfinished book/terminally ill patient to which you give the interpretation intended (compare Gardner's distortion).

Finally I have got to thank you for never so far as I recall writing me with questions, queries &c since 1) I just have not time to respond to those things which often come in in some detail & can't afford the correspondence they anticipate, & 2) have always tried to hold to the stance that the work is on its own & I cannot pursue it saying—This is what I really meant . . . (or That is not what I meant at all . . .) but mainly 3) what you accomplished without my help (read interference) is in so short a space so succinctly & well done that I am in your debt,

Yours,
William Gaddis

Regarding Broyard's *Times* review unfortunately the short shrift he gives you (in a very odd statement) is I'm afraid really meant for me: we've known each other some 30 years & I guess clearly aren't pals.

[*Weisenburger was a professor at the University of Kentucky who contributed an essay entitled "Contra Naturam?: Usury in William Gaddis's* J R" *to* Money Talks: Language and Lucre in American Fiction, *edited by Roy R. Male (Norman: University of Oklahoma Press, 1981), 93–109. Anatole Broyard (1920–90) and Gaddis knew each other in the Village in the late forties and were rivals for Sheri Martinelli's affections, which caused some friction. He was the model for Max in* The Recognitions.]

* * *

To John and Pauline Napper

Wainscott
11 Sept. 1984

Dear John and Pauline.

Some of the excuses follow but none can really excuse my not having got off even a line to you in what is an *age*. So much seems to have happened & indeed much of it has.

Most recently these past few months have been devoured by *Carpenter's Gothic* . . . good guess! Yes that's the title of my 'new' novel, why in God's name it should have taken me so long to finish & doubly infuriating since were it out today it would be selling hotcakes, its main concern being precisely the far right political USA's entanglement with the evangelicals, fundamentalists &c filling our pre-election front pages. It can't be out till next year when we've either got a new & sober Administration or Reagan's reelection, in the latter case it may well be news (as all signs point) so there's nothing to do but vote democratic & hope for the worst (Reagan). The title because in part it's a patchwork of used ideas, borrowed & stolen, with what simple materials were to hand (hammers & saws) in the way of outrage at 'revealed truth' (read Genesis), erected on a small scale (about 250pp.); but also because the entire book takes place *in* that Piermont house (where of course The World comes in by telephone) . . . some rather heavy handed satire & flashes of poor taste but it 'moves right along' as they say & should offend enough people to move it in what we are pleased to call the marketplace (supply side). I very seldom go up there but do still own the Piermont house, rented out for barely enough to carry itself but my 'workroom' still cobwebbed with most of my books & papers with no other home despite comfortable quarters indeed here on Long Isld & in NY, Muriel's dowry? but not a damned inch to store anything. At any rate every sober minute has gone into finally last week handing over to Viking Press the entire rewritten, corrected, proofread MS with vast relief.

& what took so much time? Well partly of course getting deeper immersed in the book, which started out as a 'romance' but I found needed outrage to fuel it, ergo fundamentalism &c. And life itself, mine & theirs . . . Sarah's divorce a sticky number but finally accomplished & she's now been in Paris for a year, doing design, fashion & drawing studies at a branch of the American College there (connected to Parsons) & also some side paying jobs; & though it's exactly a year to the day I haven't seen her seems to be in great shape & Growing Up (panicked of course that yesterday was her 29th, feeling the hand of Age descending (can you imagine!)). And Matthew [***]. Pretty wild for the 2 children of one of the most tried & true Francophobes you will find . . .

Well now at last blessed relief ('famous last words' as your old saw has it), we plan going to Rome for November & December, have got a room at the American Academy there which will assuredly not be lavish but at the least provide refuge from that operatic people while we sample their remains; been in such odd places as Bangkok & Libya (shades of David Tudor Pole) but for some reason or none, never Rome. And there for the moment it all stands; the heavy shadows of drink (not drunk but certainly to be cut down) & tobacco taking a serious turn & if humanly (me) possible to be ended, the new 'creative challenge' [. . .].

Willie

[*Gaddis lived with Muriel Oxenberg Murphy (1926–2008) for fifteen years beginning in 1979.*]

* * *

William Gaddis

To Sarah Gaddis

New York, NY
14 March 1985

Dear Sarah——————— here *finally* are the page proofs & good God,
I look at it & think *10 years*? for *this*? Anyhow what a vast relief to
have it out of my hands if not my life. I say I hope you "like" it but
it's not really a book to "like"—(a British publisher has just turned it
down saying it's *"too painful"*). I hope not for you & MttG; especially because I'm sure some literary "biographer" will one day—
with the ~~genius~~ talent they've got for misinterpretation, getting it
wrong (which is very much what the book's about as you'll see)—
write that the brother & sister, Liz & Billy, are "obviously" drawn on
you & Matthew. Absurd of course, but even more to the point was
when I realized, & only quite recently! that this troubled younger
brother, his beautiful & doomed sister, and her husband the man trying desperately to win a place in the world, are recreations of the 3
main characters in my aborted Civil War play—*Once at Antietam*—
which you've never read (don't, it's terrible) which I was working on
at 2nd Avenue when you were about 5 & Matthew 4, so clearly those
characters were formed before you were. But it is odd—or perhaps
not so odd: someone has said that every writer writes the same book
over & over again—to discover that somewhere in one's mind, one's
fabricated memory, that the same characters & their relationships
exist, whether the war is the Civil War or Vietnam. At any rate I
hope I've read it for the last time; it's not a book I finished in the high
spirits I did *J R* or even *The Recognitions*, but that is probably largely the difference between being 32, or 52, & being 62. I'm sure you'll
come across some familiar items—forgive me! but we take our material where we find it as you know & especially that which has
touched us closest—in fact the whole passage where Liz talks about
seeing herself as a child through a telescope light-years away, grew
out of my remembrance of the story of yours that of course touched
me closest about the girl watching her father going down the walk at
Fire Island.

with much love always,
Papa

[*Handwritten on the first page of the revised proofs of* Carpenter's Gothic. *MttG
refers to Gaddis's son, Matthew.*]

* * *

49

William Gaddis

To Judith Gaddis

24 January 1987

Dear Judith,

well this time you should really read the book to the end if only because it doesn't *end* (note no period at the last page) which in a way is what it's all about (though I don't plan a sequel) but since I'm off on this there are a few points of ambiguity which for the 'reading public' (Ch. Lehmanhaupt) I'm glad to leave that way, having always said You can't go running after your book saying what I really meant was &c . . . but after some of the reviews I've got to realize that perhaps some points were more obscure than I'd intended although (1) I thought it clear enough that Liz, bad health, talk of high blood pressure, obviously alone in the house when she goes down, that the robbery was committed earlier, her head hits the table ('blunt instrument'), kitchen's orderly enough but when she's found next morning (Mme Socrate has been told to come very early) the floor is strewn with placemats &c (Mme Socrate had seen where she kept her household $) & finally the check cashed in Haiti, obviously (I thought) she rushed back there into the dark & had a fatal heart attack, but too many read it that Paul killed her! Poor fellow, again reviewers finding him mean bad brutal &c where I found him desperate confused desolated as much or more a victim as anyone & his dependence (not simply $ly) painfully clear upon her & the last person to do her in as the FBI (& similarly dimwitted or only careless readers) adduce; then (2) is (as many inferred) McCandless 'mad'? spent some time in a hospital though what sort is only implied, may have had a breakdown? but I didn't think 'mad' unless I am which may be the good question; finally the point I think probably everyone missed so I must take some blame, wherein at the last where the woman shows up & introduces herself as Mrs McCandless this is *not* Irene but his first wife (old enough to have a 25yr old son) and that, muddy enough I admit, she & Liz each mistake the other for Irene who is never more than the constant presence haunting the house & McCandless, & Liz who in effect moves into Irene's role in her desperate attempt to rescue her own shattered identity. So there it is. I'm finally resigned to the apparent fact that I shall never reach 'the man at the airport' but perhaps some doctoral students will be kept busy with it. [. . .]

And I've been fortunate finally I must say & as you probably know from Rust & others if only *I* would just cut down on the drink & quit the smokes as I've been postponing these 10 years. So I am being dragged somewhat reluctantly by circumstances to start another book though fortune keeps interrupting: where those 12 years ago indicting 'free enterprise' abuse got me that trip to Japan, with the last book indicting just about everything else the USIA invites me to go to Australia too good to turn down, aside from all that all goes calmly though I am appalled how the time passes as one grows older. I did appreciate your message, Key West seems 1000 years ago & I've often enough thought & hoped things have gone well for you there but not written since this is quite simply not a scene that encourages correspondence, otherwise though happy to hear you sounding well & bright as I remember.

with love,
W.

[*In his first letter to Judith since August 1980, Gaddis enclosed this in a copy of* Carpenter's Gothic, *along with a note reading: "Some pain went into this as you will see but I hope it won't recall enough of yours to spoil the 'story.' No need to respond—it was, as they say (page 227) 'the best I could do'—" After they separated, Judith moved to Key West, became involved in the arts scene there, was director of a small historic house museum, and eventually became a board member of the Key West Literary Seminar.*]

* * *

To Don DeLillo

Wainscott, New York 11975
19 July 1988

Dear Don DeLillo.

Why in the world have I waited till the day your *Libra* gets its nihil obstat from Christopher Lemondrop to send you a note. It showed up in galleys in New York 2 or 3 months ago when things were ghastly (health) about the time I saw you, I looked into it then & should certainly have written without waiting to read it through because my response was immediate, it is a terrific job. I don't know all your work & also hesitate to say to any writer whatever comparing one of his works to another but in this case must tell you I find it far far beyond *White Noise*. Obviously if we take our work seriously we do not try to clone one novel to its predecessor so comparisons are indeed odious, & equally obviously the constantly shattered & reknit & fragmented again style of this new book appeals to me rather more than the linear narrative, when it's always 9 o'clock in the morning at 9 am & 3pm at 3 in the afternoon if you see what I mean; but the hard cover arrived here a couple of weeks ago & I've just read it & confirmed all my earlier impression, its marriage of style & content—that essential I used to bray about to 'students' in those grim days—is marvelously illustrated here I think & especially as it comes together at the end as we know it must, speaking of the 'nonfiction' novel if we must but why must we, except that concept does embrace the American writer's historic obsession getting the facts down clear (from "tells me more about whales than I really want to know" to Dreiser tapemeasuring Clyde's cell at Sing Sing, or Jack London's "Give me the fact, man, the irrefragable fact!") & again one marvels at what you've marshaled in this impressive piece of work. We'll be out of the country for August but may hope to see you in town in the fall, meanwhile high marks.

best regards,
WG

[*DeLillo praised Gaddis in a 1982* New York Times *profile "for extending the possibilities of the novel by taking huge risks and making great demands on readers." DeLillo would later attend Gaddis's memorial service and contribute a brief tribute to the portfolio in his honor edited by Rick Moody and published in 2003 in* Conjunctions:41, Two Kingdoms. *"Christopher Lemondrop" refers to Christopher Lehmann-Haupt and his approving review of DeLillo's ninth novel, which appeared in the July 18, 1988, issue of* The New York Times.]

* * *

To Sarah Gaddis

14 March '91

Dear Sarah.

This morning I decided to approach it all differently: daily I've got up, tea & come straight to the typewriter to take up where I left off yesterday's frustration, thinking Work Must Come First, then letters &—but what this has led to over what's now weeks is neither letters nor the work; I have never that I recall been so stuck, a day or 2 on 3 or 4 lines & even those unsatisfactory. So now at 8 am I've reversed things, at least will get one letter off to you before the day collapses. [. . .]

Well not being practical folk sitting down to apply our talents to sex greed & violence best seller success in the American Way, we have chosen an odd path for ourselves, me complaining at this end over these frustrations entirely of my own making & you there having done an honest piece of work in the so far as I know silent aftermath. Individually you get very good grades: Helen (Mrs E.L.) Doctorow with many words of praise for your book (she having written a novel), Karen Saks, all impressed by your work & wants to see you Move Onward. Louis Auchincloss the most teacherly: Well Will, I have just finished reading your daughter's book, she is most certainly a writer & now that she has exorcised you, having killed you off at the end, I hope she will go on to the wider world. And so, now given your proven talent & ability, that does seem to be the next challenge, getting away from, out of one's self to create entire fictions & characters (although these inevitably are made up of bits & pieces of one's self & one's own observations), but necessarily plot & story, where as Forster says, plot arising from character, that character must be consistent but plot should cause surprise. It has always seemed to me, though I have never really managed it, what a treat to get hold of an essentially simple situation & then watch the story write itself. For instance the one of *Gaslight*, the man marries the wealthy woman & then sets about driving her crazy, convincing her fearing & convincing herself that she is going mad & he is trying desperately to help, the only one she can trust & turn to &c. Well maybe all this is going too far but you see what I mean. A Plot. Something Matthew and I have talked about regarding his own work & medium, the movies, where it is more especially important I think, not just for suspense but that suspense must always be present (not necessarily the murder mystery sort) but simply What will happen next? To create characters the reader will, first, believe, & second, care about what happens to. Why so many movies are so ridiculously bad, the character scarcely believable but even if so you really don't give a damn what happens to him as in most of these violence prone shoot out movies, who cares?

Also this business of character & plot as of particular importance at the stage you are at now if you wish to be: having proved that you can write, publish, & get Sunday *NYTimes* reviewed, to work out & outline a 'story' & write a chapter or 2 for an advance on another novel. Not a reflection on your work but simply the times we live in that whereas a few years ago there were almost immediate paperback offers when a novel came out, now (according to my editor at Simon & Sch) far far fewer. (Any day now both *J R* & *The Recognitions* OP, out of print.) Well it's the world we've chosen & not an easy row to hoe as yr grandmother would have said. [. . .]

William Gaddis

I just learned that Mark Twain took 3 years off between halves of finishing *Huckleberry Finn*, some comfort.

> much love
> Papa

* * *

To the Editors, *Iowa Review*

> Wainscott NY 11975
> 28 September 1993

Dear Editors.

Thank you for the distinction you so generously heap upon me in your recent letter regarding your forthcoming issue on 'experimental fiction.' I fear however that in this deluge of critical approaches and categories—high modern, post-modern, deconstruction, post-structural, where I frequently see my work discussed at length—'experimental' is the one which I find specifically unsuited, due to my sense of the decline in the use and meaning of 'experimental' and 'experiment' from the blunt dictionary definition as 'A test made to demonstrate a known truth' to which I should happily subscribe, to the rather loose embrace of writing pursued willy-nilly in some fond hope of stumbling on those strokes of brilliance which that perfect poet Keats mistrusted even in himself observed with "It is true that in the height of enthusiasm I have been cheated into some fine passages; but that is not the thing."

From the start almost a half century ago I have believed (& Keats to witness) that I knew exactly what I am doing: as 'known truth' for example, that style must match content, hence the fragmentation in *The Recognitions*; language and disorder, and authorial absence going back to Flaubert, in *J R*; exercising the cliche in *Carpenter's Gothic*; language and order in *A Frolic of His Own*.

Thus it would be quite unseemly (not to say inflammatory) for me to name as 'carrying the torch of the experimental movement' writers who might well feel that they too know exactly what they are doing as I trust you will understand, as I trust you will further understand that I have no wish or intention of disparaging your enterprise, or of belittling your generous appraisal of my work. I have no short stories recent or otherwise, I do not wear T shirts, but can at least respond to your notion regarding 'the work of new and established visual artists who use text in their works' with the enclosed from Julian

Schnabel's *Recognitions* Series (there are a half dozen or so of them nicely reproduced in his catalogues &c) which you may find pertinent.

With best regards,
W. Gaddis

* * *

To Thomas Überhoff

East Hampton, NY 11937
12 May 1996

Dear Mr Überhoff.

Thank you for your inquiry: no question that that is about as dense a sentence as I have ever written, for which I apologize to Mr Stingl (but not to the reader!). I shall try to 'shed some light' which may simply confuse things further.

Overall, the 'density' is calculated to reflect the *silent spread* of *bushy frostweed,* here representing disorder & vulgarity (Ortega y Gasset's 'mass man' proclaiming his rights to be vulgar) *widening its habitat at its neighbors' expense,* i.e., Oscar's elitism & search for order, as bad money driving out good in Gresham's Law: thus the wincing defeat of Oscar's (play=ceremony of) innocence as portrayed in Yeats' poem The Second Coming wherein "The ceremony of innocence is drowned; / The best lack all conviction, while the worst / Are full of passionate intensity," Yeats being the bond that brings Oscar & Basie closer (*no small thing either* as noted elsewhere (p. 88) in the book). And so the metaphor of bushy frostweed for *the worst full of passionate intensity* (see Oscar's diatribe on pp. 96–7) demonstrating here that *survival of the fittest,* rather than *the best* ('plays of ideas'), means *no more than those fittest to survive* & quite possibly, as we see all around us, the worst.

Well! have I simply compounded our difficulties? It may be the most expeditious course just to translate the whole passage word-for-word and leave it all for some brilliant graduate student to decode in his doctoral PhD dissertation.

The 'rockets' you ask about were probably to illuminate targets (or incendiaries?) from "the rockets' red glare" in our Star Spangled Banner written during the War of 1812 (vs. Britain).

And finally, I am quite stunned by your "little brochure for the booksellers," it is extremely handsomely done, I'd never seen that picture in the overcoat before & needless to say my vanity runneth over, could I presume to ask you to send me ½ dozen more copies? (The design of the book's jacket is also marvelous but of course vanity prevails), you may imagine how I look forward to publication!

With warm regards,
William Gaddis

[*Überhoff worked at Rowohlt Verlag, which was overseeing Nikolaus Stingl's German translation of* A Frolic of His Own *(Letzte Instanz, 1996). In a rare explication of his own prose, Gaddis attempts to untangle a long sentence on page 304 as Oscar nods off while watching a television nature program on a lackluster member of the Cistaceae or rockrose family, Helianthemum dumosum, more familiarly known in its long suffering neighborhood as bushy frostweed for its talent at surviving the trampling by various hoofed eventoed closecropping stock of the suborder Ruminantia, to silently spread and widen its habitat at its neighbors' expense like some herbal version of Gresham's law in Darwinian dress demonstrating no more, as his head nodded and his breath fell and the crush of newsprint dropped to the floor, the tug at his lips in the troubled wince of a smile might have signaled no more than, or better perhaps the very heart of some drowned ceremony of innocence now the worst were filled with passionate intensity where —we share something then don't we, no small thing either [Basie had told Oscar earlier] —That's good to know, demonstrating simply the survival of the fittest embracing here in bushy frostweed no more than those fittest to survive not necessarily, not by any means, by any manner of speaking, the best . . .*]

* * *

To Christopher Knight

Key West, Fla.
25 April [1998]

Dear Christopher Knight.

I am sorry being so long about thanking you for sending your *Hints & Guesses* & for the work itself. I won't go into the somewhat bizarre circumstances that have contributed to the long delay but rather the great pleasure & rewards I had on first examining it, & have even now not yet read it thoroughly through.

However what is immediately evident is your readiness (nay, appetite!) for pursuing situations beyond their appearances (as background of American Gothic (pp. 165 fol.)) even if contradictory; or better perhaps the citations of cases, pursuing outside references; or picking up on small but vital details consistently missed by 'reviewers' (as Cruickshank/Lester (obvious) leap from CIA to industrial espionage); also my attempt at the Holmes/Crease///Hand marvelous collision. Those for random starters.

Incidentally I thought it might amuse you (177 fol.) *Jane Eyre* sequence, my attempt to find a writing style to conjure up a read-ing/visual style in such total contrast to the actual bed scene: this attempt to impose her fiction upon the reality almost coming to grief through editor's failure to get permission for the already written sequence using *Lost Horizon* only to be denied (didn't like the sex-context) at the very last minute by Hilton's estate so I broke my neck rushing through every public-domain distinctive prose passage & think it worked (though not so well as the original).

Such the pitfalls. I regret, once again, being so brief & perfunctory with this response to what I find around the top of works I've seen on mine, with on the one & happy hand reaching back to what you have made from our first encounter & I an agonized paranoid/shy (guest), to the opposite which I might have anticipated with some academic collisions under my belt now the inevitable sharp words that must emerge between those selling apples & those selling oranges.

I am incidentally heavily involved just now in a book on the player piano (the one Gibbs didn't write in *J R*) tangled for the moment in contract difficulties (my work incidentally doing immensely well in Germany (where they *read*)) and even should we all survive all (meaning *all*) the notes for the Pepsi-Cola-Episcopal case, God help us all & thank you again,

Warm regards
William Gaddis

[*A contributor to* In Recognition of William Gaddis, *Knight sent Gaddis a copy of his book* Hints & Guesses: William Gaddis's Fiction of Longing *(University of Wisconsin Press, 1997).*]

NOTE. We are grateful to Steven Moore for the annotations that appear throughout the letters. Additional and expanded notes may be found in *The Letters of William Gaddis*, edited by Moore, available from Dalkey Archive Press in February 2013.

Dogs of Cuba: The Buddha of the Vedado

Edie Meidav

FOR SEVEN YEARS IN PRISON every day he had a chair to himself. He had a chair and desk and even a private room in which to kick his heels up on the desk. Yuzniel had a friend on the outside falsify a certificate saying that he had been a geography and history teacher so he got to teach classes four times a week, which was hard for a high-school dropout, but he had no problem getting students to come to class, people always liked him, part of his problem being he was ready for anyone, having that street intelligence that makes everyone believe. Getting to move around and have private space meant everything in prison and when Yuzniel wanted something, he was diligent, at least half of why I fell in love.

We met as scraggly kids in our neighborhood with its sidewalks torn up by roots, the one where state employees work eight hours a day with machetes to cut snatches of grass so that tourists at the fancy hotels facing the seawall boulevard don't feel they've left too much home behind. Even if all the neckless men from Italy or Switzerland trip as they totter out of the hotel, their recompense is they get to lean on their mulattas, never technically hired, whose every curve is a sign of capital to come or capital spent.

It is not hard to fall in love in Cuba but it is equally easy to fall out, like that round-robin salsa the male dancers do where they twirl their girls, all with that bored face of the best salseros, the girls endlessly switching partners, the dance really about the expertise of the men though the girls' compliance masks greater skill. This may be why we have one of the world's highest divorce rates and may also have to do with the circulation necessary to any island's inner flow, the one that makes us depend on the import of foreign neckless wonders, vacation-neutral shirts tenting over their tummies while they eye their disco girls.

I did not meet my boy at a disco but instead outside school where those without mothers demanding them home by a certain time still hang out, on a crumbly plaster wall where we sat drinking and stealing time by pretending to be adults. Yuzniel teased me like a brother whenever I wore eyeliner I had swiped from my older sister but I teased him for wearing the beige slack hems of the boys' uniform so high, making him look even lankier, but despite or because of the teasing, the two of us always had radar on each other, whether in a hall or auditorium or field. We knew what the other thought or wanted, even if we pretended we were just part of our group, so no one was shocked when right before he dropped out we hooked up.

His mother went crazy three years later and stayed at the psychiatric hospital that Fidel said brought shame to Cuba because it turned out the new director let employees swipe sheets, medicines, and food until some busybody American agency snooped in to discover so many crazies dead from starvation and cold, all this at the shameful midcentury of our revolution that had never stopped. Yuzniel was less ashamed of his mother than Fidel was ashamed of the sanitarium; no one held having a crazy mother against Yuzniel, since my boy was the humble mayor of our zone, always helping even the lowest of the low.

And we did love the revolutionary slogans, that is, loved them to mock. We would see the billboards advertising the thoughtful pensamientos of Fidel or José Martí or any other hero and instead we would speak or scrawl some randiness into these holy words, the tang of teenage mischief thrumming our veins. But really there was no other place for us than Cuba; we liked to say it was the people not the government that made the place, look at all the neckless men who knew the lure, even though we all knew for us the island had become one beautifully outfitted jail. Every other person we knew was waiting in a queue to have some Miami uncle or Boca aunt send word that the time had come and the visa to America was in the mail. Of course old-timers liked saying they were diehard fidelistas, humanitarians, communists, and that revolution would stir their rice and beans siempre, but people like fooling themselves, staying in a bad situation, always telling themselves someone wiser knows best.

At first I just felt sorry for Yuzniel. His mother gone pure crazy when we knew his older sister had played the part of the jinetera, outfitting herself with jangly earrings and tight jeans before finding herself a rich Swiss man at the hotel down our street, the one that years later, after the Pope came to Havana to lecture Fidel about our morality problem, took up policies barring girls like her from entering the front door. Back in her time, things were still open. She ended up going to Switzerland so she could send remissions home to her little brother, Yuzniel being raised by their demented grandfather, the one who used all that Swiss love money to have big parties, whooping it up and only occasionally loaning a handful to Yuzniel whenever he wanted to loan someone starter cash.

Any boy in this situation would go wild. At fourteen, Yuzniel used to come to school with hair in braids tight to his head while swigging watered-down alcoholic anything out of a little silver flask with its Che face wearing off from exposure to his cheap aguardiente. Back then Yuzniel was pure edge, not yet the saint he became and who wouldn't have been drawn in? I was popular but when I got him, my neighborhood status went up some crucial notch.

Never give me advice, he told me, that's one thing, Yanet, I got to listen to my own master, I can't have anyone above me.

When he decided to quit school and imitate Juan Carlos, the guy in his tipped fisherman's hat whom we'd seen living it up down the avenue, selling drugs to foreigners, of course I couldn't keep myself from telling my boy not to head down the wrong path.

Come on, Yanet, you were supposed to be different. We were Generation Y and so everyone had Y names, though at first Yuzniel's mother had wanted to call him Lázaro because his birth had been so difficult. Difficult as opposed to what, I wonder? He was born like we all were, yanked out by a doctor's forceps a few years before the Special Period when the Soviets pulled their support and our whole island lost access to things like forceps, clothes, and soap and we were supposed to live only on rice, beans, and endless mountains of sugar.

Yuzniel did what any thinking man would do. He didn't want to go the way of our teachers whom we saw diving into Dumpsters or the doctors we met sewing kids' shoes on the street. He knew Juan Carlos was up to something and that something Yuzniel wanted. To stay in the system hoping to be some clerk making at most twenty-five dollars a month while figuring out how to survive with odd jobs on the side, you would have to be dumb. At night my boy started selling small bags to hotel tourists whose mulattas needed a little extra in order to get it on, just some marijuana and cocaine, and this despite the daily reflections of Fidel in the party paper about other countries' evils and how we in Cuba were pure and above drugs, this when about half the men you meet on any day before ten in the morning have that little insult of rum or beer on the breath, this despite the way we sip sugary coffee all day to avoid falling down the pit I started to know the day Yuzniel was caught.

You have to admire Fidel. He'd caught wind of the drugs fighting his words and so between four and five one January morning orchestrated that famous island-wide sting that threw thousands of dealers into jail. Yuzniel at first was caged with dealers but after six months the overcrowding shoved him into the rapist-and-murderer prison. First morning there, he hit on the plan of becoming a history and geography teacher so he could get out, his only goal, and got us married so we would get three hours a month of undisturbed conjugal visits.

Of course I was a little coy. I didn't want to get pregnant if I had to be alone on the outside. Still, I was working as a shopgirl, I'd come wearing the patterned stockings that only nurses and shopgirls get to wear, and he would be so happy to see me, his narrow face would light into being more like that of some big, happy dog who wanted to jump all over me even before the guard left us alone.

So I brought him whatever he needed, even the false certificate and books to study, I waited and when he was let out one year early for good behavior as a teacher, who took the bus with him to his brother's home? Who lived there with him, together with his brother and wife and their new baby until the lack of privacy just got too hard? I did eventually insist he open up some packets of the drug money he had hidden before getting caught so he could find us a new apartment, tricky in Cuba when we were allowed to trade only to an apartment of the exact same size. Only the old drug money belonged to Yuzniel, nothing else. Even the house of his grandparents had reverted to the government, given his sister's total disappearance from the family's cause, though at that time she was suffering. After she had tried divorcing her neckless Swiss man, the guy stole her clothes, money, and passport, making her rely on the goodness of the few Cubans she had met in Geneva. I thought she was crazy for trying to get back to Cuba but I heard that was her goal and who cares, anything was fine and well. Those days, things were looking up for me and Yuzniel.

With some financial lubrication, we got ourselves a place not far from his brother and our old-time crumbly wall. Fidel had just lifted the restrictions on people having their own businesses, or rather his brother Raúl pushed Fidel toward cracking the window enough that we opened our little snack shop. We hired Yuzniel's best ex-cons to work it, our triumph near the hotel where his sister had bagged her man, just a nice place for people to get a little coffee and pan con tortilla or croqueta. And we were getting the hang of the business, bribing the health inspector and electricity inspector: The whole thing was starting to take off.

61

I never take anything for granted, my boy would say each morning, kissing me. Every time I breathe fresh air, every time I take a sip of water, I realize all I could not have. Then he'd correct himself: What we could not have. Together. You waited, Yanet baby, and I will never forget. I owe you.

I would feel lucky because though it had been hard to wait those seven years—the flower of your youth! my mother, who'd made her own bad choices, never missed an opportunity to scold me—it seemed all our choices had served the right cause. Yuzniel swore he would never again touch drugs; he had done bad, knew bad, and would not get himself thrown back in the slammer. A girl could breathe easily, that was how I felt.

Which is of course the way things go, right, the point when you finally relax, things always start spilling over. In our building lived the daughter of a friend of Yuzniel's from back in high school. Because Yuzniel had been a mayor wherever he was, answering this one's debt, picking up the cell to go fix another's water issue, calmly meeting everyone's need, all of which protected him from rape in prison— no one laid a finger on me, I promise, he told me, my friends made a ring around me—because he was practically the mayor of our corner of the Vedado, this girl conceived a mad attraction for him, throwing herself at his feet when her father died. She wanted Yuzniel with a passion, a girl not even seventeen, just a light-skinned, simpering fool with a bit lower lip and a way of ducking her chin when she looked at him. Of course anyone other than me might have suspected things but she seemed too insubstantial if you didn't pay much attention to her navel ring and that smooth, flat belly.

WOULD YOU RATHER GET A PRICKER IN YOUR HEART OR YOUR HEEL? I saw she had texted him one day, the first sign to make me suspicious.

Why is Lucía texting you about prickers? I said.

Some word game she likes to play, he said, holding my gaze in that straightforward way that had passed him from jail to parole board to clean man, the kind that was enough to make your average, snoopy neighborhood vigilante for the defense of the revolution trust him.

Oh come on, I said, I cannot believe I have to ask.

Look, the girl just lost her father, he said, should I turn a blind eye on her just because you're jealous?

What, I said, you meeting in hotels? Or friends' places?

You're crazy, he said, I mean really. Why so suspicious? She's a baby. Weren't we talking about having kids soon when you know I'm not even that ready?

So I was just supposed to swallow this and go about my day, check on accounts, talk to smiling ex-cons, and not care. And no one had the right ear for my suspicions: Our lives were so entwined, I couldn't turn to anyone who wouldn't already have been taken into Yuzniel's confidence. So I burned. The next day I told him I wanted to relieve one of the ex-cons, work in the snack shop to make sure coffee was being served correctly or some other ridiculous made-up story. He took this as he took all my initiatives, calmly eyeing me and calculating, saying, as he often did: You know best, Yanet. And: Let me know if I can help.

He saw me in the snack bar that morning, standing there in my stained apron while he supposedly was heading to talk with our prepared-foods supplier, his little red Lata moving out into traffic. He didn't know I had asked a favor of my cousin, my beloved harelipped cousin I could trust with my life. My cousin with his gypsy cab followed Yuzniel and about a half hour later circled back to pick me up. We pushed through traffic to where Yuzniel was, parked not outside the supplier's house in Central Havana where the carts and smoke press on you but instead near the breezy green Parque Almendares. From the bridge above we watched Yuzniel, hands shoved in the back of his low jean pockets just as if we were all still sixteen. He was slumping down toward where they rent boats on the river that flows under the bridge.

Human nature never surprises my cousin. Unlike every other Cuban, he is no gossiper and hence was perfect for the task. All he could do was shrug and the best I could do was shrug back.

We saw Yuzniel look around, a quick hungry gaze before paying ten cents to the guy who runs the boats. I knew because once, when we were bad teens, we too had gone boating. He then started rowing one of those tin cans upriver toward the bank. Who could guess what he was doing? But then I saw the skinny little torso of that smooth-faced girl, the one I would have recognized anywhere, leaning on him as she got into the boat, making it rock until Yuzniel started rowing upriver again.

Well, said my cousin, his palms opening wide, that's one interesting supplier.

What am I supposed to do?

Maybe the harelip gives my cousin a one up on dealing with people and their deformities, moral or otherwise. He took me in before

63

he answered, weighing all potential fallout: Yanet, you got to play this one.

What does that mean?

Yuzniel's crafty. He's never going to admit it.

I waited for seven years.

Maybe that's your ticket? said my cousin, his craftiness greater than I could have expected. He went on: You want him to confess, that won't be too hard. But you want him to stop seeing her—well, men like certain kinds of flesh.

This my cousin knew intimately, given that he was the spawn of an aged Italian tourist and a too-young Cuban mother who used the money the Italian sent her not for a lip operation for her son but to buy herself too many pairs of strappy gold shoes and foreign lipsticks.

It's awful, I said, I would be young if—but this didn't make sense so I stopped halfway.

In the end, my cousin understood everything. I would say he saved the day or at least showed me what we were made of. He was the one who sent Yuzniel the typewritten card saying I had been detained. (Not technically a lie.) In this unsigned letter, delivered by a beggar paid fifty cents for the favor, my cousin wrote Yuzniel that he was being watched and that Fidel's morality police knew what he was up to. (Not wholly a lie either, even if they had been paid up not to know.) That for all Yuzniel's licenses not to be suspended—his business, the apartment—for him not to be reported again before the bureau of moral affairs, a citation that could mean another jail sentence, Yuzniel had to write a signed confession admitting to all his recent peccadilloes, as bad as those of the worst American and colonial mercenaries.

The letter went on: Because truth remains the great revolutionary purgative, Yuzniel's confession alone, if done in the correct spirit of autocritique, would be enough to emphasize the moral fiber that the parole board had seen in Yuzniel and redeem him, allowing him to continue his life. After the writing of this confession, all nefarious activities would have to cease, both moral or financial. Did Yuzniel understand?

His confession was to be left at the front desk of the hotel near the snack bar with the envelope stating REVOLUTIONARY DOCUMENT by ten the next morning. No one other than Yuzniel could write or bring the letter, and silence would confirm that the letter had been seen appropriately. However, if the letter was written in ill faith, a return to prison would be the only logical result.

You can imagine with what caught breath the next morning I leaned out of the window above the snack bar, the room where we kept our reserve stove and fridge and a sofa that had, perhaps, seen some of Yuzniel's recent actions. Did I love or hate him most as I watched him slump, head lowered, across the street and up the ramp toward where the uniformed guards nodded, letting him pass into the automatic opening of the hotel's glass doors? I cannot say. Never before had the wind fluttered the flags near the hotel so fetchingly, never before had the palm trees looked so splayed out, desperate for love. The moment stretched, that much I can say.

I am not a poet but I do listen to pop songs. If I were a pop singer I would sing a story about these flags and palm trees, the unknowing guards, and the letter that must have burnt a hole in Yuzniel's hands. I watched, sure he and I could right everything, that just the way he had finessed the cards he had been dealt, he would manage to finesse this bad deck and we would find ourselves on the other side, laughing the way we used to.

I could hold this future in my hand as easily as I used to hold my tattered red grade-school copy of the Communist Manifesto. Even if we had not yet had our kids, even if I was already in my late thirties and had drunk too much chemical water as a kid during the period you could light flames straight from the tap, I was not about to give up hope: We would have children and give them Z names, Zuzu and Zamila and Zajuan, our new snack bar would flourish, and we'd keep neighborhood kids off the street the way our parents had not.

About half an hour later, my cousin came limping out of the hotel. Only two weeks earlier the apartment above him had crumbled into his apartment, given the way our Havana maintenance teams do their work, and he still had to get his leg working from where a metal bed had fallen on his knee. One day my cousin would be OK but right then his face was dark and unreadable from my upstairs window. I came running down the stairs to get the news but of course who should I run into coming upstairs but my own husband?

Yanet, he said, softly, brushing my shoulders. Yanet, and I might have gotten the apelike message being transmitted but you see, I had frozen into the image of my husband as a saint, the buddha of the Vedado as everyone called him, a man who didn't need much and just liked to make sure other people were happy. Despite whatever I knew about how he had recently lied, I could not understand what in the end turned out to be as much an apology as a goodbye.

Here was what Yuzniel's letter said. Why do I keep it? What is my choice? Or, really, what trash can could contain such a thing?

> Let it be known that I have been an honest man in all my dealings as much as the system lets me be. I have done nothing but what the system has told me to do. As for the women in my life, the heart wants what it does and I cannot blame it for wanting a youthful woman who would have been mine had my best years not been stolen by the depravities of capitalism. This young woman threw herself at me. She fell in love with me for the good that I do unto others. Is there a morality to this? Forgive me if you cannot condone, judge me if you must, but look in your own mirror and you cannot condemn. Few among us have not been victims of our recent time and so what else is left for a person to do?

I ask you: Would you stay with such a man? And who would you blame more, Fidel or Lucía? That slut. I see her in the hall and she smiles her young crocodile teeth at me, her belly already rounding, the baby we could have had if the revolution hadn't thrown my own baby in prison. I lost the flower of my youth to a boy from Generation Y and now I have only some payoff money and this ungainly tale to tell. I'm hoping some better stories will come around my bend soon since it happens that I finally am next in line to be asked to come to Orlando by my old uncle. I am not giving up hope anytime soon. And who can say the day I step off the island will not be the very day that man finally goes to hell?

Always in Arises
Keith Waldrop

AFTER DANCING

shells, bubbles, halos, forks, chimneys

bubbles, plumes
filaments

chimneys

bubbles

echo fantasia

numbers, laying
rails, fastened to the
ties with nails

CASE HISTORY

she made him relate to her her whole life

Keith Waldrop

CASE HISTORY

shows restlessness

anxiety

ideas of reference and persecution, ghosts
in the bedroom

hard voices—fearsome ghosts—has not
spoken for five months

has to be forced to eat

scarcely moves, facial expression dull, between
question and answer long
pauses

persecuted by horrible animals that
crawl like snakes yet have legs like crocodiles

not animals at all but
unchained ocean

long arms

long legs

A DIPHTHONG

sign of affirmation, first
person, organ
of sight

CASE HISTORY

sits in the dark, sees nothing, but
imagines, later, something
earlier

BILLY UTHERFOOT

Sometimes a door stands half open, so as to conceal the next room, into which one seems invited.

In such a situation, there are two ways of entering that room, the simplest being to push the door wider and walk in.

The other is to slip in, sideways, not moving the door, not necessarily even touching the door.

That is Billy's way.

Keith Waldrop

SOUL

twaddle and minutiae

sloping water

CASE HISTORY

suffers

has to run

eats when it disgusts him

gets pleasure

doubts

was extraordinarily religious until his fourteenth year

SALIDA & SORDIDA

Two sisters on the way out.

ANTICIPATED APPARITION

uncoordinated unin-
vited
unseemly

spent, search
for symmetry, straying among
details, the animal kingdom's

other city

steady
slide *always*
down the lower side

parties

whispers

TOBOLSK

very low standard of education
principal crops rye, wheat, oats, barley, and potatoes
export of cattle, hides, tallow, corn, flour, fish, and furs
remarkable progress since Trans-Siberian Railway

no rail line from Tyumen to Tobolsk

spirits sent east to Tomsk

Keith Waldrop

CASE HISTORY

"Where," he is wont to ask, "is the Prophet-like-Moses?" Or, sometimes,

"Where is the Moses-like-Me?"

CASE HISTORY

*while crossing the street
has to fall down*

*on the street if a girl
happens to pass
crosses to her side*

CASE HISTORY

with own hand

*long legs
strong arms*

dominated by thought

Keith Waldrop

DETOURS

words

nouns like brick
night like

Mechlin lace or marbled satin
surreptitious
the light of day

hands
melodic
cross

watch now where I build
my ruin
slow

death
dying
disposal

words like dependent
origination

unheard

outside

More Little Tales of the Internet
Jonathan Lethem

#37. GUY BLEEDING ALL OVER SKYPE

HE WAS A GUY who was very much a big deal to see, in a kind of you-don't-see-him-very-often way, as well as in a then-when-you-do-he's-on-Skype kind of way. By reputation, not a guy who'd been leaving his house very often of late. Behind him was a marble mantelpiece with two flowerpots framing a mirror. In the mirror we could catch sight of the top of the back of his head but the angle wasn't such that we could see more, say the table or desk where his computer sat, which would have set up a possible infinite regress of him, back of head, front of face visible in small Skype window, plus his view in the larger window of us all arrayed at the conference table (we'd have been pretty hard to make out in particular, really). No dice. He crowded the frame, at an angle downtilted so we got about twenty-five percent forehead and brushed-back hairline and crown above and around which we only caught glimpses of mantel and flowerpots and mirror, the rest of his features, of course, crowded, receding in perspective below, and then, busy in a small margin, his face, his hands, which entered the frame to worry at a small, round bandage or plaster on the point of his chin, no big deal at the outset. We were certainly not fixated on it at the outset, not with the truly and importantly big deal implicit in getting him onto the conference call to begin with. Who ever speaks up in a room like ours packed with colleagues to say to a face on Skype, hey, you're a little proximate, wanna ease back a tad? If he was too big, let him be too big—he was big. We were small and could see ourselves there: small, arrayed, awaiting. He wasn't calling to have his approach to sitting in front of his computer adjusted by us. We were listeners.

It was maybe five minutes into what he was saying that the circular bandage or plastic kind of seemed to come off with his rubbing and worrying at it, likely the fault of his enthused declamation that his hands couldn't keep still from their nervous action of scaling and itching around the perimeter of the thing—also that he couldn't stop to notice. He sort of brushed it aside completely with the next reach-in from the bottom frame of the shot, and that was when the welling blood I guess first got smeared sideways a little. You could have taken it in the weird lighting and bad resolution for a black smear of inter-ference, a breakdown in the image smoothing, but the earlier pres-ence of the bandage or plaster cued us to the fact it was blood right away. Cued me, at least. I can't actually speak for anyone else there at that table. It's not like we were comparing notes. Maybe at that very first moment one of us might have been able to interject some-thing, but we were hamstrung by our own numbers. Who'd want to be the one to pipe up in a room like that, plus anyway maybe he'd catch it himself with the aid of the little window showing him his own image nested inside of ours (though he'd hardly used that feed-back to adjust his distance from the camera, had he?). Maybe, any-way, it wouldn't get any worse, though the fast rate at which the blood had first welled up could have put a rest to any hopes along those lines. It got a whole lot worse.

They say every one of us touches his or her face an average of seven times per minute or something like that and I guess this must have some basis because it wasn't long before he'd gone in again, and again after that. Of course some cool trickle must have alerted him at a semiconscious level but he was also completely caught up in his presentation, he was a guy who came out of a sales background to begin with and had now been in more of a development line for a while, had dropped from public view for a secret developmental pe-riod, during which apparently a certain sales imperative had been bottled up behind his covert man-of-mystery persona, and now that he had our ears he was pitching his only fractionally disclosable new product with everything he had. A talker who rarely got to talk any-more; my impression, for what it is worth. What stood out apart from the spread of the blood was a certain tic in his otherwise fairly brilliant presentation where he'd come to a perfectly apt word, *omni-scient*, say, or *compliance*, or *ambient*, and then he'd pause and frame it, as though he wasn't certain he hadn't invented the word himself. "The product has a certain omniscient—omniscient, is that even a word?" Or, "Ambient—is that even a word?" As though in his years of woodshedding secretly to develop the new line he'd forgot-ten which parts of the world he'd left behind were and weren't pro-jections of his own brain. So there was that tic—"Ubiquity, is that even a word?"—that, and the blood now smearing everywhere, daubs on his forehead and on the tip of his nose, as he quite unfortunately under the circumstances turned out to be one of those persons who enact thoughtful reflection by stroking the forehead or tugging on the nose's tip. Several of his fingers, for those moments they entered the frame, seemed pretty much to be just like a kindergartner's finger-painting implements by now, I mean, bloodied to that extent. None of us said anything. We'd gone from thinking it was no big deal to admiring him for toughing it out—here's the sort of thing, we thought for an instant, that separates guys like this guy from guys like us who sit wondering if it's even a breach of protocol to reach for the bottles of water they've placed before us around the conference table—to realizing something should have been said quite a while before. His fingers were likely getting tacky with blood, the best hope would be for it to dry somewhat and alert him with its adhesion to some dry surface, but instead he went back again and again to the well of his chin and soon had slickly painted himself to the point of resembling one of those crazy guys you see in the stands at a football game. God help you, ending up in a seat beside guys like that. It was at this point that he seemed to become self-conscious of something, not what he should have been, I guess, or he'd likely have said something, but instead he maybe had an impulse to modulate his distance from the camera at last, and so reached out, the blood-black fingers growing abruptly huge and blurred as when in underwater photography a shark's nose investigates a diver's lens, and then we found the whole screen obliterated in what I can only suppose was a single fingerprint. The guy bleeding all over Skype just went on talking.

#91. HAND-CARVED

I hope this will reach you, my darling! Though if it does I have no special confidence you will be able to read it. Perhaps when I return I will have to explain it to you. Oh, how you'll be surprised to see what I am using to send this message! You see, I came upon one of the native men at the docks, one of those who'd come out of the deep forest to make his fortune trading with the men who come in boats, but who remained very much a true presence of the deep, dripping silence of the forest, and though he was often busy jumping up and aiding with the shifting of valises up and down the ramps to the boats, for which he was apparently paid only in coins the boatmen

grudging threw down at his sandals, during quiet moments he'd re-
tire to a crate and resume his work on a mysterious effort of his hands
and a penknife, deftly whittling at something miniature in his grasp.
I grew fascinated with this man and moved nearer in order to see. It
was a tiny, perfectly formed, hand-carved Internet! His material was
some wine-dark, utterly pliant rain-forest branch, surely plucked
from some tree deep in the rain forest, one with properties known
only to members of this man's tribe, and perhaps even lacking a
Latinate name, having not yet been cataloged by our science. I waited
until he was finished, watched as he held it up, squinting in the light
now of sunset on the docks there, then purchased the elegant little
primitive masterwork from him for the equivalent of a dollar. Incred-
ibly enough, I'm using it to write this to you now, God knows if it'll
get through, and then I'll conceal it in my luggage and with luck have
it home to you in a matter of days. I want it for your collection, of
course, but I must study it as well. The poor devil's ingenious little
trinket has given me the most extraordinary new idea. With all my
love, Redacted.

You Are Country Like Me
Ngoc Doan

when rain stitches
the sky
atmosphere's proroguing

if soggy flowers   of Autumn   de-
cline   Spring's pollinating   revolvers
        pink yellow
                        and purple pink
                redder

I admit no joy
        in pigmentations, sidled-
walk   pavement   in rain
    worm-
            halves

                        *

                squirrels race fence
        birdfeeder, and pollen
                        spores accumulate on grass
            there
            we are like blue columbine
                                bursts

                as us on the lawn is

        evenings
                    see fireflies

*

there are fruit trees
and
marble slabs
uniform

not every thing is this deep
backlash slap of
                    every comment
purple   brutish
I'm content
          sometimes

     in the morning
I peel hardboiled
     eggs
in sink water steams
               and berry

this frustration
I wish that I knew
          figure
     as if—

pushing you off the bridge
     not by accident
this is us walking in the dark

*

in the beginning it's free
        you don't care enough

    our exuberance, a dream of LA

       and
   flown rapier lines on upper lips

there are stars on your ceiling
        or do I see stars

at the end of the night a song's still
        playing

   —I've   forgotten
    what I was doing

       *

it is April, so I always get what I want

    stable   coaches, riding
         loads

peter
   gilbert fills a hole   exposes
         a calf

(seed-
   potatoes,
  perihelia posies
     and cockatoo on fence

promised a man)

   peaches keep crying

the crow's waiting

to hide things that
                doesn't

    what is to need secrets—

                    *

walk that dirt
        it is dusk already

    the rabbits ride
        the horizon

wild they are

to knife
            lay your head

    duellum

        a wailing-some

rent is retch

                    *

you've seen the sun
　　　　towers of glimmering light

　　　　　picture

　　　　your levity
　　　　　　　　bareness
　　　　　　　　　　　whitens
　　　　　　the　　back-
　　　　　　　　　　　ends

　　　　the other people they go by—
　　　　　　　　　　(no scrutiny)

they are strange
to you　　　　make sense

your　disrobing　　　consent

you know

　　　　these blossom trees are
　　　　　　swept

　　　　what do you remember—

　　　　it's a day like　　any other
　　　do cry

From From a Broken Bottle Traces of Perfume Still Emanate

Nathaniel Mackey

20.XI.83

DEAR ANGEL OF DUST,

There's a review of *Orphic Bend* in the new *LA Weekly*. We didn't expect it to get any such attention, so this comes as a surprise. It's the first review it's gotten. The reviewer we neither know nor have heard of, but he seems to know the music and he has positive things to say. It's not that there's not the inevitable quibble here and there, but he does hand out a great deal of praise. One would definitely have to call it a good review. Indeed, friends are congratulating us, calling it a *rave* review. We don't go that far, happy though we were to see it, and even if it were a rave we'd want to draw back, not get too excited.

As it turned out, we were surprised not only by the review but by our consumption of it, the elation we initially felt upon seeing it, caught out or caught off guard by how happy we were to see it, how greedily, at first at least, we ate it up. It was as though it were this that we put the album out for, as though we recorded it to be reviewed, written about. There was not only the question of why we were so invested in being reviewed and in what the review said but a certain disappointment, both with such investment and with our elation's failure to live up to expectation, simply on its own terms and on the face of it, an expectation that, postexpectant as we'd have been or thought or wished ourselves to be, we didn't know (or simply hadn't admitted) we harbored. But we did, or had, and it was by that expectation that even our elation, on its own terms and on the face of it, was found wanting. Thus it was that elation mixed with or morphed into letdown. Happy wasn't happy enough. And even if it were, we weren't sure putting out a record to have nice things said about it, written about it, was what being a band amounted to.

The review, then, gave us pause, became the reason or occasion to ask, late to be doing so though it was, why we play. "It's not about reviews," Aunt Nancy emphatically said as we were discussing this at rehearsal. "It's not even about aboutness. It's not about being-about." It was a thought we needed no time to reflect on, no time to digest. We all understood what she meant, all of us in our heart of hearts having long wanted exactly that, only that, to play not for the sake of what could be said but athwart it, play without claim or caption, advancing (if advancing anything) being-in-and-of-itself, self-evidence, hub and horizon rolled into one. We countered claim and caption, coupling or conflating claim and caption, because of the elephant in the room in the review, the reviewer's reference to balloons emerging from his copy of *Orphic Bend*.

It was odd the way we tiptoed around the balloons at first. The review's bringing them up made for mixed feelings, if it didn't indeed bug each of us outright. It was our fear of their upstaging the music again. The reviewer's recourse to them as a self-crediting tack, boasting or bragging it seemed, made matters worse. Critical authority seemed to be at stake, visionary credentials even. Such were the insistence and relish he reported having seen the balloons with. Even so, we were slow to get around to it. Perhaps it was all too obvious, going, as they say, without saying. Perhaps we were loath to admit mention of the balloons bothered us, loath to admit anything in a review, least of all that, wasn't just water on a duck's back.

Though we were slow to get around to the balloons we did get around to them. Not long after Aunt Nancy said it wasn't about aboutness, Lambert ventured an equation of claim with inflation, aboutness with inflation, aboutness with would-be containment, cover. "Reviews are balloons," he summed it up by saying. We laughed, relieved it was out in the open. But once the subject had finally been broached we found we felt no need to belabor it. It was enough to know we all knew it was on the table. We briefly kicked it around and went back to rehearsal.

I'm enclosing a new installment of my antithetical opera, a new after-the-fact lecture/libretto called "B'Loon's Blue Skylight." I won't say it was inspired by the review but had the review not appeared it wouldn't have been written.

As ever,
N.

Nathaniel Mackey

B'LOON'S BLUE SKYLIGHT

*or, The Creaking of the Word: After-the-Fact Lecture/Libretto
(Djband Version)*

Djband bumped into B'Loon at a newspaper vending box. One of the local weeklies had featured a review of Djband's album *Orphic Bend*, a review whose author took pains to announce that balloons had emerged from his copy of the three-record release, doing so not only during the bass solo on a cut called "Dream Thief"—about which, he pointed out, there'd been a good deal of chatter on the underground grapevine—but at a number of other points as well. The reviewer took no small amount of pride alongside the pains he took to make this announcement, as though the balloons' appearance, multiple as it was and occurring at points on the recording not reported by others, bestowed a mark of distinction, made him elect among the elect, confirmed his acuity and taste.

The newspaper vending box stood on the corner of Melrose and Fairfax. Djband, spotting the title *Orphic Bend* in the subhead of the front-page review, had opened the door to the box, taken out a copy, and read the review, looking up dismissively when finished and humphing, "He thinks it's about him."

"But it *is* about him," an inner voice or an inner B'Loon reminded Djband, "as much about him as about anyone. Why not? Isn't the music for and about each and every listener, there to have made of it what any set of ears can make of it, there for nothing if not laissez-faire audit? Anything goes." The inner voice paused and on deeper reflection allowed, "Well, no, not anything. But where to draw the line is always an issue."

The review was filled with such wording as "insofar," "as it were," and "as if," the language of qualification disqualifying language itself. So it was, the review suggested, the balloons fled language while carrying language, bearing it to more auspicious precincts, Djband's music, and any other music, all music. "Music," it said at one point, "is language in exile, exile exponentially borne—that is, owned up to, lived up to." The review went on and on about the balloons, not so much about the reviewer, when it came down to it, as about B'Loon (though the reviewer had no way of knowing the balloons' avatar's name). It waxed alliterative and assonantal regarding "the balloons' détente between containment and contagion, forfeiture and fortitude," as though, in so accenting sound, it sought or asserted its own balloon status, inflating its recourse to sonorous air, "aeriality,"

85

sonority's infection or effects. "Sound," it went so far as to say, "is the deep, not so deep tautology of *is*, its flipped ipseity," obliquely alluding to Oliver Lake's *Life Dance of Is*.

Djband wasn't sure what to make of such pronouncements. Using language to question language seemed only a roundabout self-regard. "He thinks it's about language," Djband grumped, "that old chestnut, no more than the balloons by another name. He might as well have called it l'anguish. He thinks it's about the balloons." The review got on Djband's nerves, further mixing mixed feelings about the balloons. Could the intersection of two metropolitan avenues be called a house, B'Loon, a mixed blessing, was in the house.

Djband had been out of sorts to begin with, one of its members having awoken from a troubling dream. Aunt Nancy had dreamt an onslaught of Santa Ana winds had dried out her skin, leaving her face, neck, legs, and arms ashy. When she went to put on lotion, she dreamt, squeezing the tube nuzzling the palm of her hand, rather than a drop of lotion, albeit looking like one, what came out was a maggot. She immediately awoke, shocked by so brusque a reminder of death. She'd gotten up on the wrong side of the bed and been in a funk all day, Djband's other members, having been told the dream, in it with her.

The lotion-drop maggot continued to spook Djband, a Creaking of the Worm compounding ricketiness with unguent, omen with unctuousness. Djband couldn't help imagining an abruptly desiccated, husklike maggot, a stiff chrysalis rustling in the wind, no longer lotionlike. Knowing it meant skin would lose its luster, flesh be feasted on by worms eventually, Djband wondered what it meant regardless, wondered against knowing, not wanting to know. Knowing but not wanting to know what it came down to, body a balloon of skin with guts inside, "An offal thought," Djband inwardly quipped, at odds with and wanting to make light of the unsettling truth.

Aunt Nancy broke away and spoke. "It's not so much it all redounded to me. I'm not saying that. It's not even it was me it had to do with," she said. "It was anyone's palm, everyone's palm, the lotion came out on. It was anyone's arm, everyone's arm, the worm would eventually eat. It's not that I'm the only one whose head a sword hangs over. No, I'm not saying that. Not even close." She then took two, maybe three, steps back, blended back in. "No, not even close," Djband agreed.

Djband staggered along what seemed an exhaust wall, automobile and bus fumes attacking eyes, nose, mouth, and throat. A white sedan darted in front of a bus in time to make a right turn from Fairfax onto Melrose, black smoke pouring out of its tailpipe as it sped up, black smoke pouring out of the bus's tailpipe as well. "We'll all die together, choke together," Djband announced.

It was too much, as though, playing Monk, Djband forgot Monk's chuckling grunt, his wry wink. There was none of Monk's extreme right-hand hammering, his making the piano his toy, "Sweet Georgia Brown" turned "Bright Mississippi." It was in fact the contrary, as though "Epistrophy" had been renamed "Entropy," so doleful the note, so to speak, Djband repeatedly struck.

It didn't help that the review described "In Walked Pen" as "Monk salad," a phrase that, meant as a compliment from all indications though it was, got on Djband's nerves. It deliberately mixed its message Djband couldn't help suspecting, hearing overtones of "tossed," "thrown together," "hodgepodge." At best it was merely clumsy. It came off, in any case, in Djband's reading, as flip, too offhand, too casual, assuming unearned familiarity with Monk and Djband both. "Why not talk about a worm on a lettuce leaf as well?" Djband muttered all but inaudibly. "Why not say, 'A worm nibbled away at the romaine,' make an adage of it?" This was what Djband would have none of, a balloon of attitude meant to say, "I'm in the know," a balloon inflating itself at "In Walked Pen's" expense, Monk's expense, trivializing "In Walked Pen," trivializing Monk. "'Monk salad' my ass," Djband added.

Thus it was there was much to be annoyed about. The need for an answering salve or an answering salvo couldn't have been stronger. Neither much appealed to Djband, however. A letter to the editor taking issue with the review was anything but the water-off-a-duck's-back aplomb Djband liked to think it was an exemplar of. Salve, at the same time, couldn't help but recall lotion, couldn't help but conjure, in so doing, the lotion-drop maggot, the last thing Djband wanted a reminder of.

Djband turned its head to the right, looked over its right shoulder toward where the sound it suddenly heard seemed to come from. It was a rattling sound, as of bamboo slats knocking against each other. It was the sound of actuality falling short of expectation, the sound of a gap between ideal or imagined reception and actual reception, a discrepant rattle (discrepant rub) the review's nondelivery of ideal audition helped arise and resound.

It wasn't, Djband insisted, that there's a hearing one's mind's ear hears, a hearing that can only be virtual, a hearing no manifest hearing lives up to. This could be argued and it had often been argued but it wasn't what was going on here or it wasn't, were it at all going on, all that was going on. Indeed, Djband quickly admitted, it was in part what was going on, which was that three sets of hearing obtained: a) the hearing one in the act of composition or performance imagines, b) the hearing that in fact takes place, and c) the distance or disjunction between the two, audibly manifest now in the form of a rattling as of bamboo slats, a veritable Creaking of the Heard.

Was it that all reception, all audition, was flawed, inevitably a fall from the imaginal hearing one thought to hear and one hoped would be heard as one penned a piece or executed a run? Or was the Creaking of the Heard a veritable Creaking of the Herd, reception no inevitable fall but instead the outcome of herded audition, corralled by such would-be pundits as the review's author? Such were the thoughts that ran through Djband's head.

Yes, the latter was the case, Djband went on. It wasn't that reception was simply herded however. No, worse than that, it was *hearded*. *Hear*'s past tense's past tense, *hear* exponentially past, hearded hearing was multiply removed from the present, someone else's having heard presumed to be one's own. It's bad enough to presume to have heard with one's own ears, Djband reflected, worse to allow someone else to have done so for you.

The rattling sound made it clear *Orphic Bend* had been hearded, the review's corral evidently made of bamboo. Clunky wind chimes it occurred to Djband it sounded like, not at all graceful, not subtly insinuative, clumsily intrusive instead. "Clunk salad," Djband muttered under its breath, putting water-off-a-duck's-back aplomb aside for a moment, answering the review in kind.

"I want a big, bodacious onslaught of sound," Aunt Nancy had stepped forward again and was saying, "sound enough to beat back dream thievery, lotion-drop-maggot sleight of hand, an advent sound." She stepped back, blended in again, having had her say. "Yes, exactly," Djband agreed, "a big, bodacious advent sound." The contrast with rattling bamboo couldn't have been more stark.

Defensive, water-off-a-duck's-back aplomb notwithstanding, Djband was an ectoplasmic wall, a stone wall even, petrified by the specter of death. Either way, it was a wall from which its members might occasionally emerge. Up to this point Aunt Nancy was the one who had done so, soloist or soloistic, as though performing a piece rather than standing before a newspaper vending box.

For the moment, time was an ancillary matter, not to be disregarded nonetheless. Tacit statements of tempo implied or insisted that point or presence might be other than outright, recalling something Mingus wrote about a leaky faucet in the liner notes to one of his albums. Djband knew itself to be there more as an aggregate shake or as an aggregate shiver than as corpuscular stump, a street-corner symphony of mean provenance and prospect, time's "will tell" a window impendence blew through. It could hear itself no matter the time and the place, time nothing if not a suspended platform by turns made less than it was and made more than it was, a bevy of don't-care notes and a preterite soapbox.

So Djband stood bunched at the "will tell" window, the arthroscopic, worm's-eye glimpse into hearded audition the vending box had become. It heard itself beside the hearded rendition of itself the review purveyed, beside the rattling bamboo that was the gap between the two as well, the latter's lapse or its falling away from the former, along the rickety would-be joint between the two. Hearded audition's noncoincidence with Djband-as-it-heard-itself was only to be expected, Djband reminded itself or consoled itself, even scolded itself, angry at itself to have caught itself out expecting better.

A car's horn caught Djband's attention, a Toyota Corolla cut off by a Jaguar XJ-S changing lanes. The driver pounded the hub of the steering wheel and shook her fist as the Jaguar darted in. Oddly, it blended in perfectly, a staccato garnish to the music Djband would have been playing had it been playing, a defenestrated ragtag pomp.

All advent flew through the "will tell" window. All admonition stood streetside awaiting it, a cautionary wall Djband did its best to embody or at least evoke, an admonitory shingle if nothing more. Warning both stood and ran, a cathartic *récit* audition sought to be door to, time's indiscreet relay. Djband had seen it all. Warning stood and would always do so, it said and saw, knowing "always" to be the dangerous word it was but daring it, ran and would always run.

Djband pasted a poster on the bare wall it was, the bare shingle, the wall or the shingle it took itself to be. The poster bore After-the-Fact Caveat #1:

> Time, perfect or syncopated time, is when a faucet dribbles from a leaky washer. I'm more than sure an adolescent memory can remember how long the intervals were between each collision of our short-lived drip and its crash into an untidy sink's overfilled coffee cup with murky grime of old cream still clinging to the edges or a tidy rust-stained enamel sink that the owner of such has given up on the idea that that

maintenance man is ever going to change the rhythm beat of his dripping faucet by just doing his job and changing that rotten old rubber washer before time runs out of time.

Musicians partly come into the circle of various blame which encompasses much more than leaky faucets, rotten washers, or critics. Wow! Critics! How did they get here?

I know. It's Freudian. Faucets and old rotten washers. The innocent audiences that are sent in the direction of premature musicians—critics who want to play and some who play and study at music and can only encompass soulwise and technically about someone else what they themselves can comprehend.

It was none other than the passage from Mingus's liner notes to *The Black Saint and the Sinner Lady* that had crossed Djband's mind earlier, could "earlier," down this corridor in which time, faucet leak notwithstanding, was ancillary, be said to matter—no less dangerous, if so, than "always."

Shingle more than wall though neither shingle nor wall, it was a sandwich board the poster was pasted on, not a shingle or a wall Djband was but a sandwich board Djband in fact wore, Mingus's admonitory note gracing both boards, back and front, counseling passersby both coming and going. It was a long, detailed message for a sandwich board. Printed in large letters, it barely fit.

Djband had clearly let its water-off-a-duck's-back aplomb fall by the wayside, answering the review with the sandwich board, fighting back, answering "Monk salad" with Mingus. It was clearly involved, clearly invested, to the point of uncool even, the ensemblist equivalent of a sandwich man, anything but blasé, nothing if not caring, standing on the street advertising its message. Djband laughed at itself, realizing that insofar as to bear a message was to be a balloon it had become a balloon, balloon and sandwich man both, both rolled into one. Djband had not only bumped into B'Loon but become B'Loon, pressed and possessed by the spirit of caption and contention, the former manifestly, the latter more implicitly, bearing on which and whose caption fit. The review itself, one saw clearly now, was nothing if not a caption, nothing if not a balloon, nothing if not a message-bearing bauble, the bane of Djband's proprioceptive audition. It happened quickly, in a flash, balloon and sandwich board bound up as one.

"Myself When I Am Real," Djband reminded itself right after it laughed at itself, Mingus's title more to the point than ever before. A pointed mix of aim and arraignment, "Myself When I Am Real" said it all, could any five words be said to've said it all.

Djband turned toward where the sound of another car horn came from and saw the driver of a Mazda GLC headed west on Melrose give a thumbs-up, in approval of the Mingus quote it was clear. How the driver so quickly read so long a text Djband couldn't say but happily nodded to acknowledge the approbation. The sandwich board was making a difference already.

Djband turned sideways between the boards, lifting its arms, elevating the boards as though they were wings. It was now Lambert who stepped forward and spoke. "I want a straw to fall and fill up with air and float," he said. "I want float to be what unlikeliness does. Due to itself or in spite of itself, I want that to be what goes on, float's new leaf turned over, float's new reign and regret." Djband agreed, echoing, "Float's new reign and regret."

"Whatever comes up," Lambert continued, "it will beg the question it costs itself—float lure, float intended, float intransigence. Reed a wet stick in my mouth, I want more, flutter-tongue abandon's new almanac, float's lush life begun." Djband agreed and took up the tail end of what Lambert said, repeating, "Float's lush life begun."

"Float nothing if not a barge I'd be borne along on," Lambert continued, "I want each lick to incubate what float would be." Djband agreed again and repeated, "What float would be." Lambert stepped back and blended in again.

The sandwich board had brought an element of reduction in, Djband brought down to the reviewer's level, fighting fire with fire, balloon with balloon. Lambert's invocation of flight or flotation thus arrived right on time, albeit flotation, Djband was well aware, carried a balloon suggestion one could hardly miss. Still, lift and levitation won out over balloon rut, balloon mire, the bone "float's new leaf" picked with "Monk salad" notwithstanding, that bone the very filled-up, floating straw itself perhaps.

More no doubt than perhaps, Djband decided, embarrassed, underneath it all, by the sandwich board, needing to make a move. Disambiguating float from what balloons do was that move, float's association with balloons its new regret. Float's new reign was nothing if not a resolve to overcome inflation, nothing if not a bone proffering puncture. It remained a willingness to abide by high jive, high jubilation, a resolve to reside on high even so.

To say that at exactly that instant Djband smelled roses would be going too far. Roses did come to mind and they did so in a flash, their characteristic perfume no doubt bound up in the thought but not to the point of Djband actually smelling them. LA was way more than a stone's throw from Pasadena but Melrose might as well have been Colorado Boulevard on New Year's morning, so large did Lambert's barge now loom, float parting company with balloon.

It was a visual not an olfactory image, an address of the mind's eye, not the mind's more distant nose. Djband saw Lambert's roses-bedecked barge for an instant, easing down Melrose, Lambert atop it waving to the crowd. Yes, it was New Year's morning, float's new day begun, float's new leaf turned over, float's new reign and regret.

For only a moment were such premises afoot, parade premises. The moment they arose they subsided. Melrose was back to being itself as on any other day, Djband a sandwich man pacing the sidewalk, a modest parade if it could even be said to be that—no barge, no float, no roses. No sandwich board either, Djband quickly decided, lifting the sandwich board over its head and lowering it to the sidewalk, propping it against the newspaper vending box.

Rained-on parade was the theme but Penguin, stepping forward, would have to do with it only ostensibly, obliquely, bending away from it as what he had to say built. "I want a front-row seat at the Apocalypse," he said, quickly correcting himself. "No," he said, "I meant to say at the Apollo, James Brown on his way up, in his prime." "In his prime," Djband chimed in and Penguin went on, "I want to have lost someone or to sing and scream and shout as though I had. I want shout to mean to run around in a circle, led by immanent splendor's allure."

"Immanent splendor's allure," Djband agreed and echoed and Penguin continued, "I want the rump of the cosmos in front of me, barely up against my nose or a bit farther away perhaps, all but in touching distance, infinitesimally out of reach. I want to call out to it, calling it Regenerate Rose Reborn." Djband echoed and agreed again, "Yes, Regenerate Rose Reborn." Nose wide with cosmic whiff, cosmic what-if, Penguin stepped back and again blended in.

Before Djband could do what it would do next, Drennette stepped forward, cosmic vamp and commanding virgin rolled into one. "Yes, do remember," she agreed and exhorted, "how the smell of the cosmos's behind pervades all extension, how the smell of cosmic loins penetrates all space." "Penetrates all space," Djband thought to echo and agree but quickly thought better of it, remaining silent as Drennette, noticing the withheld echo and agreement but not needing it, continued, "Do remember how these two smells enter your nose and take hold of your scrotum." It was a footnote, a blurb, an outburst, a balloon. Djband withheld echo and agreement again. Drennette stepped back and blended in.

Djband reeled and staggered, all but overcome by wafted cosmicity, up-from-under pitch and posteriority, belt and bouquet. It was a ploy, a feinting play on exhaustion, even so. Drennette, Penguin, Aunt Nancy, Lambert, Djamilaa, and N. were each only a face on the wall Djband was, the wall Djband affected it was, the exhaust wall it earlier staggered along but now steadied and took inside itself. Immured against hearded audition, a wall against rained-on parade, Djband took a stand and stood tall against critical caption, the review's upstart balloon, cartoon acuity.

What Djband would have done next had briefly been put on hold by Drennette's impromptu boast (which is what, underneath it all but not so underneath after all, it all was). Reeling and staggering standing tall, it did now what it would have done next. It issued a collective, composite swipe of sound aimed at wiping the slate clean, a return to pre-caption premises, an airy gesturality or gist it wanted to say was what life itself is, an airy gesturality or gist gotten or gotten at by nothing quite like music, albeit to say so, to go from wanting to say, was to tie up with tar-baby balloon, tar-baby boast, as though Drennette had simply jumped the gun.

Drennette had in fact jumped the gun. That there was a gun to jump tempered Djband's recoil from cosmic waft. Reeling and staggering standing tall as though she'd held a finger out to be sniffed, a finger it knew underneath it all was coming, Djband issued a funky-butt, low-register burst, Mingusesque, a second swipe of sound, going the other way. This was also, it seemed it wanted to say, what life itself is.

Such expounding upon life, oblique though it was, attracted a crowd. Passersby stopped and looked on. They stood a short distance away, staring at Djband, able to read its thoughts evidently. They heard the music Djband inwardly rehearsed evidently, nodding their heads, popping their fingers, patting their feet. Yes, this was life, they seemed to agree, the what-is of it.

Djband knew there was no wiping the slate clean but made as if to do so anyway. Accretion was all, it knew, whatever would-be cleansing wipe a further murk or mucking up, palimpsestic supplement, palimpsestic struff. In this case, funky-butt struff spoke directly to the claim of a "détente between containment and contagion" the review advanced, agreeing with it only to complicate or contaminate it, wipe running one with swipe in more ways than one.

Palimpsestic add-on plied boast on boast, waft on waft, whiff, what-is, and what-if rolled into one.

Palimpsestic struff was nothing if not infectious. Several of the onlookers who'd gathered began to dance, squatting low to the ground at points, letting their asses graze the sidewalk. Reveling in rump cosmicity, they delighted, they let it be known, in having asses, delighted that there were asses to be had. Close to declaring ass what-is's what-if, they drew short of that, lifting skyward from the squat's low point with a pelvic thrust, saying something like what they begged off saying. Lee Morgan's "The Rumproller" had nothing on what they did or on the music they heard or thought they heard Djband rehearse.

"I want not to have seen it all," Djamilaa stepped forward and said. "I want not to have seen this movie before." "Not to have seen this movie before," Djband agreed and repeated, part antiphonal add-on, part set-aside. Djamilaa paused.

"I want," Djamilaa went on after pausing, "the clean slate I know we can't have. I want the meat of our being here truly met, true meet's tally, no mere funky-butt largesse." Djband agreed and repeated, "No mere funky-butt largesse." Djamilaa's advancing meat, meet, and romance (cosmic tail, cosmic tale, cosmic tally) went on with her saying, "I want the rose's perfume where pendent cheeks meet, funk sublimated upward, astral crevice, crease." Djband not only echoed and agreed, "Astral crevice, crease," but added, "Ass as in astral, amen." Djamilaa stepped back, again blending in.

The more booty-invested of the dancers, hearing Djamilaa's admonition, dialed it down. A couple of them stopped dancing altogether, stepping back into the crowd, content to nod their heads, pop their fingers, pat their feet.

The now more precisely calibrated serenade made it crystal clear that Djband was no Parliament, no Funkadelic, no Zapp and Roger—crystal clear even as it grew to be pearl opaque, for the review, irritant pebble to Djband's oyster, was coming to be accreted over, contained, gotten over, a tribute to palimpsestic add-on, palimpsestic struff, stick-to-itiveness. The music grew to be pearly smooth as well as pearl opaque, much less bumpy than funk.

It was now a precisely telepathic serenade, the heard rather than hearded audition every band so deeply wants. Sensing this, Djband saw no further need for the sandwich board and picked it up from where it lay propped against the newspaper vending box. N. stepped forward to flip it inside out so that Mingus's words no longer showed and then stepped back and blended in again. Djband again propped it against the newspaper vending box. The blank sides of the two boards glared in the sun.

The crowd of onlookers had grown larger, all of them nodding their heads, popping their fingers, patting their feet. Looking out at Melrose, Djband saw that traffic in both directions had slowed, drivers and passengers looking over at the goings-on around the newspaper vending box, Djband telepathically holding forth, the onlookers looking on. They too, the drivers and passengers, looked on, nodding their heads, popping their fingers, and (Djband imagined rather than saw but couldn't have been more certain) patting their feet.

Parade was back. The cars, vans, buses, and trucks proceeded at parade pace, not so much cars, vans, buses, and trucks as floats, titrating, ever so exactingly, the ideal roost and repose Lambert had adumbrated earlier.

Parade was indeed back, as much on the sidewalk, it turned out, as on the street. Emerging from the opening between the two boards of the sandwich board was none other than B'Loon, out in the open for everyone to see—the eyelashes hovering above the head and brow, the poorly defined limbs and extremities, the wistful, noncommittal mouth and all.

B'Loon, small at first but steadily inflating, grew to be as big as the giant balloons at a Macy's Thanksgiving Day parade, rivaling Superman, Kermit the Frog, Snoopy, and the rest, floating high above the sidewalk, lifting.

Everyone stared into the sky at B'Loon drifting higher. The crowd of onlookers on the sidewalk stared skyward, as did those in the cars, vans, buses, and trucks, leaning out their windows and bringing traffic to a stop. Djband as well stared skyward. Was B'Loon's lift mere exhibition or possibly more, possibly exorcism? It was hard not to wonder.

B'Loon floated higher and higher. Heads tilted farther back and hands became visors as B'Loon drifted higher, everyone more and more straining to see as the image got smaller. Less visible the farther away it floated, B'Loon soon couldn't be seen at all. Thus it was B'Loon exited the house the intersecting avenues could be said to be.

For a long time after B'Loon floated out of sight everyone kept looking into the sky. The crowd of onlookers on the sidewalk stood staring skyward. Traffic remained at a standstill, those in the cars, vans, buses, and trucks continuing to lean out their windows looking up into the sky. Djband continued looking up as well.

Everyone went on staring into the sky, lost in thought. It had all been only a bubble, a moment in the sun, a quick boon, barely embraceable, blown up to be let go.

6.XII.83

Dear Angel of Dust,

I was trying to call back time. The time I was trying to summon I'd in fact found distressing at the time but I was trying to bring it back nonetheless. I put two records on the record player, Etta James's *At Last!* and Bobby "Blue" Bland's *Two Steps from the Blues*, records that had been staples during the time I sought to call back, certain Sunday afternoons when I was a kid and my mother would play them again and again. She would usually have played Mahalia Jackson and the Five Blind Boys of Alabama in the morning, music that I heard as pretty grim, going on about a life beyond life as it did. That by itself was enough to pervade the house with a heavy mood, a mood Bobby and Etta not only kept going but took deeper come afternoon. I understood—or felt, if not exactly understood—that theirs was an even more somber church.

It was always as if time had stopped. The music and the mood brought everything to a standstill, causing me the kind of unease I'd later read Melville write about suffering during calms at sea. The music or the need for the music seemed to come out of a suspended state of some kind—not only to come out of it but to usher us into it, if or as though we weren't already there. But we were already there and always there it said or made it seem. That we were, the sense that we were, hung heavily over everything.

The music and the mood took my mother to another time and place, it seemed, a time and place given over to reflection as it touched on regret. She'd sit nursing a drink, a sad, distant look on her face, beset by some deep-seated sorrow. It was a sadness I couldn't keep from getting to me, a disappointment she appeared to feel not only with her own life but with life more generally, a disappointment that boded well for no one's prospects. She'd stack the two records, listening to the first side of one followed by the first side of the other, then turn them over to hear the two other sides and when they were finished turn them over again, start over again. She'd play them again and again—two, three, four, five, or six times. It was hard to miss the mood or what it meant. It hung heavily over the house and over the afternoon—heavily over the world, it seemed. When I went outside to find my friends and play, it went with me.

It was the same when there were people over, when my mother sat not alone but with company, one or both of my aunts, a friend or a neighbor or a few. When they got to drinking and talking loud and laughing, with Etta and Bobby in the background, they couldn't fool me. I knew it was a ruse. I knew adult life was no fun, life was no fun. Neither my apprehension of the arrest underlying it all nor my distress was diminished by their festiveness. I knew Bobby and Etta were the truth.

Those afternoons, whether sullen or festive, filled me with desolation and dread. It's odd I'd want to retrieve them, but I did. Day before yesterday, Sunday, I played the two records. I hadn't listened to them in ages. Right away they brought those afternoons and all the feelings they were filled with back. I'd forgotten how many of Bobby's songs are about crying, forgotten the reliance on strings throughout Etta's album, forgotten the poetics of plea winding through both. It was a world of adult longing the two albums conjured, a world of desperate affirmation where there was affirmation, one of dejection more often. I listened to them repeatedly just as my mother would, putting side one of *At Last!* on the turntable, followed by side one of *Two Steps*, then side two of *Two Steps*, followed by side two of *At Last!*, then starting again with side one of *At Last!*

I didn't set out to write a new composition when I did this, just to see if the music could return me to a certain mood and moment, just to relive, if I could and to whatever extent I could, my mother's blue Sunday afternoons. I did indeed call back time, did manage to recapture or be captured by those earlier afternoons, desolate and dejected as they were. It's almost as if I so succeeded in doing so, fell so deeply into that early apprehension and dread, that I had to write my way out of it, come up with a piece that, touched as it couldn't help but be by Etta, Bobby, and my mother's blue-Sunday distress, would take it to another place. In any case, I started the piece on Sunday, finished it yesterday, and we took it up today at rehearsal. I'm enclosing a tape. I call it, as you can see, "Some Sunday," meaning to draw on the utopic senses given to Sunday by Etta's "A Sunday Kind of Love."

The title echoes Duke's "Come Sunday," of course, but it was actually Monk's "Children's Song" I was thinking about, the rendition of "This Old Man," the traditional English nursery rhyme, that he plays on the *Monk* album. I wanted a folk song–sounding or a children's song–sounding phrase repeated on piano throughout, a simple, "childlike" melody built on an emphatic key variation. Djamilaa, as you'll hear, delivers on that in a big way, drawing out the phrase's evocation of childhood by seeming at times to take a learner's tack, a beginner's tack, mock-awkwardly "losing" the time only to regain it. Drennette's reliable conga throws that all the more into relief.

Please pay close attention to Lambert. He's the lead voice throughout on alto, Penguin on bari and me on trumpet offering choral support. Lambert's sound on alto tends toward tenor, without, of course, being tenor. I wanted that. "Bruised bell," I leaned over and whispered into his ear right before we hit. He got a gleam in his eye and he grinned. As you'll hear, he brings out the hollow the horn ultimately is, exacting a haunted, harried sound recalling John Tchicai somewhat. He plays hurt, I like to say. Hurt in his case, however, gathers an extrapolative whimsy, a wistful élan holding heaviness at bay, hailing some Sunday, soon come.

As ever,
N.

Glow Little Glowworm
John Crowley

SPRING CAN REALLY HANG YOU UP *the most,* Stan found himself
sing-humming as he turned off the highway and started up into the
hills, but actually it wasn't a sentiment he could say he felt. It was
certainly spring, and fully so, nothing missing to make a late April
day: The willows were green, tossing their long hair in the light airs
like teenage girls just shampooed and proud of their tresses; and the
sky had adopted that new blue; and the rushing brook by the road-
side undercut tussocks of new grass, where tiny flowers white and
blue sparkled as he wheeled by; and birds, and all that. *Robins building nests from coast to coast.* Beautiful and gratifying it was, but Stan
didn't feel the overwhelming relief and thanksgiving he once would
have, that sense that what was happening to Mother Nature was
happening at the same time in his own breast. It seemed to answer
no deep need, lift no particular burden. Just another nice day, better
than a bad day. A *very* nice day. Like so many demanding delights
and pains, victories and defeats of past times, springs were coming
and passing too quickly to engage him full force. Like a film on fast-
forward. Hadn't it just been Christmas? Stan was, he pointed out
again to himself, getting old.

Also it was still bright day, daylight saving time, when he turned
in to his own driveway at workday's end. Terry, his wife, stood as
though stoned or stunned amid the flower beds, holding a rake; around
her other tools—a hoe, a grubber, dirty white gloves—like an allegory of the season. She lifted a slow hand to Stanley as he got out of
the truck, seeming as full of the day as he was not, a mild grin on her
face: but she was ten years younger.

"So how did that house look?" she asked as they went inside
together.

"The strangest thing," Stan said. Terry washed her hands, letting
tepid water cascade over her fingers for a long time. "It looks fine
from the outside. Appealing, actually. Three stories, nice porch,
though it's wrapped in plastic sheeting just now, you know, for
winter. Original shutters on all the windows. Big garage with an

99

upstairs room I haven't seen yet."

"Marketable?" Terry asked. Stan sold real estate, mostly houses, all through the Hills, and had since he took an early retirement package from his downsizing plant.

"Well, I don't know." He looked in the refrigerator for last night's bottle of Muscadet, still half full, and pulled the squealing cork. "I told you it was lived in by these two brothers, right? For like forty years. Just the two of them. Neither ever married. It had been their parents' house. But over time—this is what the present owner says, he's a cousin who inherited the place, the only relative left—they became estranged or, I don't know, fell into some kind of enmity"— he laughed, and filled glasses with gurgling wine—"and it got, I guess, worse and worse over time, but neither was willing to move out, and so what they did was to divide the house in half. Not horizontally, you know, by floor—vertically. They put up walls to divide the space, divide even the rooms, the kitchen, into two spaces, so they would never have to see each other. They divided the staircase in two."

"The staircase?"

"With a sort of flimsy two-by-four-framed Celotex wall, right up the middle of the central staircase, so each one could get to his own half without seeing the other."

"Oh God. How sad."

"In the kitchen," Stan said, "you could see that one brother had put down a fresh layer of linoleum—but only on his half."

"It sounds awful."

"It is. I mean it wouldn't take much to at least get rid of the dividing walls, but the whole place still isn't going to be particularly aesthetically pleasing. As you can imagine."

"And one of them couldn't just leave? Or both, and leave it all behind?"

Stan shrugged elaborately, how would he know. "Solitaries," he said. "Apparently."

"Doubletaries," Terry said. "Alone together."

Stan looking at his wife holding her glass of wine thought he was right, spring was doing her good. Some sort of dry, gray quality that had been in her face much of the winter had been wiped away; she looked moist, bright, like a. Well, like a flower or new leaf. He laughed again, this time at himself. "Strange," he said.

Terry was Stan's second wife. His first had been a years-long puzzle and grief to him, consuming him and then building him up again like a bonfire only to consume him again, even long after they divorced. He still dreamed of her sometimes, dreamed of her turning away from him in contempt or boredom, naked or malformed or not herself. He was Terry's second too, her first a fine attentive guy who just one day silently decamped, leaving her with two kids, eight and eleven. They got divorced by mail. Stan in certain clearheaded moments saw that it was the two kids—both brown eyed, both witty and wise, self-sufficient but still somehow empathetic to an old fart like himself—that he had fallen in love with, childless himself, and his firm love for them had won him Terry: no surprise. He and she had been married fifteen years. Both the kids still lived in the Hills, not too far away.

"So how was the doc?" he asked her.

"The doc was fine," she said, her slow smile that seemed more teasing than it usually was. "Has a new receptionist."

"I meant," Stan said, "how did it go. Did she, you know. Have anything to say."

"Not really. Have to see how it goes. She thinks it's going fine so far but if there are side effects or whatever then you adjust. Up or down."

Terry had begun a regimen (as the doc called it) of hormone replacement therapy. Not as old as many women who began on it, she'd been suffering from menopausal symptoms since before fifty, and lately they'd got insupportable; she was continually uncomfortable, constant hot flashes, her tender parts dried like an apple (she said), and her moods black or violent. She hadn't been on it long, and said she already felt better. Remarkably better.

"Did you ask your question?"

"Which one?"

"You said you were going to ask if you were just supposed to go on taking these things for the rest of your life. Put off menopause till the grave."

"I wasn't going to say that."

"Well."

"No," said Terry. "I didn't ask. But I do wonder."

Days were getting longer, but so nowadays for Stan were nights. Not that they took any more clock time, but that he experienced more of their passing than he used to. No more now the closing of the eyes on the darkened scene and then opening them again on a brightening one. Now night came in parts, or acts: First, grateful slumber

coming easily and right off; then a muffled ballet of shifting positions
vis-à-vis partner, doing her own dance to find comfort. Realization
that he is in fact wide awake, as though it's day. Lying then on his
back, arms under his head, looking into the night sky of the ceiling;
speculation on the day passed and the one to come; sleeping again,
but soon startled awake by strange groans of pain or anguish—just
his own snores, or Terry's, who never used to snore. Awake again,
though his Indiglo watch seems to assert (hard to read without reaching for his glasses) that night's got hours left to go. So: one half hour,
examination of conscience; one half hour, political debate with
wicked fools; random memory shopping, listening to Terry's soft
steady passage between dream states, lucky her; then sudden blinking off without noticing. Dreams, which when he awakens seem to
him the point of the whole exercise, like a boring novel's finally getting under way. Tonight featuring a gripping story of adultery, not his
own but a woman's, whom he encounters in her huge, drab, crowded
house; she making it clear he is to come to her. Her husband or con-
sort just leaving her bedroom as Stan approaches, catching Stan's eye
meaningfully or threateningly as he departs; then Stan wafted will-
lessly in to where she kneels on the bed, and without preamble
embracing her, madly reckless, in that certainty of wild desire that
filled his wet dreams back when he had had such.

He woke erect and astonished.

Terry was restless beside him, which was probably (along with
that dream embrace, he felt its force again) why he'd awakened. She
rolled his way. Her skin was hot. Day was growing blue. She moaned
softly.

"Hot flash?" Stan murmured. His hand against her told him she'd
pulled off her pajamas in the night.

"No," she said. "No. The meds stop them."

"Oh, right."

No panties even. She rolled away from him again and Stan turned
toward her, his nakedness (he never wore nightclothes) against hers,
inserting his knees in the hollows of her knees but tucking that
weirdly persistent boner out of the way so as not to prod her rudely.
She drew his arm around her and slept again.

These last years they'd mostly given up on sex, it had too often
ended in nothing but her discomfort and his discouragement, and
they'd rarely felt the compulsion to set the whole float in motion.
Stan thought that she'd mostly risen to it out of a willingness to
meet his need, but if that was chiefly Stan's reason too—to meet

what he thought was *her* need—then it didn't have much of a basis. That was sad, but in a way seemed less dreadful than a younger Stan would have felt it should be. It was a lack. Sometimes Stan felt guilty that he didn't feel as bad about it as he should have; felt guilty when he found himself believing that there were more important things in a marriage, in their marriage. He wondered if Terry felt the same way. It was hard to bring up.

It was also true, and seemed sweet but strange, that since this unspoken truce or abatement, they had come to lie more often in one another's arms: front to back, as now; or her head on his breast, leg over his, warm breath on him. More kisses too. He slept sometimes wrapped around her; in former days he'd never believed he could sleep in such a way, like some god and nymph in a painting, but it turned out he could. As now he did, dreaming.

"Pheromones," Harry Watroba told him the next day.

Stan had been trying to remember the name for those chemicals that aren't smells but come in through your nose, or your sense of smell, that cause emotional reactions. Aggression. Arousal. Harry knew the word: Words were, as he said, his business.

"That's it," said Stan. "Pheromones."

Stan was selling Harry's house lot, which was not far from Stan's house in the Hills. Harry's house had recently burned beyond salvation, a sudden fire that was due (the fire chief told Stan, for his information, since he might in his business have occasion to warn home owners) to old paint cans and thinner collected in the basement. The land should be worth quite a bit, but even after the remains of the house were removed there hung over it a sorry and maybe repellent air of ruination and loss that kept even cool-hearted bargain hunters from making an offer that Harry and his wife—now ex-wife, Stan was given to know—could accept. Now and then Stan ran into Harry in the city, as he had this afternoon at the ice cream shop, and caught him up on progress, if any, or just talked. Harry knew a lot of odd things, not just words, and Stan enjoyed listening.

"In India," Harry said, "there's a kind of firefly that fills the trees at a certain season. Of course you know that fireflies flash in order to attract females."

"Glow little glowworm," Stan said.

"These fireflies all flashing on and off. Then as the pheromones connect, this is hard to believe, they begin to synchronize. More and more, until all the fireflies in one tree, in two trees, a line of trees, all flash at once, like caution lights. On. Off. On. Off."

"Insects," Stan said. The hairy antennae of moths are for picking up pheromones: He remembered that.

"Well, how about this. Did you know—it's a well-attested fact— that women in a girls' dormitory, say at college, crowded in together, will gradually synchronize their periods?"

"Really."

"What could it be but pheromones, chemical triggers?"

Harry dabbed his mustache with a paper napkin. He'd ordered a root-beer float and was addressing it with a kind of complex interaction that took into account its impressive size and his own slight one, wielding spoon, straw, and napkin in turn like a matador with cape and sword. Around them the kids from the local high school swarmed from table to table, in a pattern like the dancing of bees, expressive probably of impulses and hierarchies Stan would never know. Even when he'd been one himself he hadn't been aware much of such things, and these anyway were beings of a different order than those he'd known then. This one, young breasts hiked up by a bra that maybe was like one from his youth but quite clearly on show, straps visible on her brown shoulders; her tummy already brown too, and the bones of her hips rising out of her low-slung pants. Life's a beach, the bumper stickers said; he guessed they were dressing for it. He looked away. Harry hadn't.

"Harry," said Stan. "Don't do that. They'll catch you."

"Right," said Harry, and returned to his float. He appeared not to feel reprimanded. "But really. She's chosen to dress that way. What's she expect?"

"Well, they're not dressing that way for *you*," Stan said, laughing. "Not for some dirty old man."

"You're right," said Harry mildly. "Somehow I can't help it. I feel compelled. I feel a sense of loss if I turn to look at one passing me in the street and find she's gone, got away, turned a corner or whatever. One gone forever."

"One? One what?"

"Oh, you know. A missed opportunity to mount."

Stan laughed.

"Just doing my job," Harry said.

"Your job?"

"As a male. Listen, if we male mammals didn't think about sex almost all the time, and if our senses weren't preternaturally attuned

104

to the nubiles, well think about it. We wouldn't be here at all. We humans."

"But, Harry, you're not mounting them," Stan said. Harry was a man of Stan's own age, or older. "Are you?"

"Of course not. I don't even dream of trying. Still." He drank, the straw rattling the last of the creamy liquid at the bottom of the glass. "I feel compelled to assess. Add them up. I don't know—I think it's like counting coup."

"What's that?"

"The Plains Indians," said Harry, adopting the manner of a kindly teacher, "thought the height of bravery was to encounter an enemy, and instead of killing him to ride up close enough to give him a little tap with this special stick. The other guy was *out* then, out like in a game, humiliated, defeated. But no harm done. He was *counted*. See?"

Stan sort of didn't. He didn't think as Harry did, though Harry wasn't the only man among his acquaintance whose eyes tracked the passing scene that way. Yet just now, today, here in this shop, he felt moved: moved not in the sense of touched or affected but in the sense of being transported or carried. Carried along. He remembered what it had felt like when he was a boy, chivvied and pushed around by ardent feeling—"remembered" it in the somatic way of feeling it newly here and now. Maybe it *was* the pheromones, the massed pheromones of all these nubiles. Harry'd told him that "nubile" only meant "of marriageable age," but wouldn't that mean "putting out pheromones" too?

Why today so strongly? Just spring, he guessed.

That night Terry wanted to have the bedroom window open, though Stan thought it would be too cold by the wee hours; she insisted. When he woke later on in the usual way, he lay a long time and felt and listened: all those night noises, birds and animals and cars passing and the little river rushing through the town, that hadn't been heard in here for a long time.

Terry moved beside him in wakefulness too. He took her hand, turned his head toward hers on her pillow; she turned to him, her face too dark to read.

"The isle is full of noises," she said. "Sounds and sweet airs, that give delight and hurt not."

Stan at first heard "The aisle is full of noises," and ruminated a while to make it come out right. "What's that? Shakespeare?"

She didn't answer, only swept aside the blankets and rolled herself against his cool flesh. She kissed him, he her. Then in sudden wondrous certainty he enfolded her, and she opened her legs to admit him. It was so easy and unimpeded that he might have thought of it as *dreamlike*, like his dream of the night before, except that it was entirely actual, and Stan wasn't thinking; within minutes they were both crying aloud, barking almost, clinging to each other as to a lifesaver, or two drowners each mistaking the other for a lifesaver. It didn't last long.

For a time they lay damp and embracing, panting a little. Stan laughed. He hadn't laughed after sex in years.

"God," Terry breathed. "God, I thought you'd never."

"What. What."

"I just thought you'd never, never get." She swallowed, overwhelmed, full of liquid—he could hear it. Never get it? Never get over it? Around to it? Never get it up? How long had she been waiting, knowing that he didn't know she was waiting? For a long while she wouldn't release him. Outside the bugs and beasts seemed to have fallen silent, shocked, but Stan could hear—returning him to the world—the far-off rattle and wail, far down in the valley, of the only night train.

When morning came they awoke and almost without a word started again, as though it were a thing they did, night and day, morning and evening.

"Is it these medications?" Stan asked her afterward.

"Well," she said. She looked . . . he wouldn't have said "radiant" because that was just too, too what. But still. "It's what she said, the doctor, that it would help with, you know, the lubrication."

"A well-oiled machine," Stan ventured.

"Well, not just that, though," she said. "More than that."

"You mean, they're doing more than that?"

"I guess."

"Pheromones," Stan said. "I think you're putting out like clouds of pheromones."

"What," she said, raising herself on an elbow. "You mean you wouldn't want to just on your own?"

"Well, it's part of wanting to. Isn't it? Putting out the signals. Why people do and don't. If *you* want to, *I* want to, and vice versa at the same time." That, Stan thought, if true, was what Harry Watroba had left out: how men too put out the signals, and how theirs work or don't work on the women. If true. "A feedback loop," he said.

Terry laughed a little, indulgently, seeming to be of a mind to dispute all that but not caring to make the effort, not important, and lay back on the pillow. "Stan, if pheromones could do it, I'm awash in them all day at school. Ninth graders. Industrial strength. You can actually smell them."

"You can't, really." Stan had looked them up on Ask Jeeves. "They come in through your nose but you can't really smell them as a smell."

"You go into my lunchroom," Terry said. "The gym when there's a dance. Or a game. It's like a wall." She put her hands behind her head. "I have to get up," she said, and fell asleep.

That night, again. And though he warned her laughing not to expect much, they managed it: *three in a row*, she said, gleeful, triumphant even, something he hadn't done for thirty years: lying loose limbed grinning and feeling that hot strain of fine exertion as in days gone by, maybe he ought to watch it, though, at his age. His father had once told him that every orgasm shortened your life. He'd died at ninety.

That triple play was never repeated, but the medical miracle, if that's what it was, ran on unabated, May into June. If they bustled out of bed in the morning without locking gazes, embarrassed or confused at the new abundance, they'd find themselves at cocktail hour grappling on the couch and talking dirty. His dreams were filled with lush gardens where dewy infants played, glamorous hotels full of sophisticates who swapped teasing jokes with him in grand salons. After some more tests Terry was switched by the doctor to a patch-and-cream combo, lessening the dose, and they waited to see what effect this would have, but it seemed to have none, to subtract nothing. They laughed about her youthful reblooming, like a nature film run backward. She cried a lot too, "tears, idle tears," she didn't know why, she smiled while she cried, as though leaking more than weeping.

It was exciting and challenging, all he could say clearly about it, reaching for words he might have used at his old job to describe the prospects of a position to a new hire. Hilarious even, to be thrust again into the ninth-grade can't-wait mode, holding hands at the supermarket and making out in the car parked in front of a house awaiting them as dinner guests. But while Terry rebloomed, Stan remained what he was. It began to happen that they'd begin all right, but then get somehow out of sync, moving at odds like two cars in a thriller trying to shunt each other off the nighttime road; or he'd find himself at a loss, straining and tense, a tug struggling to turn a barge. Surely he had once known how to please her, he thought she'd liked what he did, what they did, was *grateful* even he seemed to remember, as grateful as he was to her. He could remember that she'd liked it, but maybe he couldn't remember now what *it* was. Certain nights or mornings he was made to reexperience another part of the old days: the engine failing, the movie stuttering to a stop and going dark, the silence in the balled-up sheets.

"I guess I just can't do it that often," he said to her. He remembered the rule for these moments, you never said *I'm sorry*. He was breathing a bit hard, was that OK? He put his hand to his heart. She was smiling, not altogether kindly. Hot and humid today, it looked like.

"What's the problem?" she asked. Another thing you weren't supposed to say.

"It's my age, Terry. It's nothing about you. Nothing about wanting to or not wanting to."

"You should just relax. You get upright, I mean uptight." She yawned.

"I'm not uptight. I'm an antique."

"Oh, you're not an antique yet, Stan," Terry said. "You're still just a collectible."

"Anyway I don't have the whatever," Stan said. "Or anyway not as much of it."

"Well," she said. "Come here a minute." And patted the place beside her on the messy bed.

Since so much of his work had to be done on Sundays, Stan had elected to give himself Wednesdays, or at least Wednesday afternoons, off. By Wednesday most people have stopped their Sunday-paper dreaming about houses, and not yet started on the new weekend's possibilities. It didn't always work out for him, but on this Wednesday nobody called that he wasn't able to put off. By three he was able to toss his old and rather disreputable canvas bag of clubs in the truck and go out to the country club, as free as a retiree or a dentist to hit the fairways on a weekday afternoon.

Though he had gone away for some years in the long search to find or build a life that would please his first wife, Stan had been born and grown up in the Hills and along the rivers that ran among them. At the little country club, not so much club now as public amenity open to all, Stan had learned to play by caddying for his father, watching and learning, and the game of golf had retained from those days a kind of educational quality, involving the passing on of skills and the continuance of rituals; even now Stan, when reaching the bubbler on the eighth tee and swallowing water gratefully, couldn't help wiping his chin with the back of his hand and saying, *Ah! Adam's ale!*—as his father always had done just there.

He'd just as soon have played nine holes by himself, but as he was teeing up at the first, his doctor appeared beside him, having finished nine and lost his partner, and he joined Stan for a second nine. Stan liked doing well at games but was profoundly uncompetitive; he usually went for Personal Best, which in practice meant not paying a lot of attention to the score. Today, though, an unusual intensity of feeling about the game grew up in him by the third hole, a flame of need to win. Gripping his driver, his chin out, he eyed the girt doctor, bald dome already tanned (Florida, no doubt) at the tee, impatient for his own turn to dig fiercely into the ball. Freshly angry at his irremediable slice. Dr. Beha won handily. The day stayed glorious.

"So can you explain something to me?" Stan asked with a little laugh as they sat in the empty clubhouse bar.

"Sure. Unless it's a medical question. For that you'd have to see a doctor."

Stan ignored that. "My wife, you know, Terry, has started this hormone replacement therapy. She's sort of early menopause, and it seemed like, well anyway the gynecologist recommended it for her, and it seems to do her a lot of good."

"Uh huh." The doctor seemed to be aware of what was coming next.

"It's improved her, well, her hot flashes and whatnot."

"Uh huh." Dr. Beha sipped his drink, unwilling to be helpful, Stan thought. "And your question is?"

"Well. It's certainly changed the. Well, the family dynamic." He laughed, swallowed beer for cover, wiped the foam from his lip with a cocktail napkin.

"It does do that," Dr. Beha said. "Surprises people. Spring awakening sort of thing. Is that what you mean?"

"I guess."

"Young again in all respects."

"Well, that's I guess the problem."

"Aha."

"I mean *she*'s young again, but I've stayed the same."

"How old are you, Stan?"

"I'm sixty-three," Stan said; as usual it felt like a lie. He looked around the bar and not at the doctor. "This has all taken me a little by surprise, to tell the truth, and at some times I haven't risen to the occasion."

"It happens," said the doctor. "Just advancing age, I'm afraid. But you get concerned, naturally. Which doesn't help. It gets so you can't think about it even for a second or it fails. *Everything OK down there?* And woop." He illustrated with a drooping forefinger.

"Not that you can't get it up," Stan said. "You just can't count on it."

"It's common. Would like me to refer you for counseling? Sometimes a change in attitude."

"Hm." In the tiles of the bar floor a comic stick-figure golfer was inlaid, his legs tangled, wild swing gone wrong, club bent, divot flying. It had been there for decades.

"Are you interested in trying an erectile-dysfunction therapy?"

"Well, I hadn't. I mean."

"You know about Viagra."

"Well, of course. It's unavoidable. Bob Dole on TV. Jokes everywhere."

"It is," the doc said, folding his hands together somewhat medically or professionally, "a really quite remarkable breakthrough. Actually does what it claims to do, safely, few or no side effects even, for most men. It's like an elixir of life, the thing the Chinese sought for centuries, drinking gold or eating mummified tigers' hearts. Old men are taking young wives off to Niagara Falls, knowing they can perform. Stan, I've prescribed it for paraplegics, and it's worked for them."

Stan, looking within, as people tend to do in the course of conversations like this one, sensed an odd vacuity or absence down there where the old tripartite unit ought to be felt. Maybe he really was getting superannuated. *My get-up-and-go got up and went.* Or maybe his wasn't the attitude that needed changing. "It seems, I don't know, a little shaming," he said.

"Oh cut it out, Stan." Dr. Beha finished his drink, shook the ice in the glass, and sipped again; then put it down. "Come by the office," he said. "I have a passel of free samples. Try it out and see if it's for you."

*

Stan knew himself to be a hypochondriac, or at least frequently fussed about his health, but his hypochondria consisted mostly not in talking himself into believing he was sick but in obsessive recountings of the good reasons why he surely wasn't. Sort of a glass-half-full hypochondria, Terry thought. The idea of a new pill with sudden major effects and unknown consequences set off his alarms, even as it stirred his hopes. Dr. Beha said—as on an afternoon of the following week he handed over a blister pack of four pills—that he understood porn stars used it, to reliably get wood (their term, good Lord). Dr. Beha had a way of being cheerfully frank, no harm in it really; before he'd done Stan's vasectomy long ago he'd told him that it was usual at this point to give some psychological counseling, but he'd never seen that it made a difference, and so with Stan's permission he'd skip it.

Get wood. Of course Terry couldn't be told; he'd have to keep it from her; she mistrusted any resort to pills, she hadn't wanted the HRT at all until her situation got so bad, and he was sure a sex pill would turn her off entirely, she'd be disgusted with him for falling for it. But then what if he had a bad reaction in her presence, fainted or something, how would he explain? What if he counted on a night's certainty of its working and then it didn't? How much could worry about the pill's effects actually offset the effects? Driving the deeply familiar curling road back up from the valley in the softening light, Stan fell into that late-afternoon flow of word and image, logic-less and dreamlike. He pictured himself, or saw someone like him, fired up and eager, grinning as he popped his pill, young wife in a baby-doll so happy for him. Nubile. His old-coot habit of letting something lie where he'd put it down, or putting it carelessly away, on the assumption he'd remember later what he'd done with it—what if he hid his new pills and then forgot where he put them? Hold on a minute, honey, I'll be right there. Stan turned downward onto the village road, feeling like the town would be shocked to know what he had in his pocket, if it could only know it; but why would he think that? Maybe it was in every old couple's bathroom drawer.

> *Said the old coot on his way to Niagara*
> *To his young wife, "Just can't wait till I shag ya!"*
> *He's sure he'll get wood!*
> *But his memory's no good*
> *And he'll find he forgot the*

Stan swerved a little sharply to avoid an SUV appearing before him at a turning, using up more than its lane. Ugly fat-ass cars, why were they so selfish, alpha male at the wheel, Stan realized he actually knew the guy. Heart quickened, he settled down and made it home.

The pills were pretty things, kite shaped and softly rounded, a dusty azure. The long, microscopically small list of warnings and side effects stirred Stan's fears, he'd need a magnifier to read them, and so didn't. He revolved in his mind the right time to swallow the first of the pills—apparently it took a while to kick in, so to speak, longer in fact than any sex act he was likely to be capable of, hopped up or not, it'd be all over or given up on well before he got the help; he'd have to take it in anticipation, or expectation. Or hope. Would he remember that he'd put them in this old travel shaving kit? Some other place better?

"Hi, babe, you here?"

It was Terry, entering the house on little cat feet, she trod lightly on the earth, disconcerting sometimes actually.

"Yes! Be right there!"

"How was *your* doctor?" she called, coming closer.

"Oh fine."

"The thing you were worried about?"

"That? Oh nothing. He said treating it would be just a bother, it'll pass."

"Oh." Terry at the door of the bathroom regarded him, smiling just barely, her thoughts unreadable. She wore a loose cotton sundress he hadn't seen on her in years; once he'd told her he thought it was sexy, which amazed her. What was sexy about it? It was sexy, he'd said, because it looks like it would come off easily.

The summer solstice had passed but the sky was light till late, by now you were used to it as though it had always been so; the last dim blue at nine o'clock and then stars and then a golden moon appearing in their bedroom window as though taking turns coming on stage.

In the dark of the morning Stan got up to pee, and on an impulse dug out the pills from where he'd put them, and took one. He went back to bed and lay open eyed on his pillow, waiting. He heard thunder, or thought he did: trucks down on the road? No, there it was again, thunder, a low, far-off throat clearing. First of the spring. Harry Watroba had told him that in many American Indian languages birds are related to thunder. Because when they go away in the fall the thunder stops; it begins again when they return. Makes sense. Thunderbirds, arising at its rumble, up from the dark mountain's slopes into the red air. You could see, from these ramparts, the lightning dully flaring. No, said Harry: bombs. The bombs are falling out there, see, coming closer, the birds fleeing.

Stan awoke as though shaken, feeling weird, not himself, and couldn't think why. Ill? Fever? None of that.

Oh, yes, the pill.

He was erect, as often after morning dreams, but good Lord the thing was hard as a broom handle, feeling to his touch to be not his but as though affixed to him. It seemed to be of no mind to go down. Stan felt like giggling. And now what? Tap Terry on the shoulder, make her look?

She rolled over and woke. "Oh God it's late. I have to get up."

"It's Saturday," Stan said.

"Oh right. Oh good." She rolled back, and went back to sleep. Stan waited, sensing an impatience in his magic power, like it might evaporate if unused, but if it worked as promised he could worry about that and it wouldn't have any deflating effect, and so he didn't worry. For a time he lay quietly and listened to her breathe, wondering where she was and what she was doing. She had the most startling and unlikely dreams; sometimes waves of chills would pass over him as he listened to her recount one. *Eldritch* Harry called those chills. Awaking again from brief unconsciousness he snuggled up to her, and started in. "Oh," she said.

"Hi."

"Hi there." Smiling, a smile clear and open like her son's, just the same. Stan kissed her throat, touched her here and there, tried to assess the response he got. It seemed to be going well. Moist and open. Certainly his own side was good, no problem, he nearly laughed. He bent to her ear, whispered things, then gave attention to the parts of her he could reach, looked into her eyes. He was inside then and she was moving beneath him; she seemed, though, somewhat thoughtful or doubtful; he wondered if it was possible for her to discern a difference, from within. She twisted, grasping his arms in her hands, working. All right, he could probably go on for hours, but it began to be clear she wasn't writhing in delight or the struggle to get off. No, definitely cooling, like molten lava in a nature film ceasing to flow, turning dark and stony. Now she was actually pushing him away, teeth gritted and a wild sound in her throat. What? What? She pushed his chest, pulled back her hips, and Stan popped out, astonished, horrified; his knee slipped off the side of the bed and he went over, barely managing not to land on his ass, though ever after when these events passed through his mind it seemed that's just what he'd done.

"What the hell, Terry! What are you, what."

"I *hate* that," she said, eyes alight with anger. "I hate it when you do all that. You know I hate it."

"All that *what*?" Stan cried. What had he been doing? Just the stuff, the usual stuff. Sex.

"All this mem-mem-mem," she said, waggling her fingers in the air to suggest the inappropriate or witless or insensitive things he did and had done and done. "All this, all this myeh-myeh-myeh you do." She gave up and fell back against the pillow. "Ack." For a while she only lay staring at nothing. Her rage and her bareness consorted badly. It was the first time in all the years they'd lived together that she reminded Stan of his first wife.

"I *try*," he said, "to do what you want."

"You never knew how to do what I want."

"Never?"

She said nothing.

"Why didn't you tell me?" Stan asked. He stooped to pull on his shorts. Tucking in the rejected tool, its head now hanging, but still engorged. "Why?"

"I did tell you."

"You didn't tell me," he said. "You only ever told me—sometimes you let me know what you *didn't* like. That's different." He waggled his fingers at her, miming her disgust. "*No mem-mem-mem.* Well, I don't know what you mean by mem-mem-mem," he said. "Myeh-myeh."

She laughed a little, relenting, and moved within the sheets.

"You can't teach somebody something by negatives," he said. It was a key doctrine of Human Resources, in which he'd worked so long. Terry'd heard him say it before, he wondered now how often. "Can't get somebody to do right by telling them they're wrong. There are too many ways to be wrong. Over against one way to be right."

"I didn't want to teach you," she said. "I wanted you to just know."

Breeze lifted the lace curtain at the window in a gentle arc.

I wanted you to just know. Well, that made a kind of dreadful sense. She said no more, he sat down on the bed, the two of them in

114

the strange air of having said unsayable things.

"This was all along?" Stan asked.

Terry sighed, covered her eyes with her hands.

"I'm not inside your head," Stan said. "I mean there's always a certain amount of guesswork. I did what I thought you liked. I can't feel the effects of it."

"I'll make coffee," Terry said.

Stan watched her climb from the bed, draw on a pair of sweatpants and yesterday's shirt. She wasn't looking his way. "I love you, Stan," she said at the bedroom door, but not looking back at him where he sat. "I always will."

He listened to her feet on the stairs, the old stairs crackling faintly as she went down.

What the hell, he thought, now what the hell. What an awful thing to do, no matter what. Wasn't it? A wave of some black cataclysmic kind seemed to rise up behind or before him, then recede, but not vanish, no, not ever after now.

He noticed that the daylight growing in the room seemed a strange shade of blue. Just spring advancing? No, couldn't be. He turned on the lamp by the bed, and its bulb burned blue as a Christmas light.

What was he supposed to do, was he supposed to do something, mend his ways somehow? What were his ways? *Myeh-myeh-myeh.* He clapped his cheeks in his hands and muttered what Terry's books called an imprecation. And then another one.

Once in a college art class that Stan had taken for no real reason, the students were told to hold up their portraits or self-portraits to a mirror; when a portrait was reversed you could suddenly perceive all its faults, the face hilariously misshapen, wall-eyed, broken-jawed, all wrong. It was hilarious and also mortifying. Also you didn't know what you were supposed to do to fix it, or, if you began again, how to do it better. Just keep trying, the teacher said. Give up your preconceptions and really look.

He didn't want to have to do that. Wasn't he too old to? He sat immobile a long time, the unreal blue day brightening; not thinking, not doing anything. His organ had recovered from its humiliation and Stan lowered his shorts to look at it. Wood. It rose from its base at an acute angle he hadn't seen since adolescence, as though straining to take off. Big help you are. The odor of coffee arose from below, as it always did, as it would.

*

Stan worked hard that summer, his busy time. The dot-com bust cut into sales but not as badly as everyone feared; in fact, for some reason or reasons that Stan couldn't analyze, house prices around the valley went up, and the eagerness of buyers was apparently intensifying. Sometimes Stan felt the unnerving sensation of big engines revving up in preparation for a takeoff, and wondered what he'd got himself into: He hadn't expected his postretirement job to be a demanding one, full of urgent labor.

Even the house that Terry had come to call the Tragic New England House, the Ancient Wrong House, tall gaunt place divided in half by warring brothers, began to get offers. The cousin who'd inherited it brought in a crew at one point and ripped out all the two-by framing and the plasterboard and Celotex so that potential buyers could at least see what they had to work with. Stan stood within it looking at the unscabbed wounds where ceiling plaster had come down with the divider walls, at the floors tiled or painted to the middle and no farther, a black line of mildew where for years the wall had stood. Forty years of not parting, not reconciling either, getting by, and now the sad makeshift exposed for what it had been. Tragic New England, land of embittered making do. A living-room window had been split between the halves, rag of curtain on one side, narrow blind on the other; whole now, showing a nice view of the river, actually.

It sold for not a bad price, just as summer was ending.

Through this time Stan took no more of the blue pills; it was obvious what the drawback of these was, which the manufacturers had certainly foreseen, grinning as they watched their sales climb: If worrying about performance is what's diminishing your performance, and the pill fixes that, then worrying about how you'd do without the pill would be enough to cause failure all by itself. So better stock up, take 'em early and often.

No. And for Stan the necessity to keep them secret only increased the impossibility that they'd help in any way with the big process that it seemed he was on, that he and she were on, which couldn't have a secret plot, a concealment, at the heart of it. So it was up and down—as Stan would reply (wry smile) to an imaginary questioner who asked how it was going: up and down. Whatever it was that somehow made them a bad match in bed meant it continued knotty, sudden surprising ardor sometimes that wiped away worry, at other times ambivalence and what-now-ism that produced cascading failure, sometimes worse than that, a sadness never expected, not by him.

Meanwhile Terry went on flourishing, growing younger, wrinkles erased, skin gleaming; watching her undress and hop into bed was like one of those movies where someone's sold her soul to the Devil and been given things she shouldn't have, delighting in her new and luckier self while the audience knows it's going to turn out very badly. Though to say that out loud to her without being able to laugh with her at it too—he couldn't. The HRT regimen might keep her in youthful shape for years (*years:* like a bell the word struck in his breast) and so they had to *work on their marriage,* anyway he had to. It was as on your wedding day when you say solemnly that you will take it on, whatever comes, without knowing really what you might be assenting to: as though all the labor that followed that day now lay once again ahead, all of it to be done as it had been done but done differently.

He was trying to change his life. He knew he must. His good, beautiful life.

Another bottle of Muscadet, another incipient spring. She was preparing to make nettle soup for the first time, an experiment that Stan was enthusiastic about, anyway he was on her side concerning it. She wore gloves, to keep from stinging herself.

"So the doctor," Terry said. "There's news."

She wasn't looking up from her washing and cutting, which made Stan attentive.

"About HRT," she said. "It seems there are research results."

She moved without haste around the kitchen. It was a talent she had, in tough moments, to keep at work in that calm tea-ceremony concentration, even as she said hard things.

"What results?"

"The HRT increases risk of breast cancer, Stan. Like quite a bit. In fact they had to put an end to this huge study because the number of women getting breast cancer went over the stopping boundary."

"Stopping boundary?"

"That's Dr. Florenz's words. She said: Too many. So you stop the study."

"OK," said Stan cautiously. "And this means . . ."

She turned on him then, ceasing her all-alone-in-a-room mode. "It means I have to stop. Everybody's going to stop, unless they don't care about the risk."

"Well, of course," Stan said. "You have to stop."

"So that's the answer to the question," she said.

"Which question?"

"Whether you take them your whole life long. Now we know."

Stan made the *tsk* sound, blew air, drummed his fingers on the tabletop. Complications, well, you could have guessed. How strange that medicines could do this, he thought, upend your life, float your boat, upturn it too. He cleared his throat to say something about that, then didn't.

"So it's back to the hot flashes and all?"

"I don't know. I guess. What a drag."

She went back to cutting nettles. "The cooking takes away the sting," she said, as though to herself, gathering the green stuff. Stan watched her, her beautiful absorption. "I don't know how."

He felt a sudden spasm of grief for her, all that youth regained, only to be given up again, maybe, probably. Would that reborn sex drive now evaporate?

Not the time to raise that point either.

He lifted his glass and looked through the pale wine at the pale sky scribbled on by still-leafless branches. Perhaps, without a choice, they'd soon be returned to the calmer waters they'd been sailing on not long ago. Which actually he couldn't think would be so bad. But—this occurred to him—it might seem bad as a place returned to rather than a place arrived at. Returned to with new *baggage* as they said now.

You can't unknow something you have come to know.

He thought: How is it that we live in ignorance of the things to come? We don't anticipate, but we can't, can we? A treatment, a pill advertised everywhere, a gift, or not. For the first time Stan seemed to see that these developments ever arising in time weren't opening outward the life he would live, he and she, as once they had seemed to do; instead they were filling it in, gradually or abruptly, like discoveries filling in the blank *terra incognita* in an old map; and they would go on doing so, lands and peoples, until in the end there were none.

Landscapes on a Train
Cole Swensen

The window is the open train; open now on whiter air. Other measures drift.
Quick the lost, and how the window fast. How the green comes back
Unnumbered strong. Sweep the green off sky. Far name lies on fair. Holding
Fair the stone wall unwound. What green does to rain.

Landscape is always also a painting. Again a small thing broken that is
Breaking from hand to hand. Each one. Passes to another the growing,
That then gone is one more. And then one more station on a station of roads.
And is crossing a road, a sequence of goings. The road in its offing, along
Which belongs, a church made of far distance severs. And one more station
Standing on the platform. And so we say no other we. Are the line of poplars.
It is the poplars that populate the field.

Disappearing road. It curves and goes. Cows along a road. A graze it comes.
Close if green grazes the eye. Why this precise or this green or this exactly
Why. Who was a landscape painter who. And then suddenly died. Had in hand
A whole, and so aloud that all the birds flew off they arise, they alive alive oh
They cry. And off they are from there, neat stacks of cut wood in the middle
Of the glade. The red bricks of rare houses climb.

A church in the middle of a field is a tree. Is big and that's older. Was killed
By a river. Some body of water in the corner of an eye. Poplar poplar.
Hundreds of swans. White is a minute. Is settling inward. In darkness is. A
Tiny gash. Swan in and swan all over. Light striking the arc of it. Or anyone's.
Or any animal is adamantly new. Emphatic crows in the field. Three of them.
Then thousands are the dark. Are alone the traveler folded. Intricate folding
Apart.

Light keeps up. Light on building, light builds on. On the inside of the
Window. And so the train hurries past black trees in their vivid tongue.
Cut clear in form. Most colors amount to this without names. It happens
In the sun and there is little else.

Houseboats on the green, the overhanging and embankment flashing. A river
Back up to the sky. Another boat going blue. Evening results in a motion
Of sorts a sort of splintering air. Lights in a train that passes its little windows
Through a sieve. Little houses in the sky. In the rails, verge. Flowers on a
Bridge. All white is one way back, all white birds. All white moves.

Old stone building on a hill already weight, is still some hill, a hill taller
Then and stone. Blind until gray until white. They felled the trees and left
Them lined up side by side a small white bird, a lamp in the other lost
And another, and then each one of the hundred yards apart lighting
The length of the river causing dark.

White gates standing open, open directly onto the river, river a bridge
In brick and stone and matching white boat, the boat takes part, creates
An equation that stands between boat and gate: an equivalence sealed
By a white horse running toward a white house, its front door open in the rain.

White arches along the river that is. A river having towns. They weigh it
Down. River of trees that return (nothing ever dies in the sun) made of
A collection of crows that cuts. Another small stream defines the green
Of the meadow that is. This. Meadow drenched in overmuch season extant
Season entire. And so the invented surface of water: effect of light. Bright
Wash across buildings facing the face across. A face is all that is crossed by
Light. As it hardens and shines.

Lights in parallel lines like trees but cold. Lining like roads the roads
Are gone. The trees on. And the lights turn on in long rows. Double rows.
Once there was. A swan lost on a road. And so on. A map on the wall
That forms the end of the train. We go on. In the other going more.

Little inlet, little coast and another both, whistle a train, long, a train
Is a sound is always by definition in the distance so those onboard are gone.
More pears that won't in exquisite cloud of white, off-white, off-cloud,
Standing cloud, cloud at rest and poise. And large. A large white bird, aquatic
Cloud along an inlet headed inward. With the silence of a window.

Blue heron in slow motion over half an ocean the ocean is slow and it rises
Blue wing gray against water, water is nothing in the sky but the swans one
Often alters among lakes and inlets let in an ocean thrown away again is
Water unnamed.

Marsh out of a rock hoed, marsh flush with rivers where a new stone fence
Almost glints which is all this sun on sun on water spills. White new greens
With that young light under trees a stone house underneath a magnolia
Nothing could not be a whole five of them for at least a day or so a day of
Them. The plums. Among. All flowering things sworn.

Tree broken. In half a tree. In half, a history will see all sorts in the dark, the
Sharp, to see a whole, and then why not the forest as day now falls. On two
Cows next to a flowering pear and a flowering plum. Which lightning might
Intersect. There always is a little slice. A matchstick. Falls as a reflection
Quietly perfectly burned all across the marsh another grave another yard
This one flowering as all coming down hard in the stones they can't avoid.

Woodland Pattern
Ted Mathys

Jack-snipe in stick shadow.
       Light failing to show against light,
dark against dark. When wide-eyed
      in oaks I praise the sun's

power to pervert a basic reality
      I pass from nakedness
into pattern. A copperhead waits
      in dry matted leaves.

Its black-and-tan crossbands
      in conflict have canceled out
boundaries of form. Effacement proceeds
      under circumstances wherein

such effacement serves the wearer.
      Come, Thayer, disgraced
father of camouflage, our animals
      have dismantled their silhouettes

but I'll stare at this oak canopy
      as your outline reappears, ghostlike.
The crown of a chickadee at nest hole
      just merged with the dark beyond.

After choice of position
     it's about discipline,
especially in snow, new tracks
     should follow existing tracks,

especially now. Exposed routes
     should never end in your location
but flower all over the tundra
     like a drunk midnight argument

or a statesman's arc diction,
     tensile, looping digressions
that drag us blind and euphoric
     through the history of coloration,

desperate to entertain ourselves
     with the promise of a woodland hut
constructed with resolute authenticity
     inside a claim to innocence, a hut

we'll never find, draped as it is with earth,
     grass and gravel woven into shrimp nets
in a Greek key pattern, to hide us
     from our predators, who are us.

"His experiments are jugglery,"
      Teddy Roosevelt says of Thayer
to inaugurate the public
      denigration. "He'd put a raven

in a coal scuttle and call it concealed."
      From the sanitarium, Thayer knows
the ex-president can't see
      that a colorblind wolf quick behind

a prong buck sees every sky as white.
      He can't see how the buck's white
rump tufts arc high when it leaps
      a fence and the wolf loses his quarry

to clouds. Never will the president concede
      that nature endowed the flamingo
not with vanity but an ability to melt
      into blood-orange sunset.

The failure of American imagination
      is the failure to see that the opposition
has had as many centuries to perfect his part
      as the predator to perfect his.

Grassland zebras and vessels at sea
            can't hide. It's better to cut
the bearer of color to pieces.
            Thayer wanted to evade

the torpedoes of expectation
            and knew that to do it openly
would kill him. His grand plan
            was to live in Emersonian ideals

and love with a trueness of form
            concealed in the commonplace.
But there are some ideas so big
            no amount of patterning

can render them invisible.
            Warships and forequarters
painted in black-and-white dazzle stripes
            slice a single visible thing

into meaningless fragments. He confused
            expectations about his type,
course, and speed, but his desire was too big
            to hide where the water meets the sky.

The poem needs to teach you
        how to read it, the painting
how to see it. Unless of course
        you are not the final destination

and the work's role is not to enable you
        to read what otherwise might be
illegible, but to prevent you from seeing
        what otherwise might be visible.

"Use of course not these crude colors,"
        Thayer implored Churchill,
"but the exact tones of the suit I now send."
        The poem is a uniform

though its form is not uniform
        but patterned—woodland,
desert, snow—each work adopting
        a specific position within a culture

already congested with meaning.
        Each word a splotch, within which
is condensed the entire set of concealed
        principles that supports it.

The phantom army constructs a jeep
       out of burlap. Under a vault of stars
Ellsworth Kelly and fellow conscripts
       arrange inflatable troops

in action poses along the Rhine.
       They are sworn to betray,
even to superiors, nothing more
       than a serial number. At dawn

Germans waste their attention
       and ammunition on the rubber
regiment below the railroad bridge,
       who hiss as helium flows out of them

and they collapse back into artifice.
       Statistics say phantoms saved
10,000 men, which was no consolation
       to the real infantry, who believed

that after months of the unspeakable
       they were at last being relieved
by the nameless new Americans
       looming about town.

None of this applies
      to cave crickets. White
in the absence of light,
      as if buried beneath the earth's

surface is the terminus of color.
      As if there were one rogue star
straining against the cover of darkness,
      and the new century's project

was to pull its hue up through
      everything we touch. Sugar
refined from cane to brown
      to white. Wheat

milled of bran and germ, bleached
      into a white bread sandwich.
Clay passing through kiln fire
      to end in a porcelain bowl

in the museum's glass vitrine. Eyeing
      the pure object, I was confronted
with my reflection and wondered
      if he was a man I'd ever known.

Ted Mathys

To fully embody an art
        requires disembodiment.
Warhol's final work was
        Self-Portrait in Camouflage.

Floating in a lake of black ink,
        his pallid Polaroid head
is silk-screened militaristic
        olive, black, and gray

in Woodland Pattern.
        He glares through the forest
of color, directly at the viewer,
        as if to play on the platitude

that we will exit just as we came—
        across his boyhood skin
side effects of scarlet fever
        once spread blotted splotches

of pigment in Woodland Pattern.
        Portraiture demands interiority.
Camo is soul in surface.
        The legacy lies in reproducibility.

"Nothing is what it seems"
        is exactly what it seems,
a primary cliché
        skating over the ambiguous

pronouncements of poets.
        Thayer places a mirror
in a depression in snow.
        To the Society's amazement

the reflected blue sky
        dissolves into the color
of the shadow in which it was nested.
        "Cliché has genesis in fact"

is in fact a metacliché,
        doubling the virtual
into an authentic experience,
        negatively. "I miss you."

The red flash of a cardinal reveals
        for a moment the hidden
surface of the mirror.
        Some call this phenomenon love.

When the world falls apart
      it falls into usable parts.
Modern camouflage was pixilated
      by an act of Congress.

In the lab at Fort Benning
      the digital was found
superior to the traditional. It mimics
      dappled textures and boundaries

found in natural settings. Sound
      and scent can bend
around corners, but sight is straight
      and quick to the point:

The values of digicam are discrete
      but they add up
to a continuous system. We were
      culpable, living as we were

in words. In the alphabet's
      limited data set
continuous emotion is perceived.
      All poems are digital.

Concealing coloration
      in the animal kingdom is
elegy. When his first son dies
      Thayer renames

his second son after Emerson,
      retreats to document how
the partially terrestrial grouse
      is crisscrossed to erase

what is near or distant. When infant
      Ralph Waldo dies
Thayer hikes Monadnock
      for the hundredth time

ripping out handmade signs
      that read *private property,*
stay out. He forgoes his beloved summit
      for the interminably various

forest floor, where he can feel
      the spirit of those creatures
he knows are all around him
      but he will never see.

Seven Stories
Jedediah Berry

HEIST

THE KIDS AT MY MOTHER'S HOUSE are new recruits, and I don't know their names. They look tired in their heavy wool coats. One kid examines maps pinned to the basement walls. Another shovels coal into the furnace.

I take a call from Central on the old basement phone. The handset is big and heavy in my hand. After the usual exchange of codes, the line goes to static.

A truck pulls into the backyard. Canvas flaps over its sides don't quite conceal the rows of old toys. And inside those toys?

I run outside; the kids have to stick to their own mission. The driver is hitching my grandfather's old lawn mower to the back of his truck. When he sees me, he leaps into the cab and drives off, spilling teddy bears and board games over the lawn.

I'll have to take the glider, but that's on the top floor. I head up the stairs and into a border outpost. I fish through my pockets for my papers. They're missing, but nobody asks for them.

At the top of the outpost, we have a view on the whole valley. G is seated at the control panel. He pours me a mug of coffee and shows me the morning papers. Page after page of black-and-white comic strips: nothing but pratfalls and big sandwiches.

SILENT AUCTION

I descend from my mother's attic and emerge in an alleyway in Damascus. S warned me not to come alone, but this is a quickly developing situation.

A fish merchant stands at the corner. I can see rubies through the mouth and gills of one fat trout. "That one," I say, and the merchant flips the fish into a paper sack. A few rubies spill, but the merchant doesn't see. I pretend not to notice. There are more gems inside the fish.

I glimpse S through an open window above. A burlap mask has been placed over his face, but I know him by the scar at his right temple. How did they find him?

The merchant starts yelling. I don't have any cash, and he doesn't want the junk from my mother's attic. I leave the fish and run, but the man keeps yelling. A boy on a bicycle pulls up beside me and says in English, "Cover's blown."

Spread out across the central square are pieces of furniture from my brother's bedroom. Local men and women, along with a few tourists, examine the desk and the dresser, the shelves, the nightstands. They stick small black numbers to the things they want. My brother is asleep in his bed. He always sleeps late.

The boy on the bicycle gives me a handful of the black numbers. I go to my brother and kneel beside him, but his face and hands are already covered.

APPOINTMENT

The city was an American city. The car, an American car. The girl was missing, and time was running out, but it felt good to use a stick shift again. I wondered how that monster of an engine sounded to the dreams locked up in their houses.

At the top of a hill, I let the engine idle. A pool of water glistened among the trees at the bottom. The agent known as the Dandy was seated on a bench, feeding scraps of bread to the moon's reflection. He saw me and waved, a little uncertain.

I thought: *No more deals. No more dancing around time bombs.*

I threw the car into gear and drove down the hill, straight at the Dandy. The car shook at the descent, at the power of its own functions. I heard bolts loosening. Pressure gauges hit the red. The rearview was an earthquake.

The car came apart, each piece moving out and away, an assembly line in reverse. I plummeted with only the steering wheel in my hands, but I could still hear the radio. Ornette Coleman was tearing a saxophone to pieces.

The Dandy, terrified, held up a sheaf of documents. I wasn't close enough to read them. I was getting closer.

SHOTS FIRED

I'm called in after hours, to inspect the damage. The detective pulls the coat out of the closet with a gloved hand, shows me the bullet hole in the right breast. The hole is charred at the edges.

"No blood, though," he says. "No body."

I tell him that's because no one was wearing the coat at the time.

The detective is stunned. I show him the back of the coat, the hole there. And the hole in the coat hanging behind the first coat. And the hole in the next coat. Seven coats in all, and the bullet passed through each of them.

"Monsters," the detective says.

I point out a hole in the wall at the back of the closet. "What do you see through there?" I ask him.

He puts his eye to the hole and says, "It's like the goddamn bottom of the sea."

I instruct him to keep watching, then head into the hallway. It's good these local yahoos called me in. They have no idea what they're dealing with.

S is beside me, opening a can of peaches. "Status?"

"We're looking for a room with deep cover and underworld ties. No windows, one door, full lockdown."

S drops a peach slice into his open mouth, like he's a dolphin, and he's also feeding the dolphin. "Worse than I thought," he says. "You suspect—?"

"The American? Yes. Or one of his chief agents."

S's eyes go wide. He sets the can on the floor and leaps down the nearest laundry chute. There are protocols.

I put my ear to the first door that gives me a suspicious look. I hear gurgling, and maybe a Teletype transmission.

I kick the door down. My brother is here, asleep in bed. I check him for wounds. He's covered in popcorn, but no sign of struggle.

The only light in the room comes from the aquarium. I hunker down and peer into its depths. Past the dancing seaweed, over the ramparts of the plastic castle, a school of silvery fish zigzags, then disperses. And there it is: a little gray submarine, motoring over the sandy floor, pinging us with its sonar.

"Mom?" my brother calls, half awake.

I wave my hand at him, shushing. He sits up and looks at me. He doesn't know my code name, and calls me by the one I grew up with.

I wave at him again, signaling for him to cut it. The submarine is moving fast now, and the pinging grows louder. Its torpedo bays are open.

I grab my brother and pull him under the bed. "Cover your ears!" I tell him.

We stare at the shadows moving across the floor, and wait for the blast. I pray that the detective is still watching. That he trained himself never to blink.

PAPERS IN ORDER

The documents we'd stolen were printed on jigsaw puzzle pieces. E had been working since dawn. She was good, but at sundown the puzzle was only halfway finished. I ordered takeout, opened two beers, and joined her at the table.

S came into the room, swinging his arms. There were tears on his cheeks. "My father," he said.

I put my arms around him. I didn't want him to knock over the puzzle. "I know," I said, though I didn't know.

"He just got smaller and smaller," S said. "It went on for weeks. We lost him in the laundry."

I squeezed his shoulders. "Who did this?"

E got up from the table. "It was the American," she said. "He did the same thing to my sister."

We geared up. Our motorcycles were old but they sounded good. Without speaking, we knew where we were headed. Those blinking red lights on the horizon: a communications array! How had we never noticed?

We took the tunnel under the river. Soldiers stopped us at the checkpoint halfway. None of us had our papers. S said, "Now we'll see who's been feeding the piper."

A soldier brought us a flask. "Drink from this," he said. "It keeps the weather out."

S and I took deep gulps, but E only smelled it. The soldier looked offended, snatched back the flask, and put his hand on the butt of his pistol. Then he looked at the ground and shouted, "*Schnell, schnell!*"

The tunnel was filling with aquarium water. Green pebbles, plastic mermaids, and crawdads oozed up out of the drains. We rolled out, and I heard E laughing. She'd made this happen, called it in days ago. The perfect distraction.

"I love you," I told her.

She couldn't hear me over the noise of the engines. "What?" she shouted.

"You can see Jupiter tonight," I said.

I pointed, and there it was. Big and orange over the clouds, watching us with its one weird eye.

AUDITION

Some local cops were behind my mother's house, shining their flashlights into the trees. They didn't have search warrants, and they hadn't bothered to knock. I put on my best suspenders and headed outside.

The cops had changed into civilian clothing, but I wasn't falling for it. I grabbed one of them and drove his face into the dirt. In high school he'd been a bully, or the cousin of a bully.

The other cops started backing away, like they didn't want trouble, but I went in swinging. I had the superior training. They went down before my fists could find them: I was blowing them over with pure rushes of air.

The last cop standing put his hands up. It was R. In eighth grade, we'd had a band together for a week or two. "Dude," he said.

I patted his shoulder, and we took the shortcut through the woods and headed downtown. I showed him where I kept my chopper. "Just one of the benefits," I told him.

We followed the Hudson River down to the city, flying fast and low. Trains swept by on the east side, and I knew that E was on one of them, preparing her mobile base of operations.

We landed in Brooklyn, and the party was just getting started. We were famous here! R got behind the drum set and the cameras rolled. Central would be furious with me for doing a video, but I needed a new cover.

An enemy agent I'd seen in Kabul months before was behind the bar. He nodded at me, not bothering to keep up pretenses. I said, "This your night off?" He poured me a double and then showed me the little vial of poison.

"Fifty-fifty," he said.

Too late to back out now. I downed the drink and closed my eyes, then opened them. The agent watched me, like not even he was sure what was going to happen. Then he laughed. "Get up there," he said.

R was already banging away on the drums. I grabbed a guitar, and wondered whether we had a bassist, whether our band had a name. I knew only three chords. The kids were screaming for blood.

THE AMERICAN

I remember how the American used to come around the house when I was nine or ten, blending in with my parents' friends. He drank beer in the kitchen, talking loudly about whatever game was on television. He always had a different job: construction, deep-river salvage, accounting.

I was drawing a lot of castles then. The American told me about the portcullis, the murder hole, and the oubliette. He knew so much! Sometimes he'd be up later than my parents, and sometimes he'd have a girl with him. I saw them on the patio out back one night, sitting together on one chair. He whispered something into her ear, and she laughed.

Once he took me with him in his pickup to get a pizza. He said, "Your mom was the coolest, back in the day. We'd drive around in that little car of hers, with the top down. What a lady."

I didn't know what to say, so I told the American that I liked his Superman T-shirt.

"It's yours," he said, and he took it off right there, craning out of it while he drove first with one hand, then with the other, blind for a moment. The shirt was huge and full of holes. It smelled terrible. But I'd said I liked it, so I had to put it on.

Another time, I came home from school to find the American at the house. No one else was there. "Let's walk," he said. We walked around the neighborhood. I saw friends in their backyards, and I hoped they didn't see me.

"I could use someone like you on my team," the American said. "I've got plans, big plans. There's a place for you, if you want in."

I didn't know how to refuse him. It was just like the T-shirt. I told him that I wanted in.

I went to meetings in the basement of the public library. Coffeemaker, a few people wearing ties, a few drifters. Maps on the walls, stacks of documents on a fold-out table. The American came sometimes, but usually he was too busy, and the woman I'd seen with him

139

on the patio ran the meetings in his absence.

We discussed pressure points, electrical systems, the benefits of meditation, propaganda, small island nations, archaic card games, chemistry, seduction, protection rackets, 1960s French cinema, firearms. I was always behind, and I had to pretend like I understood what the group was talking about. When I approached one of the other members of the group, the older brother of a friend, and asked him if he could help get me up to speed, he looked at me like I was an insect.

Eventually I stopped going to the meetings. I pursued other interests. For a while I played the recorder at historical reenactments. I went hiking and got lost on purpose, to practice my orienteering. The American stopped coming around, but as the years passed, I saw signs of his work everywhere. Few would have recognized his hand, but for me there was no mistaking it. It was there in the weather reports, in the stock numbers, in the comics. He sometimes appeared in newspaper photographs of politicians and business leaders, always at the edge of the frame.

Finally the other side reached out. Coded messages in snack boxes, windblown pamphlets on the sidewalk, smoke signals on the horizon: the usual recruitment tools. My training began in earnest. They knew from the start about my association with the American. I told them everything I could remember from those meetings in the library basement, but they either nodded like they already knew all that or told me that I'd probably been fed lies. That the American had foreseen even this moment.

Now we trace his movements by satellite, and by the subtle seismic activity he leaves in his wake. Sometimes it feels like we're making progress. Usually it feels like we're just the clueless guests at his birthday, the ones who weren't told it was a costume party.

The Superman T-shirt is still in my top dresser drawer. I haven't worn it since the day the American gave it to me, but I can't get rid of it either. Its smell grows more sour every year.

On the Monstrous

A Portfolio

Edited by Peter Straub

EDITOR'S NOTE

ONE HIGH POINT OF THE 2012 International Conference on the Fantastic in the Arts, held in Orlando every March and which I try never to miss, was an evening panel, on the last night of the conference, about the nature of The Monster. China Miéville, Theodora Goss, James Morrow, and I, along with Kelly Link and Suzy McKee Charnas, offered widely varying takes on the subject, and Bradford Morrow later asked me to request brief essays on the monster and the nature of the monstrous from various of the participants. Here are the intriguing results.

China Miéville   Theodora Goss

Peter Straub   James Morrow

Theses on Monsters
China Miéville

1.

THE HISTORY OF ALL HITHERTO-EXISTING societies is the history of monsters. Homo sapiens is a bringer-forth of monsters as reason's dream. They are not pathologies but symptoms, diagnoses, glories, games, and terrors.

2.

To insist that an element of the impossible and fantastic is a sine qua non of monstrousness is not mere nerd hankering (though it is that too). Monsters must be creature forms and corpuscles of the unknowable, the bad numinous. A monster is somaticized sublime, delegate from a baleful pleroma. The telos of monstrous quiddity is godhead.

3.

There is a countervailing tendency in the monstrous corpus. It is evident in Pokémon's injunction to "catch 'em all," in the *Monster Manual*'s exhaustive taxonomies, in Hollywood's fetishized "Monster Shot." A thing so evasive of categories provokes—and surrenders to—ravenous desire for specificity, for an itemization of its impossible body, for a genealogy, for an illustration. The telos of monstrous quiddity is specimen.

4.

Ghosts are not monsters.

5.

It is pointed out, regularly and endlessly, that the word "monster" shares roots with *"monstrum," "monstrare," "monere"*—"that which teaches," "to show," "to warn." This is true but no longer of any help at all, if it ever was.

6.

Epochs throw up the monsters they need. History can be written of monsters, and in them. We experience the conjunctions of certain werewolves and crisis-gnawed feudalism, of Cthulhu and rupturing modernity, of Frankenstein's and Moreau's made things and a variably troubled Enlightenment, of vampires and tediously everything, of zombies and mummies and aliens and golems/robots/clockwork constructs and their own anxieties. We pass also through the endless shifts of such monstrous germs and antigens into new wounds. All our moments are monstrous moments.

7.

Monsters demand decoding, but to be worthy of their own monstrosity, they avoid final capitulation to that demand. Monsters mean something, and/but they mean everything, and/but they are themselves and irreducible. They are too concretely fanged, toothed, scaled, fire-breathing, on the one hand, and too doorlike, polysemic, fecund, rebuking of closure, on the other, merely to signify, let alone to signify one thing.

Any bugbear that can be completely parsed was never a monster, but some rubber-mask-wearing *Scooby-Doo* villain, a semiotic banality in fatuous disguise. It is a solution without a problem.

8.

Our sympathy for the monster is notorious. We weep for King Kong and the Creature from the Black Lagoon, no matter what they've done. We root for Lucifer and ache for Grendel.

It is a trace of skepticism that the given order is a desideratum that lies behind our tears for its antagonists, our troubled empathy with the invader of Hrothgar's hall.

143

9.

Such sympathy for the monster is a known factor, a small problem, a minor complication for those who, in drab reaction, deploy an accusation of monstrousness against designated social enemies.

10.

When those same powers who enmonster their scapegoats reach a tipping point, a critical mass, of political ire, they abruptly and with bullying swagger enmonster themselves. The shock troops of reaction embrace their own supposed monstrousness. (From this investment emerged, for example, the Nazi Werwolf program.) Such are by far more dreadful than any monster because, their own aggrandizements notwithstanding, they are not monsters. They are more banal and more evil.

11.

The saw that We Have Seen the Real Monsters and They Are Us is neither revelation, nor clever, nor interesting, nor true. It is a betrayal of the monstrous, and of humanity.

Monstrous, Monstrosity, Monster, and the Little Man Next Door

Peter Straub

EXCEPT IN THE CASE OF the little man next door, the monstrous is where our suppressed yearnings take us, and the monster is the form they inhabit. While humanity is the sum of everything we have and are, monsters give us the opportunity of exceeding the human, going beyond it to occupy strangeness, grotesquerie, power, selfishness, para- or supernatural capacities, size, and massivity. And strangeness on the level of great size and massivity effects a dislocation and disorientation that can be both unsettling and joyful, though not at the same time.

I am interested in a fruitful disorientation produced by monstrosity, but I'm not at all immune to the shocks of mingled dread and pleasure experienced by the abrupt appearance on a movie screen of Godzilla, Frankenstein, Dracula, or poor Larry Talbot, the werewolf of Universal Studios. Monsters of a literal kind exist to be feared, worshipped, and destroyed. Although they have great metaphoric potential, they are not in themselves metaphors—to treat them as metaphors is to ruin their narrative capacities. It spoils all the fun too. You don't want to be deflected into hand-wringing over colonialism when you could be tiptoeing down a gloomy passageway with a torch in one hand and a sharpened wooden stake in the other, on the hunt at the beginning of the grand final movement. In such cases, even the desire for metaphor enfeebles.

Some might say: So you are asking us to behave as though we think these creatures are real? Well, yes, exactly. Behave that way, within yourselves. You'll get further. We are speaking of a shock, a moral shock, that at its best jolts you out of conventional perceptual habits and drops you in the midst of terror, wonder, awe. *This too exists, this out-of-scale strangeness. The world is wider, wilder, and less predictable than I ever knew.* This recognition is useful and true.

If an even momentary glimpse (as though, for example, through the window of your neighbor's house) of out-of-scale and terrifying

145

monstrosity calls into question a great many common beliefs and assumptions about the nature of physical reality—as though at best it momentarily reveals a contiguous world that is capable of disastrous leakage through the shared boundary—if, that is, this "glimpse" expands our notion of truth by revealing some of its components as (let's say, thinking about what we glimpsed through the window of the house next door) insufficient, certainties are shaken or detonated, security is exposed as a myth, and daily human life subject at least intermittently to a haunting sense of incompletion and provisionality. The question then becomes: Which kind of life and world do you prefer, the stable and known, or one in which fear, mystery, and a greater range of moral and intellectual speculation have become available?

We keep saying we prefer the first, and (leaving aside that guy next door) choosing the second. In a simpler, more straightforward America, urban arcades and small-town sideshows gave employment to bearded women, microcephalics, people covered all over with hair, people inordinately short or tall, the astonishingly obese, persons in fact with unusual deformities of every kind who earned a living by displaying their abnormalities to a parade of ticket buyers: the freakishness of actual freaks, both at a safe remove and right up front. The elephant girls, alligator men, dog-faced boys, and unsettling mutations in jars sent the punters home marveling, contemptuous, excited, disturbed, shaken. The carnival grotesque, a domestication of the monstrous, often included a geek, the original kind of geek, who did not obsess about Batman comics or Orson Scott Card novels but instead killed chickens with his teeth to earn money for the alcohol he needed to do his job. It is safe to say, I think, that in spite of my first sentence, nobody ever consciously yearned to be a geek.

Yet . . . would it not be possible to know, at the lower psychic frequencies, a perverse, half-fledged desire for the absolute moral freedom of such utter shame and degradation? Nothing more will be lost, nothing can be gained, and one consequence is an entirely sure-footed clarity. To be a professional of shame invokes a deep, essential paradox, that the systematic negation of hope automatically creates a profound dignity. (Dignity keeps on surprising me. The slave, not the master, possesses it, as does the silent beggar, and not the well-off citizen who strolls past without a sideways look.) The sideshow geek is not a monster, of course, for the same reason that the world's tallest dwarf is not a giant, no matter what he feels like when he gets home and locks his door. The scale might be right, but the size is all wrong.

Sideshow freaks evoke a complex, sometimes skeptical wonder, but they cannot inspire awe. Except within other sociopathic losers, neither can serial killers. Although I think both of these categories have so sidestepped conventional human patterns as to be approaching monstrosity, the freak via the grotesque, the serial killer through his negation of moral awareness, they become truly monstrous only when transmuted by imagination into some form scarcely recognizable, the Sasquatch, say, or the bloodthirsty giant at the top of the beanstalk. The sense of a kind of sublimity should never be too far from an actual monster, who by definition commits "monstrosities" and expands the boundaries of what we call the "monstrous," on a scale that obliterates or at least destabilizes previous concepts of what it might be possible to witness within a human life, also within human history. For me, the psychic conditions established by this sudden destabilization produce an ongoing uncertainty, insecurity, wariness, openness to the extraordinary, and suspension of formulaic assumptions that amount to a far more accurate response to the world in which—are you ready for this?—the man who lives next door is capable of doubling, tripling, quadrupling in size and becoming a creature of roaring darkness who snatches you up, secretes you in the folds of his rough, stinking garment, and bends over to whisper those fatal words all of them, every last one of the next-door monsters, is obliged by his nature to tell you: *I love you, love you, love you, and if you ever tell anyone about me, I'll be forced to kill you. Don't make me do that, little one. Understand? Because I love you so much, if you should happen to tell another single, solitary soul about me, I'd have to snuff out your miserable, puny life. I promise, before long you will understand. We love each other in this special secret way. You'll see.*

But you don't see, you will never see. You can't. You really just cannot do that.

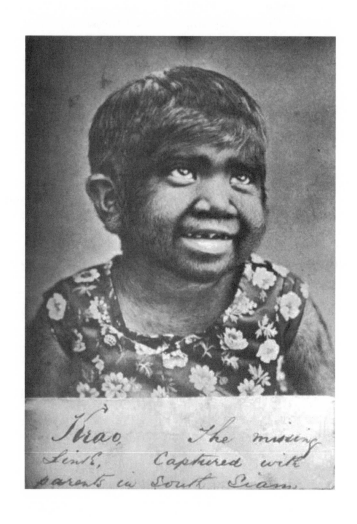

Krao. The missing Link. Captured with parents in South Siam.

Listening to Krao:
What the Freak and Monster Tell Us
Theodora Goss

I HAVE A FAVORITE MONSTER. Her name is Krao, and she was what scholars would now call a freak. It seems ironic that "freak" should have become a scholarly term, a technical designation for performers in the freak shows that became so popular at the end of the nineteenth century: men and women with congenital abnormalities such as Joseph Merrick, the Elephant Man; or Chang and Eng, the Siamese Twins; or Krao. After all, it is also the term of the school-yard bully: You're a freak! Like monsters themselves, it is double. It is both an insult that emphasizes the freak's outsider status and an acknowledgment of power. Although freak-show performers were social outsiders, they were also professionals who could gain a measure of social and economic power, directing their own careers. However, in the late nineteenth century, the heyday of the freak show, the medical term for those born with congenital abnormalities was in fact *monster*.

Krao is my favorite monster because she represents so effectively the central characteristics of the monster, while making us question our preconceived notions of monstrosity. Those notions have largely been formed by early twentieth-century movies: Our monsters are Boris Karloff's nameless creature, a lumbering corpse brought to life by Frankenstein; Bela Lugosi's Dracula, preying upon beautiful Englishwomen; and the Creature from the Black Lagoon. Based on movie depictions, we have come to think of the monster as frightening because it poses a danger to us or those we love. Even when we pity the monster, as in James Whale's *Frankenstein*, we agree that it must be dispatched. After all, it is a freak, an unnatural creation, whether of science or the supernatural. We use the term "monster" more loosely to refer to whatever frightens us: Hitler and Jack the Ripper are called monsters, and their crimes are identified as monstrous. That use of the term allows us to distance the dictator and serial killer from ourselves. He is not like us: Like Dracula, he is outside the natural order. However, as Krao demonstrates, the monster is a monster

149

precisely because we cannot distance it from ourselves. It is not outside the natural order but both inside and outside, both other and us.

Krao was about as different from the movie monster as one can imagine. She was first exhibited in 1883, when she was only seven years old, by the showman G. A. Farini. She had been brought to England from Siam, where she had initially been exhibited by her parents, who had found it more profitable to sell her to the showman. Her distinguishing characteristic was the fine, dark hair that grew over her body. Like Jo-Jo the Dog-Faced Boy and Julia Pastrana, the Bear Woman, both popular freak-show performers, she had been born with hypertrichosis, a condition that produces excessive body hair. But to Farini and his audience, she was half human and half monkey: living proof of Darwinian evolutionary theory. Throughout the years Krao performed on the freak-show circuit, advertising posters stressed her identity as the "Missing Link." She performed all over England and internationally. Monstrosity became her profession.

Nineteenth-century science is distinguished by a mania for categorization, a desire to understand nature and culture by dividing them into categories (geological eras, biological species, human races). Monsters are monsters precisely because they cross the boundaries of those categories, bringing their stability into question, so it is with trepidation that I offer a set of attributes that define and characterize the monster, attributes we can understand by considering Krao, as both woman and performer.

1. WHAT MAKES THE MONSTER MONSTROUS?

We are not so different from nineteenth-century scientists: We understand the world through categories, which are often oppositional. We distinguish good from evil, civilized from savage, human from animal, man from woman, adult from child. Perhaps it is because we are bilaterally symmetrical, divided ourselves into right and left. Traditionally, these oppositions have had cultural significance: The civilized man has been privileged over the savage, the animal, the woman, and the child, all of whom have been associated with the forces of unreason. These hierarchical oppositions underlie the identification of the left hand as sinister and the burning of witches, who were mostly women, by the Inquisition. They also underlie the British imperial enterprise, which sought to forcibly civilize supposedly childlike, animalistic savages—and when it could not do so, justified their extermination.

But monsters cross categorical boundaries. Frankenstein's monster has the intellect of a man and the impulses of a child, raging like a seven-foot toddler when his needs are not met. Dracula is female as well as male, reproducing through the vampire bite to become the mother as well as father of a vampiric family. The animalistic Creature from the Black Lagoon walks like a human being and falls in what might be love. Categorical boundary crossing, or hybridity, has marked monsters from the beginning. Classical monsters are either animal-human hybrids, such as the minotaur and sphinx, or combinations of animal parts, such as the chimera. Medieval monsters described by travelers to distant lands, such as the dog-headed Cynocephali or headless Blemmyae, also confuse categories, having the wrong body parts, or body parts in the wrong places. In their hybridity, these monsters symbolize a time before categorization: They stand for the forces of primordial chaos, which the hero and saint must battle.

Krao's performance also crossed categorical boundaries. Although advertising posters depicted her as a loincloth-clad savage, in her appearances she was often dressed as a middle-class Victorian child, with her arms and legs left bare to reveal their hairiness. Newspaper accounts stressed her perfect command of English and her good manners. These accounts involved a narrative of civilization. Although Krao had been born an animalistic savage, her time in England had turned her into a proper English girl. This narrative supported the British imperial enterprise and its underlying ideology—natives could be taught to be Englishmen. However, it also involved a boundary crossing that brought into question the distinction between civilized and savage, human and animal. What did it mean if the missing link could curtsy and say, "How do you do, sir"? One journalist, disappointed that she was not as hairy as he had expected, wondered who was the true missing link: Krao or the fashionably bearded Farini. The monster is monstrous precisely because, by crossing such boundaries, it reminds us that the categories are human rather than natural: that we have made them up, and that underneath lies boundless primordial chaos.

2. WHY ARE WE FASCINATED BY MONSTERS?

We fear the monster, as we fear Frankenstein's creation, Dracula, or the Creature from the Black Lagoon, but we are also attracted to it. That is because the monster allows us to escape from the categories that structure our understanding of the world. We are attracted not only to the monster, but also to what it represents: the chaos underlying meaning.

Perhaps that is why monsters have recently become romantic heroes. Jo-Jo the Dog-Faced Boy has been transformed into Jacob from the *Twilight* series, the werewolf who is a potential love interest. Dracula has been replaced by the rock star Lestat, or Edward Cullen, a younger, sparklier version of the vampire. These characters are not safer, more palatable versions of the monster: They are logical expressions of the monster's dual nature. Jo-Jo, in reality a Russian man named Fedor Jeftichew, performed with Barnum and Bailey, as did Krao later in her career. He drew large audiences and, although he barked and growled during his performances, was said to be as gentle as a puppy. The fascination with monsters exhibited by late nineteenth-century freak-show audiences resembles our attraction to the literary monster: After Dracula bites her, Mina is most horrified by the fact that she does not want him to stop. We are drawn to the darkness that the monster represents, because that darkness is also freedom from the constraints of our ordinary lives.

Audiences were certainly drawn to Krao: She became one of the most popular freak-show performers, and one of the highest paid when she later joined Ringling Brothers. As she grew older, her performances became more sexualized. Her costume was designed to reveal her hairy body, which implied her sexuality by reminding audience members of the hair that proper Victorian woman kept hidden: both pubic hair and hair on the head that was customarily pinned up. The long hair on Krao's head was deliberately left down, signaling her sexual availability. However, that sexuality was complicated by her beard: She was both feminine and masculine. The sexuality she represented was transgressive, both because it crossed gender boundaries and because her hairiness implied that she might have been produced by the mating of a human being with an ape. As an adult she received marriage proposals, as did many freak-show performers; however, she chose to marry Farini.

The complicated audience response to Krao is the response that monsters evoke: We do not simply fear them. We also want to see and touch them. Sometimes, we fall in love with them. They represent both what frightens us and what would transform us if we gave in to their allure. Dracula's bite turns Lucy into a monster, but it also frees her to express her repressed desires—to be the self she has always been, under her civilized veneer.

3. WHAT CAN THE MONSTER TELL US?

The monster always *means*. Its body is a text that can be read, but how it is read depends on the reader. For *Beowulf*'s medieval compositor, Grendel represented outer darkness, the chaos that exists outside the social order of Heorot. For John Gardner, he was the outsider who could perceive the underlying corruption of society. In early nineteenth-century political rhetoric, revolting Jamaican slaves were compared to Frankenstein's monster for turning against their masters. In our own cultural discourse, he has become a symbol of science run amok—we protest genetically engineered Frankenfood. The monster always exists in a narrative, but the narrative changes over time.

Krao existed in a narrative: late nineteenth-century evolutionary theory. Within that narrative, she was a reassuring reminder of how far her (white, hairless) audience had evolved from its animal ancestry, but also a disturbing reminder of its connection with that ancestry. Her narrative was made explicit in advertising posters that proclaimed her identity as a Darwinian missing link, but could be rewritten in accounts of her performances by journalists who pointed out that she was not particularly simian—just a polite little girl with a lot of hair. For modern scholars, she has a different significance, revealing the ways in which British imperial ideology was both supported and undermined by freak shows. Krao's hairy body always *means*, but what it means depends on the significance we assign to it; its meaning is produced by social and historical context.

Although the monster exists in a narrative, it is rarely given a narrative: In literature, as in real life, monsters are rarely allowed to speak. Frankenstein's monster is a notable exception. By allowing her monster to tell his own story, Mary Shelley implicitly asks us to consider whether he is a monster at all. Her intention in this respect was likely political: She was the daughter of two parents centrally committed to giving the voiceless a voice. But in general, the monster means *for us*; it is rarely permitted to create its own meaning. If

153

there is one important change in our cultural approach toward the monster, it is this: that in contemporary literature and life, the monster is more often allowed to speak. The vampire Lestat gets to tell his own story, and our own freaks, human beings with hypertrichosis or other congenital abnormalities, appear on talk shows. This openness to the monstrous is part of a development in our attitude toward what we define as other.

I wish Krao could speak. There are questions I would like to ask her: What did you see when you looked in the mirror? Did you miss your parents, your country? How much control did you have over how you were advertised, how you performed in front of an audience? Why did you marry Farini? Did you want children? Were you afraid that they would be hairy, like you? But Krao is as voiceless now as she was in her lifetime, available to us only through accounts and images.

We need to be careful in how we apply the term "monster." We should not apply it sloppily to the latest serial killer or dictator. Such misuse implies that human beings do not imprison, torture, or kill wantonly, although historical evidence shows us that indeed they do. It conceals the true horror of the serial killer's or dictator's acts, which is that they are committed by human beings just like us.

Monster needs to be used in a more specific sense, to identify what crosses the boundaries between self and other, stability and chaos. Then it can become a useful term that helps us to examine and interrogate the boundaries themselves. And we need to listen to our monsters, to hear what they are telling us. Once we start listening, we can learn what the monster sees in the mirror and hear the other side of the narrative: the story of Grendel, or Frankenstein's monster, or Krao. That perspective can allow us to reevaluate how we assign designations such as monster or freak. It can expose categorical boundaries as human constructions and assist us in creating a society that is more accepting of difference—in which we recognize that the division between self and other has always been arbitrary, and that the freak and monster are always ultimately about us.

A Taxonomy of the Teratoid:
Self-Aware Monsters, Oblivious Fiends, and Elusive Demons

James Morrow

IF I RAN THE UNIVERSE, a book critic would never presume to dismiss *la littérature fantastique* as puerile, jejune, or escapist before consulting with those who believe themselves to be nourished by it. Upon conducting the necessary interviews, these nonpartisan journalists would quickly discover that aficionados regard the genre not as a vehicle of escape but as something quite the opposite. It is a medium of arrival. It brings us home. Henry Jekyll's basement, Victor Frankenstein's "workshop of filthy creation," Caliban's island, Gollum's cave, the Gill-man's lagoon, King Kong's jungle, the Wicked Witch of the West's palace: All such labs and lairs, these domains of the deformed, these stomping grounds for monsters, are where we belong—not for our whole lives, certainly, but at least until we get our bearings.

In "The Child and the Shadow," an essay concerned largely with Hans Christian Andersen's fable of a professor's detached and autonomous shadow, Ursula K. Le Guin critiques our tendency to equate *le fantastique* with escapism. For Le Guin, "the language of fantasy" engages with the phenomenon of evil far more honestly than does "realistic fiction" aimed at preadolescent or YA audiences. Too often, Le Guin argues, supposedly true-to-life children's literature serves up the bromide that "there's a little bit of bad in the best of us and a little bit of good in the worst of us," a notion she calls "a dangerous banalization of the fact, which is that there is incredible potential for good and evil in every one of us."

Le Guin goes on to assail books for young readers that treat our daily abysses as solvable conundrums, like questions in an arithmetic book. "*That* is escapism," she writes, "that posing evil as a 'problem,' instead of what it is: all the pain and suffering and waste and loss and injustice we will meet all our lives long, and must face and cope with over and over and over, and admit, and live with in order to live human lives at all." Near the end of the essay Le Guin notes, "To give the child a picture of the gas chambers at Dachau, or the famines of India, or the cruelties of a psychotic parent, and say, 'Well, baby, this is how it is, what are you going to make of it?'—that is surely unethical. If you suggest that there is a 'solution' to these monstrous facts, you are lying to the child. If you insist that there isn't, you are overwhelming him with a load he's not strong enough yet to carry."

Although I've never had much patience for the famous evangelical Christian exhortation to hate the sin but love the sinner—I find it smug at best, destructively arrogant at worst—this formulation arguably enables us to think intelligently about the phenomenon of evil and the domains of the deformed. The same impulse that behooves us to detest the monstrous (when by "the monstrous" we mean, with Le Guin, real-world cruelty, violence, bigotry, and injustice) also inclines us to embrace the monster (when by "the monster" we mean a creature whose physical or spiritual aberrancy condemns him, her, or it to the status of outsider). This is as it should be. Our love of Quasimodo, the Phantom of the Opera, Frankenstein's shambling experiment, John Gardner's vision of Grendel, and the cast of Tod Browning's offbeat movie *Freaks* speaks well of us. It may even be the saving grace of a species not otherwise noted for its generosity of spirit.

In *Danse Macabre*, Stephen King's delightful report on his personal poetics, the author recalls his primal encounter with the Gillman of Jack Arnold's *Creature from the Black Lagoon*, "a scaly, batrachian monster" that lurks in "a wide pond that seems an idyllic, South American version of the Garden of Eden." For the seven-year-old King, the experience involved a kind of metaphysical commerce. "I knew, watching, that the Creature had become *my* Creature; I had bought it . . . I knew that, later that night, he would visit me in the black lagoon of my dreams . . . Seven isn't old, but it is old enough to know that you get what you pay for. You own it, you bought it, it's yours. It is old enough to feel the dowser suddenly come alive, grow heavy, and roll over in your hands, pointing at hidden water."

As King's dip in the Black Lagoon suggests, there is always something exotically arcane, something beautifully outré and darkly glamorous, about a beloved monster. We instinctively recoil from a Timothy McVeigh, a Charles Manson, a Ted Kaczynski, a Jeffrey Dahmer, or a Jerry Sandusky not merely because their deeds partake of the monstrous, but because the worlds they inhabit seem bereft of the aesthetic. They are monsters unworthy of the name. Their souls, peeled, yield only a void. McVeigh and company instantiate what Hannah Arendt, taking the measure of Adolf Eichmann, memorably called the banality of evil. Perhaps there are difficult cases—does Jack the Ripper speak to a certain romantic sensibility even as he nauseates us?—but in general we know where to draw the line.

SELF-AWARE MONSTERS

Those of us who practice the art of fiction are forever scrutinizing the fine print on our poetic licenses. It turns out that we're allowed to stand Hannah Arendt's insight on its head, creating transgressors who know exactly what they're about, thoughtful fiends who would rather die than be thought ordinary. As far as I can tell, such monsters are largely a literary conceit. The Marquis de Sade of Doug Wright's play *Quills*, the Humbert Humbert of Vladimir Nabokov's novel *Lolita*, and the Demon Barber of Stephen Sondheim's musical *Sweeney Todd* don't remotely correspond to the sorts of miscreants who populate reality—and yet the convention of the self-aware monster is so delicious that we can hardly do without it. As John Irving's Garp remarks, "Fiction has to be better made than life."

Self-aware monsters take pride in refusing to deny their depravity. *Quills* is not long under way when de Sade spits on a curate's Bible and says, "This monstrous God of yours: he strung up his very own son like a side of veal—I shudder to think what he'd do to me." Humbert Humbert also acknowledges his wickedness, periodically expressing remorse over having stolen Lolita's childhood, most especially in the novel's final beats. "I was a pentapod monster, but I loved you. I was despicable and brutal, and turpid, and everything, *mais je t'aimais, je t'aimais.*" (Of course, Humbert's guilt doesn't prevent him from indulging in pathological apologias. "Why then this horror that I cannot shake off? Did I deprive her of her flower? Sensitive gentlewomen of the jury, I was not even her first lover.") Sondheim's Sweeney Todd is not as eloquent as the monsters contrived by Wright and Nabokov, but he unreservedly adds his own name to the company of the damned. On the eve of his murder spree, the Demon Barber offers his best friend a lucid if nihilistic rationalization for his imminent crimes.

No, we all deserve to die,
Even you, Mrs. Lovett, even I,
Because the lives of the wicked should be made brief,
For the rest of us death will be a relief,
We all deserve to die . . .

In my novel called *The Philosopher's Apprentice*, which I've described as "Frankenstein meets Lolita on the Island of Dr. Moreau," I likewise attempted to plumb the soul of a self-aware monster. Spawned by genetic engineering, Londa Sabacthani comes into the world devoid of a conscience. It falls to the philosopher of the title, a failed PhD candidate named Mason Ambrose, to implant a sense of right and wrong in this unfortunate creature. Things go swimmingly at first, with Londa wrestling profitably with classic moral dilemmas and engaging fruitfully in role-playing exercises drawn from the history of Western ethics. But then Mason makes a fatal miscalculation, exposing Londa to the Sermon on the Mount, whereupon her superego swells to grotesque proportions. At first my heroine's hypertrophic conscience inspires her to perform benevolent acts, including the establishment of a utopian community dedicated to improving women's welfare throughout the world. Later, her skewed moral compass leads her to a dark place, and she ends up hijacking a luxury liner with the aim of rehabilitating—by any means necessary—its plutocratic passengers.

Londa suffers from many illusions about how the world works but few concerning herself. She is rarely blind to the ethical implications of her behavior. When she takes the side of the angels, she knows exactly what she's doing, and later, when her soul begins to rot, she still enjoys a salutary perspective on her sins, dutifully ending her reign of terror by programming her own clone to assassinate her.

OBLIVIOUS FIENDS

For reasons that Carl Jung would understand better than I, the writer who organizes a novel or play around a self-aware monster will, more often than not, leaven the conceit with a secondary demon of atrophied imagination. It's as if the author is saying, "See, I know perfectly well that Hannah Arendt was correct about evil—but who wants to see a banal fiend at the center of a work of fiction?"

In *Quills*, Wright juxtaposes the overtly sociopathic de Sade with the ostensibly virtuous, wife-raping physician Royer-Collard. In *Lolita*, Humbert's poetic and cultivated obsession parallels the prosaic and pornographic pursuit of the same nymphet by his quasi-Doppel-gänger, Clare Quilty. Sondheim counterpoints Todd's inner torment with the machinations of the insipid and respectable—but equally vile—Judge Turpin. And as *The Philosopher's Apprentice* evolved, I decided to burden Londa with an enemy of quintessential oblivious-ness, the Reverend Enoch Anthem, who blithely pilfers tissue from aborted fetuses, turns their genetic blueprints into full-grown adults, and conditions these angry "immaculoids" to torment the parents who presumably canceled their prospective lives.

But it was surely Leo Tolstoy who, in *War and Peace*, painted the definitive portrait of the oblivious fiend. After Napoleon Bonaparte, at an adjutant's urging, gives an order to hurl more firepower against the Russian center at Borodino, the omniscient narrator offers a damning analysis of the emperor's mind. "And not only for that hour and day were reason and conscience darkened in this man who, more than all the other participants in this affair, bore upon himself the whole weight of what was happening; but never to the end of his life was he able to understand goodness, or beauty, or truth, or the mean-ing of his own actions . . . He could not renounce his actions, ex-tolled by half the world, and therefore he had to renounce truth and goodness and everything human."

Of course, many historians would take a more charitable view of Napoleon's soul. Tolstoy is no more purporting to offer an unbiased depiction of the emperor than the Russian Orthodox believer Dos-toevsky was attempting, in *The Brothers Karamazov*, to objectively limn the Grand Inquisitor of the Roman Church. But the passage serves to remind us why we love our self-aware monsters, from Mary Shelley's philosophical fiend to Gaston Leroux's Opera Ghost to Doug Wright's unrepentant sensualist. Misguided though they may be, these creatures struggle to sustain Tolstoyan "reason and con-science"—at least insofar as they can apprehend those ideals. The same cannot be said for either Napoleon at Borodino or Eichmann at Auschwitz.

ELUSIVE DEMONS

Among my favorite guilty-pleasure British horror movies of the 1970s is *I, Monster*, Milton Subotsky and Stephen Weeks's gratifyingly artsy reimagining of *The Strange Case of Dr. Jekyll and Mr. Hyde.* The film stars Christopher Lee as Dr. Marlowe, a physician who methodically injects his patients with an experimental serum that reverses the poles of their personalities. Under the influence of Marlowe's drug, prudes become wantons and bullies turn into weaklings. The primary narrative is intercut with scenes of Victorian upper-class males discussing relevant philosophical issues in their gentlemen's club, notably Rousseau's theory of innate goodness versus Freud's more pessimistic assessment of human nature.

The title says it all. *I, Monster.* To be human is to have a shadow side. The most elusive demons reside within, denizens of our private Black Lagoons, a circumstance we would do well to acknowledge at all turns. In her Andersen essay, Le Guin frames the issue in terms at once personal and political. "Unadmitted to consciousness, the shadow is projected outward, onto others. There's nothing wrong with me—it's them. I'm not a monster, other people are monsters. All foreigners are evil. All communists are evil. All capitalists are evil. It was the cat that made me kick him, Mummy."

In my view the greatest fictive meditation on elusive, unassimilated evil is Herman Melville's *Billy Budd.* Now, of course it makes no sense to regard Captain Vere as a fiend. Indeed, he is benevolence personified, virtue dressed in Royal Navy blues, far closer to the angelic Billy than to the satanic Claggart. This is surely a necessary observation. But is it sufficient? In her astute review of Peter Ustinov's movie adaptation of *Billy Budd*, film critic Pauline Kael notes that Vere is "not so much a tragic victim of the law as he is Claggart's master and a distant relative perhaps of the Grand Inquisitor." Kael then offers a sobering elucidation. "Sweet Starry Vere is the evil we *can't* detect: the man whose motives and conflicts we can't fathom. Claggart we can spot, but he is merely the underling doing the Captain's work: it is the Captain, Billy's friend, who continues the logic by which saints must be destroyed."

The evil we can't detect, the monster we don't see, the unassimilated shadow. At the end of the day, each of us is master of the *Indomitable*: We are all Starry Vere—and beyond the bright constellation of our starry selves stretch vast tracts of dark matter, a terrain populated by entities that have no names. The undetectable demons from our unobservable ids are not inevitably the ones we should most fear, but we ignore these beasts only at our peril, lest we too participate in the monstrous logic by which saints must be destroyed.

Two Elegies
Robert Kelly

ELEGY FOR THE WEATHER

Chemical ring
mystery bond:
coupled at the level of the hip
who cares if nobody reads this
everybody is welcome
and welcome is all that matters
to welcome and to praise—

hier bin i ! cried Bruckner
that's all a word can say,
here I am ! loud and boisterous
at your door, a bottle
under each arm, threaten
to stay inside you for days
or years—my endless
opera—words are the true
invaders of the house,
Occupy your mind.

I touch each one
I am the dancing master
of this disaster, I ripen
consequences on the leafy
stems of what you think,
I interfere.

Be quiet, *vates*,
your tune will come,
your drone become the epic
children suffer through
in school, your radiant
imagery their tediums—
can that word have a plural,
are you even listening?

This is about the doubt
resident in saying anything
the bluebells on Betty's lawn
her tumbled columbine—
it makes you think, *ça,*

it puzzles you with otherness
that smells suddenly
like your own skin—
remember skin?—
                              the touch
he rants about
is more quick than silver,
tarnishes, doesn't last,
isn't even toxic, or not very,
but stains the brain
like walnut juice from hard
green pebbly rotundities
used to rain down on the lawn
before the hurricane
and my poor tree went down.

Reminds me of your voice
on the phone call from midnight

Robert Kelly

promising emotion's
slow eternity—I remembered
deer tiptoeing on the lawn
always afraid, always vanishing.

Believe them, tumble
into language as into
the arms of a lover
who promises everything, who
might one day even be a friend,
endure.

    Endure. The policy
of the stone is best—
listen to pure reverberation,
accept thirstily unchanged—
o god the thirsty stones

accept what is poured out
over you, the hand
that picks you up
or lets you fall

back where the world—that
presumptuous gravity—
wants you to be.
                Glisten
while you can.
                  Wake up, stone,
I summon thee

and who better to wake
than what is firm and certain
made of many elements

all turned one?
                    Word,
be stone. Stone, be man.

Now the caravan can start
splay-footed in the desert.
Camels, lions
leaping onto The Woman
hurtlessly boisterous
—that word again
that can't be me—
intermediate rapture
postgraduate *ecstase*
the kids leap off the dock
as the ferry hauls away—

I'm thinking of all her perfumes
the mere disclosure of chemic bond
—read the manual—
scattershot glad-to-be-home
in you, I love your lap—
so many martyred
for being other—
                    motherless despots
alarmed at the merely human world,
teach them to be meek, breezes,
teach them milk.

Is there any way to anything,
a road to learn all this?

Sparkling stardust you call sulfur
I call dull yellow she calls
her cat peeing on the rosebush root

he calls getting even with the world's cruel thorns
that spike our joys with intoxicating pain

—meek danger!—begin to lay on
the antidote, lovesick art, bring
Prussian-blue Crayolas and rough paper
bring graphite chunks and fumes of turpentine
bring lipstick from your sister's drawer
and granddad's ancient Zippo lighter—
now you're talking—wheel flint to flame—
smear color on the tepid world
by minutest observation
of particulars—songbeat
heard on leaf—stilled
in conversation—listen
between what's said—
waterfall turns into Nile
can reach unlikely oceans
—landlocked philosophy
of rational men—Engels
in his heart knew better
for Compassion without Wisdom availeth not
—let him praise at least
the comforting angels of the lower air
those girls

   —I watched the wake
turbulent spread wide-wedged
in the bay behind us, the view
haunted by spray from windward,
daunting tomtom of the engine
churning us through the *formless*
accurate, the sea—
    that's just memory,

what else is in your wallet—
tense the word, brace it
but the shank of the screw snapped though,
a fresh breeze, steel bears our weights
reluctantly—mirrors
are the strangest of all metals
they hold us all—
but if once the sight of her
shatters glass as it breaks my heart—
pish-tush, you have scant
heart to break, amigo—
por favor lo hacer sin corazon

enough border-talk, give me moon-oil
give me gratifying Friday midnight
and spoonfed Sundays—belle
époque come every day—
nesselrode pie and busy aftermaths—
wake in clover—time for prayer
to keep this sorry craft afloat
headed straight to New Jerusalem,
clouds my sails
the crows my captain.

Something had to change
the debilitating habits of his dream
spilled into matins, reflections,
all those dark prequels
the night is full of

and then the phone rang—
it was a mystery story
yearning to be told—
about hang gliding and Christ on Corcovado

and how to spend money
in poor countries ethically,
how to solve equations with two unknowns
and no bedspread—
look, a lizard on the ceiling!—
in Delhi that time too hot to breathe
you mean you sweated
with the effort of each breath
yes, that's more like it
but where are the birds today
I've seen not one—
call the doctor—add ambergris
and oil the pulpit
that old dry wood
needs all the jism it can get—
oil of semaphore, grease of separation—
but I did hear crows
they were excited they were giving warning
they were loud they were here—
be still while I catch your breath—
clouds shield us from disaster
in blue transparency our lives are sealed.

SYRIAC ELEGY

1.

The import of rosy flowers
on a green bush. Very green.
Mandibular impulse at peace—
no engulfing needed now

though there are those who swallow
mirrors and the walls left bare
the shadows slinking homeward
from the rowdy fair. Late summer!

Clouds of organdy, air a challenge,
heavyweight atmosphere knockout punch,
hide me in your bosom, child,
I am the annotation and you are the text.

2.

You must have already guessed the flowers
what kind they are (you know how
little I know, so few names, Botany 101
so long ago) so you can tell by the shade of green

the woman I'm not thinking of, the church
I never visit, the music rattling on
in the back of my head, the chipmunk
glimpsed in the breezeway. Or was it a rat?

3.

What was all that about mirrors?
Do you mean those women from Miami
who stand nervous at the ocean's edge
worrying about Cuba or their husbands,
the intractable mercies of human life?
Or do you mean the ones so beautiful
their images march with them everywhere
to satisfy a famished audience's eyes?

Or something in between. Something dark
in the hallway just after dawn, a gleam
and then it's gone. And it's inside you
and you know that's all you'll get of this day
that one little sheen against all your doubt?

Hold on. There are dolphins in the sea—
it's not all sharks out there, the gulls
woke me and the Christians came home.

4.

Peace, sister. The eyes have it.
Pink of the roses quicksilver of the glass
over the dusty window—same old story,
leaden plates engraved with artless forgeries—
look old, be old. The cashier
does not even bother to look up.
The invisible man buys Kleenexes
already his tears are on the way.

5.

Book of Lamentations.
Lost mirrors.
Children waiting to be born,
oh I've heard it all.

Non credo. The moon's
voluptuous sarabande,
monthlong striptease,
and when the clothes
are flung away there's
no one there, the sinner
on his knees before no cross.

How much can a lover stand?
A breeze, a difference.
That's all we ever want.
Sit down beside me
and tell me all your lies
and see if I can tell
your skin from my own.

Five Poems
Rae Armantrout

EXPRESSION

Give me your spurt
of verbs,

your welter
of pronouns

desiring to be spread.

Bulge-eyed, clear-
bodied brine shrimp

bobbing to the surface.

I prefer
the hermit, trundling off

in someone else's
exoskeleton—

but we all
come down,

to self-love,
self-love which,

like a virus,

has no love
and has no self

PERSONHOOD

1.

Imagine the recent dead
gathered in a parking lot
or lobby

wearing Victorian clothes
to distinguish themselves
from the passersby—

a flash mob.

They can't take themselves
or one another
seriously. It's hard

to hold on
to an idea

2.

Clearly, each
orange parasol

of poppy,

having opened,
is one.

But effort is not
cumulative.

It figures
second
to second.

A self
is a lagging

indicator

Rae Armantrout

BELIEVING

1.

When did you first learn
that the bursts

of color and sound
were intended for you?

When did you unlearn this?

2.

Believing yourself
to have a secret identity
can be a sign
of madness.

On the other hand,
the lack
of a secret identity
can lead to depression.

Many have found it useful
to lie down
as men
believing themselves
to be little girls

or as girls
believing themselves
to be mermaids
stranded
in their own bodies.

Rae Armantrout

OCCURRENCE

Here's something about me.

I get up when sleep
becomes unbearable,
when dreams repeat themselves,
minor variations
on a randomly selected theme.

I go to bed
when consciousness becomes unbearable,
when the house repeats itself
and the television offers
to think for me.

Layoffs accelerate
turnaround.

Aliens may try
to communicate with us
using black holes.

Here is what we know
about God.

If we are made in God's image,
God is impatient
without really knowing
what he wishes
would occur.

Rae Armantrout

KILTER

Since I crop up
in sentences.

Since I can see
through your eyes.

Since I've been moved
into a mouse

in a cartoon
and then come back,

I can survive death.

*

This lateral
drift,

off-kilter

(as if one
saw double)

signals the approach
of sleep?

Luxembourg Gardens
Aurelie Sheehan

THE GRAY CHAIRS MUST HAVE floated down from another galaxy and alighted in the gardens, spread near the pool like petals. Most were lined up on the north side of the pool, by the marble steps and one of the many plots of flowers. "Lined up" isn't quite accurate, though, because of the chancy or haphazard nature of the clusters, the ghost conversations.

Wilson remembers the chairs as gray, gray against the fire riot of the gardens. But the website is referring to them as green. *Green?* Green is what the trees were, the unfurled lawns. Green was the wave of palms in the pots on the sand surrounding the pool and before the palace, the pool where the children were and where he was, a foolish child himself in the face of all that glory. Her.

A grayish green perhaps, at best—a greenish gray.

It was eight months ago. Not so long.

My name is Wilson and I have lost control. I do not know if the chairs in Luxembourg Gardens were green or gray.

He clicks to another website, and then to another. Darkness falls. He is, as usual, alone in his apartment. This is where Wilson comes at the end of each day, after his nine clocked-in hours, or, on luckier days, the gym or the bar. His job does not represent, though he's often suggested as much to concerned family members, a career, and the apartment is not, though it once seemed to be, a home. Wilson struggles to even exist. His memories are all that hold him together.

Yes, the past few months have been strange for Wilson. He feels that perhaps he is a nothing-nowhere man now, when before he was Wilson Manor, a man but also a building.

(My father told me on the phone that he used to walk me around Luxembourg Gardens when I was a baby, or anyway that he'd done so at least a couple of times. My father's voice betrayed this: He was looking at the horizon behind his property, and he was smiling. Not the smile of a photograph or a joke, but close to if not a little less

manic than the smiles we wore as we stood under a tent in his backyard the day after my wedding celebration and finished the keg, father
and daughter, Irishmen both. Gave it a try, anyway, our plastic cups
filled with mildly stale, still cold but warming beer. Stared into the
lucky rain like we were staring across the sea. It fell in a visible mist,
a multitude of dots, a hue, between his gardens and us. This was
early August in the hills of Western Massachusetts, and the green
was everywhere, was plenty, had taken over (a far cry from Tucson's
strangled summers). There was a second and much larger white tent
in the middle of the field. In the gardens were greens of many colors,
and two varieties at least of purple. To know the names of things:
This is not something I did then nor do now. But as time stretches in
its ample and terrible way, even the names of things seem a possible
consolation.

Listening to my father's voice on the phone, I could see us on those
paths in Luxembourg Gardens. In front of my eyes: my father and me
and the baby buggy, white broken stones underfoot and under the
wheels, the uncanny beauty of the gardens as if this were literally
heaven itself, as if we could engage in a dream.)

(Does everything have to die? Is cause and effect necessary? It seems
too much like a British TV mystery to find a body in the shrubs, two
feet sticking into the path, toes up, baguette tossed aside, timepiece
broken at 2:14.)

Until now, Wilson had exactly this much faith in God: a little bit.
There was something too occult about God, he thought. He went to
church occasionally regardless, for a series of tentative reasons. Wilson
was gently blown toward church. If the wind blew from another direction, he might just as easily go on a bike ride, or to a coffee shop.

Still, he was familiar in a pleasant, vaguely urgent way with the
ritual, and aware that he usually felt better when he left the church
than when he went in. He appreciated the space itself, the building.
The service was filled with speech or song, but the church felt silent
to him in an essential fashion. Lately he'd started talking back to
God, as if he were addressing an invisible friend, or as if he were at a
wedding reception, talking to a vacant seat. "I am here, or I *could* be
here," echoed in return, a din, a magnum opus of solitude.

What the fuck is going on?

What the fuck is going on!
What the fuck is going on!

(The occasion of the phone conversation with my father: I'd just returned from a trip to Paris. After we spoke, I could say with certainty that I'd been to Luxembourg Gardens at least three times. Back
when I was a baby, with my father, and mother most likely. Then
with my husband, five months after our wedding. The first day of
that trip he gave me (a little late, yes) an engagement ring. He gave it
to me in Shakespeare & Company. We were wearing trench coats
and it was raining and we were jet-lagged and I was pregnant. We
were in the fiction section, A–F, and he'd carried the small box in his
bag in the plane, a nervous wreck until he could hand it over. I have
the ring on now. I can picture us, heads bowed by the bookcases, but
I don't remember the actual words he said, "Will you marry me?"
being unnecessary. Then a third time last summer, with my husband and our child, a twelve-year-old force of nature, a hip-hop-hat-
wearing, Orangina-swilling adventurer. This time, the three of us
stayed at the same hotel near the park as the two of us had on our
honeymoon. We bought croissants at the same *boulangerie*.)

In fact it really kicked in at a wedding reception, all this—the new
nothing-nowhere stage in Wilson's life—the wedding reception of
his sister, Claire, two months ago, a "Christmas wedding." It was
Wilson's first big family event since the spectacular breakup, when
Alyssa said the following immortal words: "I think our growth as
people will improve now." Our growth—as people? As opposed to—
as plants, or lemurs? *And I'm a little sad about the idea of improving growth period*, Wilson muttered to himself, continuing a
conversation with another kind of invisibility, lo these many months
later.
    In their adulthood, Wilson and his sister didn't speak much, al-
though when they did it was always with good cheer. Still, at the rehearsal dinner she'd held his hand urgently, intertwining her fingers
with his and looking deeply into his eyes, glassy eyed herself with
vodka tonics or hope, or a little of both. She'd finally gotten that ass-
hole out of the house, and now she'd found this new, also-divorced
lad who liked yard sales and had a career of his own. It all fell into
place somehow, thought Wilson blurrily. *When you're young, you*

179

worry people will leave, and later you worry they'll stay. He'd been blubbering dubious aphorisms, these Improved Growth days. Having finished everyone's Jordan almonds at Table 2, he focused on the odd purse of the woman sitting to his right. What if women carried odd things in their odd purses, instead of mundane crap? What if lives were swift modern novels, where swaths of connection are left undeveloped, or may be crystallized in brief moments or even objects? This blue vase is my life thus far. This green apple is my very childhood.

He had felt that, as a brother recently Grown as a Person, it was his duty to drink a goodly, chipping-in and lending-an-oar portion of pinot noir, which tasted something like consecration, after all. "Who Let the Dogs Out?" was followed by "Last Night a DJ Saved My Life," followed by "Relax," followed by "Pumped Up Kicks," which, being kind of a downer, returned two couples to the table. Wilson liked the song, could feel himself running and a generalized ethereal being and nothingness in the syncopation. Across the dim, artificially glamorized dance floor, he sighted his cousin Lucy, whom he'd always thought was sincere and funny. And there was an uncle he'd known his entire life, and a raft of elusive spouses—people he could walk up to and chat with if he had the notion, and they'd have to stay and listen, at least for a while, because they were, after all, family. Wilson grunted, a laughlike *huck* in his throat.

Then he made some kind of slight error in judgment. Among the sparkle and heave of electricity and DJ'ed throbbing sound, shouldering the tender weight of familial connection and the wild abandon of recent heartbreak, Wilson jumped up and proceeded to kiss everyone at his table, a game of Duck Duck Goose, six squishy cheeks, and then he tottered and spun himself out toward the stage: He hadn't made a toast yet. He began running, running, running, and as he leapt like a veritable stag up toward the stage, to say something cheerful and Grown, and also essential and profound, he lost his way, his balance, and then Wilson was on the ground, holding his bloody nose in his hands. He'd not jumped, *per se*, but hit the stage front with his nose.

(There was a boy on the train outside of Paris, an ethnicity not my own, maybe he was African, or Middle Eastern. He was fourteen or fifteen. He had a protruding upper lip, like the lip of a man I once knew. It was sexy on the man, biteable, an ever-so-slight deformity, a vulnerability or deviance from the norm. I watched the boy on the train. Every few seconds, he'd blink rapidly and deliberately—a tic. He did not look happy. He did not look at me, though I was staring. And it is hard to describe the feeling I had, looking at him and thinking of the other man, dead now. It felt uncomfortable, at least, as if I were doing damage to the boy by looking at him, as if it were untoward. But he did not know I was watching him or thinking of someone I loved long ago.)

(I will write, but I must never say anything incorrect or angry about my family, and I must never betray any large, reckless feelings that are unresolved or messy, or that are so big and wide and stormy they fill up the sky.)

I am a Melancholy Narcissist, thinks Wilson, staring at his nose in the mirror on a Thursday morning, still feeling the psychic effects of that wedding caper. First the pinot noir guzzling, then the flurry of rapture, then the profound timelessness of pure humiliation: catching a cab to Urgent Care with his cousin, coming back after the cake was cut, still blinking rapidly against the glare of capitalist healing. It was already weeks ago, that grim family drama. There is a kind of gorgeous new plane or vector, a nonlinear acknowledgment, a twist to his face now. *My face is filled with potential. It has been changed.* Who knew a face could change? The Melancholy Narcissist needs to go to work, says Wilson to Wilson. If nothing else, the nose looks Baudelairian.

Wilson's apartment is a multiplicity of tans, the triumph of American Bland. Although he has had time to shower and drink coffee and stare in the mirror, his bed remains tragically unmade, the not-so-mussed sheets of the single man.

He dreams of gray-green chairs arrayed alongside the bank of a pool, alongside a fountain. He dreams of gray-green chairs scattered in a forest.

(The original idea for the story came from a dream about a vector. It was a Very Important Vector. I could see the vector in my mind. In the morning, I tried to draw it. In the dream a more famous writer wrote the story about the vector, it was pretty much already written, I just needed to crib from the dream, to own this thing. Although I started the process with much heady enthusiasm and boldness in the days after the dream—I had found a solution, I had been given something spectacular—it became increasingly clear that the idea wasn't a particularly good one. Well, it was good—as an idea, but not as a story, the kind on paper.)

Devin is Wilson's friend, at the newspaper shop. Devin is handsome, thinks Wilson. What if my life were Devin's? I could have a large extended family. I could have the hawk eyes and fever of the immigrant. Wilson puts *The New York Times* on the counter. He pulls a dollar out, and some change.

"Hey, dude, what's going on," says Devin.

"I've got some thoughts," says Wilson, and then he leans in with a faux yet also fearfully earnest new intimacy. "Let's swap lives. Everything would be different then."

"Funny fellow, my Wilson—but I would be a fool to swap lives with you today."

"Why is that?"

"I, Devin, am going to a concert at the Nutcracker Center. On Friday, three days from now."

"Let me come with you!" says Wilson, surprising himself to the point of nausea, surprising also Devin.

"It would be an honor," says Devin, backing into the cigarette stand.

Was it so wrong, to admire the work of a young ingenue, a Canadian songsmith? *After all, I was young once.* In his cubicle, Wilson rakes his hands through his hair. I was young, I was young, he moans (though he is only twenty-four). He is interested *journalistically* in being Devin, or seeing Justin Bieber, or both, or either. He could start a blog about . . . being himself . . . in this new world. Is he sincere? Is he—does he have a word for that essential thing he might be, underneath it all?

He remembers his life with Alyssa. It *was* a life, an entire snow globe. In that place and time he was young, and he was sincere.

It was sad the way Devin stared at Wilson and said those things about maybe they could get a ticket with nearby seating and he'd see what his brother said vis-à-vis going together, and then the way he lifted his arms—at last, great beneficence—to the woman behind Wilson, with the bottle of water and the fitness magazine.

Sexiness is a flint, an opening. It is a sense of action that might be or should be taken. For Wilson, floating along on his tan river of tanness, there is no true movement or sense of impending movement. Occasionally there is wan hope. This cubicle is not even a metaphor, it is reality, thinks Wilson, before he gets ahold of himself, straightening up in his chair.

(Did I make a fool of myself last night? Why, yes, I did. First: My clothes were simple cotton, not at all worthy of a special occasion. At the bar I wedged myself into the mound of cushions like a child with a keening feeling. I immediately identified a yearning within myself, a wish for her to love me and the realization that if I *wished* it then it could not be, that the wishing always pushes away, or the wanting pushes away, certainly. How about if I try this, a doe-eyed look? *Please, pretty please.* I must have appeared, at best, like a cliché librarian. Legs crossed, one wrapped around the other, arms without purpose. Sometimes I put one arm on a cushion, dangling the hand over in the airscape. Or I'd put my hand in my lap, a stroke victim's hand, or reach for the champagne flute. *Slosh, gobble, slug.* I'm so dainty! I think we could easily, in fact we *should* drink all night. Much was going on in this librarian mind of mine, amid the cushionage. And yet she remained calm, the object of affection. She held her glass upright. Never a look of uncertainty, although she did say: *Every day I feel existential depression,* and then backtracked: *Doesn't everyone?* I twisted my napkin. Perhaps my nurse champion self needed to come into play? The duchess on the moors, ready to investigate, to run briskly with dark cloak, to be wistful and brave and first-aid ready?

We scurried to our Official Event ten minutes late, the extent of our revolution. But for a little while it was like being in a gondola, the beloved gazelle who lived near the beloved penguin (that was me), crooning under the plentiful sky, Italian songs and short murmurings that had to do with crucial life points and survival schemes. I believe in islands, in seas, I believe in moonlit escapes and small eternities.)

*

Aurelie Sheehan

(My father sat on my patio in the shaded rectangle between the house and lawn. Our yard is a burdensome collection of too-large trees, dead trees, and distorted trees, and the lawn itself is sparse, as is frequently the case in Tucson (without extreme intervention). He was looking toward the yard, holding the binoculars in his lap. He raised the binoculars and I looked where he was pointing them. Two brownish-black birds were standing or hopping on my lawn. His looking revealed them to me.)

Wilson at work. Probably best to lay out the office, or perhaps talk about his multitudinous and colorful coworkers. What is the essential core of the work experience? Perhaps we should speak of the microecology of his desk, chair, computer, and patch of rug. And in the center, Wilson's brain, connected by silly string to his fingers, at this moment clacking away at the computer's keys, answering an email. *Jay, you're absolutely right, the newsletter wouldn't be complete without a "Staff News" section. I'll see if we can squeeze that in next to the giving form. Back at you later this a.m. with a new version. W.*

He has three other emails that will also be easy to dispatch, yeses and nos and one Thursday at ten works for me. He only gets the dreariest of junk mail on his office account, e-circulars from suppliers and mailing-list wholesalers. The computer is his little world, indeed. He stares into it as if into a clear pool, a gorgeous still lake. He is the reverse-reverse of Alice in Wonderland, prototype of a twenty-first-century dullard. At the bar, Wilson thinks, he would not be worrying as much about Really Living as he does here.

He receives a new email from his boss. Will he come there?

Wilson goes there.

The boss is often stern but sometimes goes on tangents in which she speaks jocularly about weekend plans. She has strict dark office attire: She always wears black stockings, black boots, and black skirts, but she will occasionally wear a white blouse or a white-and-black-striped blouse. Today she is wearing a white-and-black-striped blouse. She fires him. Two weeks notice. But she says, as if it is a gift and not a way to get him immediately out the door, that he can use his vacation time for those two weeks.

"Why?" Wilson squawks, having known nothing of this, no premonitions of any kind.

The boss places her hands together before her mouth and mumbles something, as if she were a CIA agent or a football coach, attempting to keep her words unknowable, especially on any hidden cameras.

(With my father, there has always been gardening—or there has been gardening from the time I was eleven on. Our new house in Weston had a wide, rolling lawn, and in the middle of all that grass my parents dug a garden. Laid down railroad ties, weeping squared-off logs you could stand on, rock back and forth on with your heels in the air. My father rented a Rototiller, and they unfurled a roll of chicken wire. This garden you could see from the kitchen window, it was everyone's garden, a public garden, with a strawberry patch appended to the end near the house, a square of low-slung plants with unlikely hearts in the gray, dry soil of Connecticut (I didn't even *know* dry then). Harvesting the strawberries was my job, and my brother's. Clearly a quid pro quo situation, you pick them, you eat them, striking me at the time as parallel to or symbolic of so many reconciliations with the adult world. But my father also had a secondary garden, all his own, hidden from view—a potato patch, Irishly enough. Here was a big boil under the earth: so innocuous up top, but underneath an explosion. The potatoes were a secret within a secret, and he conned my little cousins into digging them up one Labor Day. *He who finds the most potatoes wins!* This is not just a raw memory; it's a smaller-scale legend.)

(To be absolutely alone in winter: This too is life. To be in a field of snow at twilight, the stark velvet of death, the everlasting and the snuffed out. I experienced this in Wyoming once. Two golden houses on the horizon made the night colder and bluer. The first stars were visible in the thick, black sky. In the distance, cow shapes, by the creek. A car came and went along the nearby highway, someone else's life. I raised my boot and stepped into white.

Here at home in the desert, I have a postcard of a Monet leaning on my lamp. It's a winter scene, a magpie on a fence, a small, intrepid bird in a world of snow. A farmhouse is in the background, behind a stand of trees, and everywhere is the suggestion of silence and time. Snow has covered the field and the wall. The wooden gate is not completely covered but it is still, all is stilled but the dark bird, not a frantic bird, but alive. I hear incremental shifts in the surfaces. Return to life, in the sunlight.

185

A picture from my childhood, not a postcard, but in an album somewhere and in my mind: My family is standing before what appears to be a snowdrifted chalet. We are in wintry garb; I'm wearing a poncho. We hold skis. We are in downtown Norwalk, in front of a backdrop behind a building on the edge of town. And here is the question again: Is life a disaster because it ends? Does end always bring tragedy? It's a simple shot, a lark, a seven-year-old girl, a three-year-old boy, a mother, and a father, somewhere in history.)

The city in which Wilson lives has a specialty foodstuff: the walnut. Walnut pie, walnut-and-chocolate-chip cookies, walnut risotto, walnut hamburgers. At the airport: walnut key chains and mugs and lanyards. The city mascot is a chipmunk.

Wilson had ambition, in the past. He had ambition prior to his trip to Paris with Alyssa. He had it even two months ago, before the wedding. Walking along the street, feeding indiscriminately on walnut-flavored chips, he thinks again of Devin. Devin has a private self. The hidden selves of some men are small, white dishes, gleaming. Wilson eyes the newspaper shop where his friend, or previous friend, or never-friend, works. Should he go in and ask if he's had any luck procuring another ticket? But he could tell, for Wilson isn't a social idiot, that it was a no-go type of situation.

"My God, at my age," Wilson says to himself, as he eats and veers around the city's sunny streets, amid all these people with jobs and lovers.

By the time he gets back to his tan apartment, he's sunk from disbelief into reckless depression. Rent is due in two weeks. He'll be able to pay September's rent, but what about the bills, the phone, the electricity? Not Having a Job is a profound and immediate state, very much unlike Devin's life—a life of concertgoing and low-level, ravenous, hour-stealing labor. Wilson is separating out not just from Devin but from everyone. He ransacks his mind for the names of any friends who might, like him, be without employment. But he only thinks of Jeff G., who it was rumored had become a born-again Christian, after running through alcoholism and minor drug use. Isn't it a recession, though, thinks Wilson dully—wishing there were others like him. A great luminosity of unemployed persons.

*

(My father is in the habit of getting cancer these days, or heart flutters or blood-pressure problems. It began when my daughter was four. They irradiated him. They put seeds of radiation in him, ugly flowers. Late-afternoon sun streamed in the dark house after dinner, dust in the air like an ascension, all the people tryptophaned out, or just inebriated—we handed the girl in her pink, puffy dress from person to person. A brief amusement for her, to sit on every lap. A few laps in, she came to my father—recent nuclear waste dump. I did not jump over the table and tackle him, although part of me wanted to pull her away pronto, with dispatch. She was only on his lap for a few seconds. My father: humbled, humiliated, wised up. He did not squeeze her to him, as he might have otherwise. He was a ticking time bomb, a bloom of death. And then without knowing it I was getting up, walking over, lifting her from his lap.

My father and his wife live two thousand miles away, far enough to keep things from me. I do not know if he is ill again, or how seriously, until he is ready to tell me.)

(My husband says I sometimes have a dicey memory. I'll concede that my memory is not completely realist. It's not abstract either. I think I am more of an impressionist rememberer, or perhaps a surrealist rememberer.)

Wilson is sitting in his (well, his for now) apartment, and he is feeling tense. Understandably. He has not written a letter for a long time, but right now he has a piece of paper, a pen, a stamp, and an envelope, all lined up before him. Over on the cocktail table by the TV is his laptop, but Wilson has turned off his laptop. It is the site of nonmail. He has nonmail coming in from all over. *Dear Alyssa*, he's written on the top of the piece of paper before him, and he's also written the date. He is staring at his handwriting. Surprisingly handsome writing, if he says so himself. It looks like the handwriting of a Victorian fellow who might well have something to say, and is, most likely, gay. But Wilson is not gay. Wilson isn't even close to gay. Wilson doesn't even like the word metrosexual when it comes to himself, or anyone else, for that matter—it's such a stupid word and, really, concept. Why isn't there a similar word for women who happen to like—what?—cars, sports. Wilson would really be fine with being gay, if he was gay. So why is he not gay, despite his attraction to

Devin? Because his attraction to Devin is not, actually, sexual. Wilson would never write in the nude, but he remembers the way his body looks from when he was in the bathroom five minutes ago. Wilson's crisis includes his body, and so he spent a little longer than usual staring at himself in the mirror after his postwork, post-job-at-all shower. No one besides himself has touched his body since Alyssa left, in October. His body looked more or less the way it always did, except for the nose, of course. He did a jokey arm curl, and then busted out into the full Grecian: one leg on tiptoe, and the almost-gonna-throw-the-discus twist of the torso.

Much time is passing, he thinks to himself at his desk, before the nearly blank piece of paper. Night is falling. Through the loaming and dusk and on to twilight. Through all the stations with names, into the no-name place. My name is Wilson, and I am not a building. My name is Wilson, and I am not Alyssa's lover or even friend, and I do not have a straight nose, and my sex life has been reduced to the ethereal and the basely personal, and I do not have a job either.

My name is Wilson, and I am *not* a publicity coordinator.

(His face is slightly askew, which is a thrill, because the best statues show signs of wear. The ground under Rome has shifted, and so the white-marble visage tilts. Or: The maker is prehistoric, or perhaps Picasso. How smart, to pre-crack the stunning face. One doesn't care for surfer beautiful. Perfection must get old in a different, duller way. Oh, this skewed beauty. I have also noticed a slitted look to his eyes, as if he has not yet woken from a dream, or as if he's been crying, or staring too long into the sun. But today, luckily, I haven't been drinking. No helpful schemes come spilling out, and I am unimpeachably lacking in the crassness category.)

(*Things I've Forgotten*: I've forgotten why I had to stay after school and write the repetitive sentences. I've forgotten if it was me, or my mother. I've forgotten who X was, in the list of things I did with men. I've forgotten my brother's face at the dinner table of our childhood. I've forgotten what we talked about. I've forgotten the plot. I've forgotten the exact words. I've forgotten the novel I was writing. I have plans, though, to edit out the naughty bits, to obfuscate time still further so I'm not implicated.)

*

Later still Wilson returns to the websites. Maybe the chairs *were* grayish green, after all, or greenish gray. If the chairs were grayish green, then what of his recollections of Alyssa—how could this whole sector of his life be recollection now, a basket of thoughts and some stray vases and forks amid the tans of his apartment? If he closes his eyes . . . in the dark he can remember being with her.

(I wish now we'd spent one more hour per day in Luxembourg Gardens. We were in Paris four days and went to the park every morning to eat breakfast by the pool. We had Orangina (the cheap man's mimosa), croissants, and coffee from McDonald's (the cheap man's café au lait). Four days, four extra hours a day: If I had that, would the memory of Luxembourg Gardens have burrowed in, would it be more likely that I'd always remember?)

In the days like heaven, Wilson remembers there was a bee that kept coming near, in that garden, back with Alyssa. A young couple sat on chairs closer to the palace, preparing to take wedding pictures. A photographer had arrived. Then came the gendarme. Bride, groom, photographer, gendarme—they talked among themselves for a long while. Then the photographer packed up the tinfoil umbrella and the stands and boxes, and everyone left.

(My father's voice on the phone again. He is making beef stock. He's bought the bones and has deglazed the pot. He has pulled the last root vegetables out of the garden, the beets and horseradish. He has harvested kale and okra and potatoes. He had a good gardening season, the best in a long while, he tells me. It is autumn now, and soon he will be putting his gardens to bed, and his gardens are as beautiful as the ones in Paris, but more on the wild side. There is mist and sorrow along the edges of his field, a weird and sultry beauty. Myself, I had a bad gardening summer. The tomatoes wilted and died, all six plants. I did harvest three cucumbers, but they had grown too big and I didn't know what to do with them. Cucumber salad? Cucumber soup? I stare out at the bleaching Tucson sky and imagine the

189

aroma of beef stock in October in a cramped kitchen in the Massa-chusetts countryside.)

*

(Emotions are manifesting themselves in my body now. I get a feel-ing like a grasshopper is lodged between my ribs if I think of my father, mother, and brother. There we are, The Little Brute Family, as in Russell Hoban's children's book. In my shoulders and in my heart is where I feel the *You Fool!* feeling. After parties, or more gen-eralized. I want this story to succeed. Life is a story.)

I must take control, thinks Wilson, a tear streaming down his face.

Résumés, dating, reconciliations with the past: He has a busy near future. Yet he is now feeling a wave of calm, lying prostrate on his bed of singleness. He didn't like his job anyway. It was time for him to leave his job. He loved Alyssa. It was time for Alyssa to leave him. What does "it was time for" mean exactly? A superstition, belief in fate, Monday-morning quarterbacking?

I could be a fireman, or a journalist, or I could go back to school and study literature or geography. This is just a transition moment.

But the transition is making Wilson think about what is under the surface.

Perhaps I could get a new job, as a rememberer.

(I'm not there, I'm writing about being there. My teeth buzz from the chocolate cupcake my husband and I split earlier. I'm drinking Earl Grey tea with sugar and lemon—not my many-years method of milk in my tea. I've already had coffee. We had coffee with the cupcake. Yes, I'm using megacaffeine to help me sort this out. Pretty soon it's time to move on to white wine and sole and spinach and rice, and darkness, and our daughter returning from her adventures, away from us. When we went to France we were forty-eight, fifty-four, and twelve. To say the ages makes it seem ominous, time bound. This weekend, I'll call my father.)

Wilson goes to his favorite coffee shop. Inside or outside? Outside appears to be the location of still too many love affairs and business meetings, and so inside he will go. He waits in line, staring at the bonbons and the pastries. He is not thinking of pastries. When the time comes, he orders a cappuccino. He waits at the Waiting Place. A woman with an athletic demeanor, but more a yoga-athlete demeanor, sends his cappuccino in a short spin toward him on the counter. She glances his way. Her eyes are large and bronze-brown, and narrowed. She recognizes him, smiles slightly, and then turns away to the next task. Wilson picks up the cup and saucer—there's a lovely leaf design in the foam. He smiles at the woman's aura, her wake. He brings his cup to a small table by the wall in the back of the café. He places the cup and then sits, adjusts the chair, leans back, crosses his legs. He lets the motion catch up to him, a kind of focusing or stilling, as with a top. This is where he will stay.

Wilson wears his own family like a hat also: a wide-brimmed woman's hat heavy with fruit. An invisibility.

I shall now think like a man, he tells himself, in a gruff interior voice filled with comic potential. At least in his mind it seems pretty funny.

(I do not remember being there in a buggy, but I believe it happened. Wilson holds an image of Alyssa in his mind. It is almost like being there, almost as if they are together always. Wilson feels he is on to something, in his café in the walnut city, jobless at the moment but employable. A man with skills, if not a straight nose. In my closet I have rabies tags for cats long dead. Last night I dreamed my cat got outside and a strange man captured him with a net. My cat wasn't a cat in the dream—he was a red bird, a cardinal. The man handed me the net with the cat inside, and when I took it from him, I made some kind of error. The cat was caught, snagged, and I heard a small crunch within the netting. I'd hurt him, a lethal blow. I lay on the floor next to the dying red bird, my cat, on the cool tile of our living room.)

Luxembourg Gardens, again and always. The riot of white gravel under our feet, a river bringing us to this place. We are giddy, excited, passports on our persons, croissants in tiny bags, Orangina, and coffee. We head to the pool, to watch boats and sit on the green chairs, or gray chairs, to set up breakfast and stave off bees. In the glorious light of early August, mornings without end, a breeze ruffling the surface of the pool, flower gardens in riotous bloom, our steps are hopeful as we approach. The white river invites us into the past—now, somehow, also the present day. The past crushes us, a fine crushing. I can smell the most outrageous flowers, the fine last bits of who I am smashed up and squeezed. The gardens swirl, pear and palm trees, blossoms of every color but mostly tea-rose pink, yellow, white, purple. Everywhere, everything, three hundred and sixty degrees, dizzy.

Letters So That Happiness
Arnaldo Calveyra

—Translated from Spanish by Elizabeth Zuba

UN GALOPE ABRÍA RAMADAS hacia el este de las tunas; no podíamos saber quién era, qué era, tan así, tan a campo traviesa; y luego, los perros, todos, que ladraban y parecían acometer algo de bulto por su furia momentáneamente ensimismada. Apagamos la luz porque la luna. Y por más que escudriñábamos, se ahogaba ese no saber en la blancura extrema sobre el campo. Papá dijo que las gallinas; a mí me apagaste una suposición con un "no será nada"; pero antes de que él saliera con la escopeta ya volvías de las piezas del frente diciéndole que era Billín, nuestro hermano.

Y ya no te vi sino cuando apareciste de entre los ligustros, con los botines embarrados, del tajamar esplendente, con él por delante, retrasándote, tú retrasándote para que te copiara la suavidad del paso y no se nos despertara en el pie del sueño, hasta que se entró en la cama.

A gallop parted lean-tos to the east of the cacti; we couldn't have known who it was, what it was, so much like this, so much through the field; and later, the dogs, all of them, that barked and seemed to mob something with some momentary daydreamed fury. We turned out the lights because the moon. And for all we searched, that not-knowing in the far white out over the field was drowning. Papa said the chickens; you turned out my doubts with an "it won't be any-thing"; but before he left with his rifle you had already come back saying it was Billín, our brother.

And I couldn't see you until you appeared from between the shrubs, your boots all muddy, from the resplendent creek water, he ahead of you, keeping you from gaining, you yourself keeping your-self from gaining so that he would mimic your smooth gait and we wouldn't wake up at the foot of his dream, until he got into bed.

* * *

Ya van para veinte años en el color del fierro.

Recuerdo la cocina en el hervor del frío de bolsillos y la boca en el humo cantando del buen día.

El gato o el fogón rumiando hasta no entenderlas, las palabras de arar, o de moler el maíz, o de ir al pueblo, y la taza ávida y bocona probando antes que nadie el sabor del candeal, y la escarcha de rocío coloreando la teja hasta la gota.

Cuando tocabas la campana ya algún muchachito viejo viruejo de picopicotuejo de pomporerá enfilaba por la calle de los paraísos. Eso parecía bastarte, te sacabas el delantal del desayuno y el menudo blanco redondeando en las rodillas de tu guardapolvo se alejaba unos pasos.

¿Y de cómo nos repartías el amor no te acuerdas?, ¿de cómo no cambiaba el descanso de tu rostro en el día de campanada subiendo?, ¿de cómo no cambiaba el azul de tu encontrada cuando ibas con todos nosotros al buen día del aula?

They're already going on 20 in the color of iron.

I remember the kitchen in the fervor of my cold pockets and the mouth in the steam singing good morning.

The cat or the stove ruminating to the point of gibberish, plowing words, the grinding corn or going to the village words, and the eager cup and huge mouth tasting the eggnog before anyone else, and the frosted dew coloring the tile right up to the trickle.

When you rang the bell, some little boy blue go blow your horn was already heading down Paradise Way. That seemed about right, and you took off your breakfast apron and the small bull's-eye rolling around the knees of your overalls distanced itself a few paces.

And how you handed your love out to us, don't you remember? how the quiet of your face never changed through the climbing bells day? how your finding blue never changed when you went with us to the good morning of the classroom?

* * *

Soñé con la casa color de tormenta. Estaba yo conmigo una mañana de 1943. A las ventanas se remansaba el balcón esperándolo todo. Estaba descalzo, con la luz que me hacía cosquillas para que saliera de ella, y el sol no estaba a las baldosas sino que ya era en el río de dos riberas. En una, yo. En la de sombra, si se la miraba a los ojos, retumbaban nuestras voces hacia el fulgor de remos en el pasar azul. Y de nuevo era en el patio que estrellaba naranja en instante de cascotazo entero sobre cachurra monta la burra y el finado Urquiza como el ánima del rey del *Hamlet* les arengaba *in hoc signo vinces* en la respuesta agorrionada.

Yo hubiera querido esa poca luz pasando a la altura de los ojos pero alguien murmuró que igualmente había que encenderla, y me levantaron de cabezal de agua y se bailaba con una soledad de la isla jacarandá.

"Tienes que amar mucho," me dijo la rama. "¿Y esto?," le dije, y no pude sino despertarme.

Era la rama con la luz.

I dreamed about the storm-colored house. I was there with myself one morning in 1943. The balcony backwatered at the windows waiting for everything. I was barefoot, with a light that tickled at me so I would run from it, and the sun wasn't on the tiles anymore but already in the double-banked river. Me, on one side. On the shaded side, if you looked it in the eyes, our voice thundered toward the radiance of oars in the blue passing. And it hit the patio again and blew up instantly orange pelting hard over leapfrog and the dead Urquiza like the king's soul in *Hamlet* urging *in hoc signo vinces* with his sparrowed reply.

I would've wanted that little light passing by at eye level but someone muttered that you'd have to light it just the same, and lifted my head from the water headboard and danced with a jacaranda island loneliness.

"You have to love a lot," said the branch. "And this?" I said, and all I could do was wake up.

It was the branch with the light.

* * *

Como si estuviera por llegarme a cada instante esta compaña de siempre, en la cueva del invierno de una friolera, junto al perro que encontramos en tu día, subo a la loma que se apura a que yo regrese para darte las margaritas alegres.

Es gozosa la llegada de pulmones, gritarte que asomes con tu falda de patatas a ponderar flores y mandarlas en seguida a los santos.

Y después era día de otras cosas, y a una hora de ese día nos dábamos cuenta de que no sería tampoco tu día, de que no cumplirías años.

¡Pero qué alegre ademán la biznaga ardiendo, y ponerse en cuclillas el sol, y abanico de lámpara, y recordar versos de memoria, y tu niñez de nosotros desde nuestras espaldas como el estante más alto sobre puntas de pie abuelita qué horas son, en tu homenaje!

En este día de seguida con sol alto de invierno me quedo aquí oyéndote la mañana que me trajiste a lomas, a desniveles de aguas, el otro cumpleaños de los dos.

As if I were almost ever there this same company, in the cave of a shiverer's winter, together with the dog we found on your day, I jump up on the hill that hurries to take me back to bring you merry daisies.

The lungs' arrival is wonderful, yelling for you to come out with your potato skirt to ponder the flowers and send them off to the saints.

And later it was a day of other things, and at some point we realized that it wouldn't be your day either, that you wouldn't turn a year older.

But what a happy gesture the burning bishop's weed, and the sun crouching, and a fanning flame, and recalling verses by heart, and your childhood of us on our backs like the highest shelf on tiptoes, Grandma what a time it is, in your honor!

On this protracted day with winter's high sun I stay here listening to you the morning you brought me to hills, to declivities of water, the other birthday of both.

* * *

Kikirikí grita una hierba entre los dos pulgares.

¡Mira hasta qué lejos el yuyal se encresta!

No es el aire que pasaba, no. Ni el andador de loma que se ensaya a solas a no voltear los niños.

Y las cañas locas por la música y el silbido de la perdiz que le contestan, ¡cómo se esconden y en el eco de vuelta se dislocan, suben!

¡Mira hasta qué arriba en la veleta la cresta colorada del kikirikí!

Cock-a-doodle-doo whoops a blade of grass between two thumbs.

Look how far out the weed patch crests!

It isn't the air that wended, no. Or the hill's baby walker practicing keeping the children from flipping over.

And the music-crazy reeds and the partridge's whistle that answers back: how they hide and then dislocate and rise in the return echo!

Look! The colored crest of the cock-a-doodle-doo so far up in the weather vane!

* * *

La muchachita guardapolvo blanco venía a la cocina a darnos el buen día, no esperaba la campanada de entrar al aula.

Una mañana me encontró llorando, y me di vuelta para que no viera lo que lloraba. Ella se apuró en la mentira hasta el punto porque otras niñas andaban por ahí con miradas de irse sacándonos la lengua.

Tenía la facilidad de subirse a la cara las margaritas silvestres sin arrancarlas, ¿no recordarías su nombre?

The white overalls girl came to the kitchen to wish us good morning, she didn't wait for the classroom bell.

One morning she saw me crying, and I turned so she wouldn't see what I cried. She hurried straight through to the end of that lie because there were other girls around ready to stick their tongues out at us.

She had a talent for getting up easily on the faces of wild daisies without ever picking them, wouldn't you remember her name?

Immortals Having a Party
Mei-mei Berssenbrugge

1.

You could be a person or you could be immortal, a wave in the environment.

How to describe energy without matter, without dimension or gods?

Through space, the world has passed; a year has gone by.

The word for earth, world is year, which moves in time like water in water; it does not pass.

Their word for cosmos is year.
.
We say time contemporary with creation, our births, the birth of our daughter was constitutively blessed by the presence of gods, say goddess, divines.

At our age, world grows into time faster than light, an energy in the medium of love, no quanta, rays, waves, no gods or geomantic force, angels, not even ghosts of those who loved us, who were present at the origin, co-creating; now light without light.

Light is reversible.

2.

Air in air, my mesa comes into being in world, like love in divinity.

In winter we move south, where flowers can blossom; lightning flashes there, rain; every story happens.

There, life was created by gods and revealed to my family through celebration, cosmic time coming forth as beautiful pattern-time without age.

Before a juniper tree existed, time in which it grew after drought did not exist.

Time rushes forth with the appearance of any new thing.

It makes an orientation in four directions and above and below, marking clouds' movement and potential for rain, the sky with morning star in winter, when time proceeded so slowly.

I wake at dawn and see the full moon eclipse in apricot shade setting into the Jemez, cerulean-blue sky, dark caldera.

I go to the mountains; sun through trees seems to activate air as a material substance; emerald moss is ground now; it's spring.

One log crosses a narrow place of the pond, reflecting on a still surface; a sapling doubles, tangled trees, the lighted air doubles in a world above and below.

Mirroring by love founds place; atmosphere saturates as an old woman reenters beginning time that floweth not, but stays with me by my walking and looking.

Where sacred manifests in a place, landscape unveils.

Every fragment as transparence shows through a structure of being.

For us the homonyms are experiences, and living is at the same time of open, emotionally transhuman structure.

An angel, a young avatar appears.

The substrate, what I mean by open, is parallel, connotative, as gods narrate.

For them, the state of things, as of pond molecules reflecting light and exerting gravity isn't intrinsic, but created by states of other things that manifest with our perceptions and prayer.

199

Mei-mei Berssenbrugge

3.

A "tiny" garden below the mesa symbolizes isled rivers of the immortals, a symbol miniaturized as if by distance or contemplation to concentrate presence.

With symbol I find my way through entropic time, exhausted space, to the garden.

In the presence of a juniper, cocreating the general, the universal, I experience that.

Even in winter, it ciphered a pervasive mood and motivation with such an aura of fact, mood was more like matter opening to values that are no longer contingent.

I find openings through the centers of flowers, the voice of a girl, through memory of black dragonflies weaving and breathing at dusk.

It's personal, like drawings on a wall of dragonflies in a realm or substrate more like an imaginative sky?

* * *

The shape of the pond is like the character for heart; its flow is slightly restricted; muddiness heightens reflectivity of the surface, glass water; bird on a rock doubles by the far shore.

There's a feeling of love, for which reflectivity is the substrate.

Space is denser fluctuating light; emotion turns into information underlying all particles that reflect and gravitate, which are coherent, virtual, connected, not just in time that precedes and gives weight to spring.

For immortals, emphasis is not always on spring itself.

They seek prophetic signs of the substrate: greening branch, a cluster of white flowers, wood thrush, more like an awareness, orientation, than any season.

4.

There's an absolute, which manifests in the world, making it real.

Sacred means saturated with being.

She believes, as she celebrates gods, she keeps close to the real, because existence, nature, is the creation of "others," so we envision entities we don't know where space and objects have intention: sunbeam on a mushroom in woods, sighting a rare animal.

Then I try to infer the intentions of others' love.

I spontaneously feel loved in dense forest, but wonder at the rigor of summer drought, forest fire, earthquake?

My mind exchanges data with holograms in the field, then waves of quanta, narration, distribute where I walk.

Here, moonrise across white feathers of sleeping owls; mind moves from chaos to increasingly entangle with a goddess as protagonist for trees and their shadows on a cliff face.

Love may appear as beings attached to space around her, water in water, narrative anteriority, and it assimilates through mothering, healing others.

With symbols, she reintegrates the passage from virtual to formal, beginning again with life's sum energy, a place: eye of a spring in dry country.

Unoccupied territory still shares in larval chaos.

She imagistically transforms uncertain space into a cosmos from watery time, the preforms of plants, stones, animals by drawing them.

She draws a spring overflowing its bowl.

Prayer and memory share this sum unfixed, as in woods of "unbounded ambiguity," of the potential to awe, like timing when music shapes the voice of the immortal, magic time that reverses and recovers.

The Connoisseur of Pain
Michael Reid Busk

IT WAS ME ALONE AT CUFFY'S, swilling corn beer and waiting for the mouse. I was underwhelmed and oversexed, woeful and old, and not half as drunk as I wanted to be. Football was over, spring training was a month off, Castro had shut down the Tropicana, and cops and hobos were finding friends of mine crushed and shredded and burned in places never mentioned in *The Hollywood Reporter*: the bilgy beaches of South Bay, the Manchester on-ramp to the 405, Rancho Cucamonga.

The TV above the bar was as dead as the moon, and three stools down, a rube in a bowler and topcoat too heavy for March was eyeing me like he was a razor and I was a strop. In the corner lounged the Looney Tunes crew, carrying on like they do, tittering like hussies and sipping their bitty cones of gimlet and sloe gin fizz. It was just the rabbit sitting, two-legging a stool against the wall, his big rabbit feet propped up on the rim of the pool table, the pig and the duck and the bald hunter laughing at everything that came out his mouth. About my head a zeppelin of a fly was circuiting lackadaisically, and I swatted at it with my splinted paw, which had swelled up big into a soft club.

"Thomas," the rabbit called to me. "Thomas, come nostaligize with an old man." The others goggled my way, and the pig gave me a white-gloved thumbs-up. As I waved Bugs away, the Ivy Leaguer in the bowler asked if I'd ever heard of William Jennings Bryan, and I debated the merits of frying pan and fire. But finally the rabbit said, "But, Thomas, it's my birthday." I glanced up at the nudie calendar tacked above the bourbon shelf, where about half the days were x-ed off. "The eyes," he said. "The eyes of March."

With my splint and my beer, I shuffled across the clapboard's peanut shells in the dishwater-blonde light, setting myself down on the edge of the pool table by the rabbit's feet. He didn't take them down. The pig blew a kazoo and offered me a party hat. He was the only one wearing one. I told him thanks but no thanks.

"You were there my first Hollywood birthday," Bugs said, jiggling

202

his wrist and its Mickey Mouse watch at me. "Remember this? Mickey's still ticking. You were the best roomie ever."

At the name of the Disney poster child, Daff heaved an empty Tom Collins glass at the wall opposite, almost braining a raccoon playing darts, Pork took the kazoo out of his mouth to cup his hand around his snout and boo, and Elmer muttered, in the King's own English, "I loathe that man." Obliged, I slammed my bandaged paw on the table, and through the pain grunted, "May his mother rot in hell."

"Hey, T-t-t-t-tom," said Pork, "is it true you were the one who p-p-p-p-p-painted the devil horns on, on, on . . ." He was treading water, not wanting to say the name. "On that jerk?" he said, raising a stubby white-gloved finger at Bugs's watch, whose faded Mickey still sported faint red crescents behind his ears.

"Just trying to be accurate," I said.

"Hey, Tom," said Daffy, eyeing me but raising his hands toward the hissing raccoon by way of apology, "what he get you for your first LA birthday?"

"Arrested." All I remembered of that night, the summer of '37, was a motorcycle with a sidecar, a gun-toting priest, a truckload of rotting bananas, and four very angry Chinamen throwing me off Santa Monica pier. But the Looney Tunes crew tossed their heads back and cackled like hatchlings waiting for the worm.

"Bugs Bunny," said Elmer in his tea-and-crumpets accent, "a man with a criminal past but not a criminal future."

Bugs shook his fist. "To the moon, Elmeh," he said. I wasn't sure if it was an impression or not: If you closed your eyes, Bugs Bunny sounded just like Ralph Kramden. When I asked if he'd gotten any presents, he said, "The good sirs at Warner sent roses and carrots this morning. And Daff here got me a tie bar, which I'll be wearing on the red carpet after those Oscar nomerations come out. And I bought myself a Studebaker."

"Don't you already own a Studebaker?"

"That one's green. This one's blue. Besides, it's a new kind. Avanti."

"Hey, T-t-t-t-t-tom," jackhammered Porky, that sweet sausage of a lackey, "what happened to the p-p-p-p-p-p . . . what happened to the hand?"

"Grand piano. Three stories up."

They all puckered at me like my words were made of lemon juice— the Looney Tunes bunch risked life and limb on set less than Lucille Ball, and the worst thing probably ever happened to any of them was a fleck of carrot in the eye from all Bugs's munching. What my paw felt like was cheap meat, pummeled to hell then set to simmer in a Crock-Pot.

"We were in Barbados on a shoot," said Daff. "Two weeks. Just got back last night."

"Don't talk to me of Barbados," said Elmer, who took off his flap-eared hunter's hat to show a cap of skin so red he looked like a Roman cardinal. "The place was nothing but mosquitoes, heatstroke, and the clap."

"You were just palling with the wrong crowd," Daff said to Elmer as he rolled a cigarette. "I had a great time."

"You *were* the crowd," said Elmer, throwing his hat at Daff.

"I bought a shrunken head from a medicine man," said Bugs. "I hung it from the rearview of the new Studebaker."

"You heard about Igby," I said.

"What about Igby?" Bugs asked.

"Found him legless in a storm drain in Hawthorne."

"D-d-d-dead?" asked Porky.

"No, just peachy." I should've taken it as a omen not to come to the set that morning when instead of Gracie next to me there was the early edition of the *Hollywood Reporter*, with a front-page headline IGBY BERT BINDLE MURDERED, and an accompanying photo of Igby, who looked less like a frog and more like green-egg hash. Gracie'd underlined the grisliest parts with an eyebrow pencil.

"I blame the French," said Bugs.

"Don't joke," I said, grabbing one of the pool cues and poking Bugs in the neck. "He was one of us." The cue chalk left a blue polka dot in Bugs's white fur.

"Guess I'll have to get it dry-cleaned," he said, trying to brush the powder off his fur, trying to brush away my comment. Bugs always had trouble feeling bad for pain that wasn't his own.

"He ever get anything after *Mr. Toad*?" asked Daff, striking a match on Elmer's hunter's jacket and setting the tip of his loose cigarette afire.

I shrugged. "Does Campbell's soup count?"

"Are you in m-m-m-m-mourning?"

"He wasn't my mother."

"But somebody was his mother," said Pork. I hadn't thought of that.

"Two is a coincidence, but three is a spree," said Elmer, absent-mindedly removing his hat and scratching his head. "Christ," he shouted, jerking his hand up from the burn.

"Four," I said. "Beaks. No one's seen him in two weeks."

For the first time since I'd seen him that day, Bugs's feet touched the floor. "Beaks?"

"Sorry," I said. "Thought you heard." Pork's face was plastered over with his white gloves. Daffy's cigarette was dangling from his bill, but he wasn't smoking. Beaks used to have a regular poker game at his place, a shoe box in a pagoda in Chinatown; he said he lived there because the Chinese made the best jerky, and since Beaks was a vulture, I guess that made sense, but we always suspected it was more Oriental powders and not Oriental meats that kept him there. He spoke very slowly, very perfectly, and his sense of humor was a meat cleaver—unserrated, sharp, heavy. He was the best poker player I'd ever met.

Bugs's egg-shaped eyes were pooling with tears. "What did Beaks ever do to anybody?"

"What did any of them ever do to anybody?" I said.

"What about Jericho?" asked Bugs, gripping the edge of the pool table, eyes bouncing around the room, looking for further signs of the End Times.

"Jerry's fine," I said. "Jerry's always fine."

One hour, two beers, and no painkillers later, the bar was picking up, the William Jennings Bryan guy was gone, and me and Cuffy were deep into a game of German whist, talking wounds. He pointed to his left pinkie, forever buttonhooked and the color of a screaming baby. "*Stalag 17.* Tire iron."

I lifted my tail, thrice kinked near the tip. "Two mousetraps, one 3 wood. Cameras weren't even rolling for that last one. Jerry just thought it'd be fun."

Cuffy pulled down the neck of his A-shirt. Below his collarbone was a patch of raised pink skin that looked like Jersey. "*Twelve O'Clock High.* Steam burn from an engine on the fuselage."

I nodded. Steam burns were the worst.

Bad luck good luck bad luck man, Cuffy, kraut-type bruiser, like me born orphan in Baltimore, went west, ate eggs, bench-pressed on Muscle Beach, gained some small fame on the silver screen in the rah-jingo flicks of the late forties and fifties, a natural Nazi thug with his chrome dome and blond handlebar, but shit out of luck when World War II epics gave way to teenybopper dreck and faggy beatnik mopers. His was the usual decline: littler and littler dirtbag Venice bungalows, rotgut rye, diner waitress whore wife, Mexican tar, the orchard wars, porn acting, bearbaiting, arson, until one night when he blacked out, woke up in a schoolyard in Watts, quit the bottle, found Jesus, sweated and shook himself cold turkey off the smack, cut ties with his own personal Jezebel, begged up the money to buy a bar, and started turning a decent profit with the Tinseltown crowd. Judging from the stock floor chatter, the big burger of smoke clinging to the ceiling, the menagerie of boys and badgers and ladies and lemurs all tossing back whiskey like water, I'd say he was doing all right.

I played a spade and flexed my wonky back left foot at him. "Steamroller."

He lifted his head to reveal a collar of rope burn around his coffee-can neck. "Rough love."

"Speaking of," I said, "you hear news about the ex?"

He jerked his noggin at the nudie calendar and grunted.

"Ah," I said, and took my foot off the bar. "Miss March. I see."

The first sign of Jerry was a thonking at the base of the door, and when it finally opened a crack, my partner squeezed in with an industrial bolt slung under his arm. "The bolt is mightier than the door!" I roared, and the crowd of bigger beings parted. After swinging the thing above his head like some mad Viking, Jerry charged through the gauntlet of wingtips and pumps, then into the clapboard floor he braced pole vaulter–like the end of the bolt, which bent a hair then flung him barward. I stuck up my tail and he springboarded off it, somersaulting toward Miss March, whom he kissed on the tit before kicking off and backflipping down onto the bar. He bellowed, a burning trail of vowels that lit into the air and singed the frivolity of flirting bigger creatures, except for Cuffy, who beamed with his hockey player's mouth, gave Jerry a splay-fingered clap, and in a silver jigger glass poured him a rum and grenadine. Jerry always liked it sweet. He had a name for the drink, but it couldn't be repeated in polite company. I reached over the bar, yanked out the LA phone book, and told the windburnt surfer on the next stool to scram.

"Walls," I said, sliding the phone book onto the stool as Jerry stepped off the bar, just as smooth as Aladdin onto his magic carpet. He started slurping the jigger through a coffee straw.

"Hoss," he said, tipping an imaginary cap at me.

"Half past five beers, Walls."

"Don't scold. You sound like a schoolmarm. I was out." Out meant whores. "How's the slapper?"

"About how you'd think after a one-ton thing fell forty feet on it. But you should see the other guy."

"That's right," he said, miming a piano scale. "Other guy's firewood."

"Doc got me morphine, Walls. Gracie picked it up from his office, out back of the soundstage."

"Pills or drops?" he coughed, finishing up his rum and grenadine.

"Drops."

"Good," he said, waving Cuffy away for another drink. "Drops hit you faster."

"What's that on your ear?" I said to him, licking my good paw then wiping at a patch of dark crusted hair.

"Smidge of this, maybes," he said, jiggling the jigger glass, his whiskers bristling at my touching.

"Can't be. It's already dried."

"If I'd wanted a bath, I'd a asked for one." He squinted over at the corner of the room. "Why's Pork wearing a hat?"

"The rabbit's birthday."

"First time I met Bugs, I says to myself, there is somebody would suck poison off the pavement if he thought it would make people like him."

"I have met people with a steadier hand at the emotional tiller," I said.

"You know he can't read?"

"What? Bugs?"

"Couldn't make out the directions on a box of shampoo."

"Who said that? I lived with him nigh on two years."

"Grip buddy of mine at Warner. Anyway, think about it. He never looks at menus—it's always either the spaghetti and meatball or he just asks the waiter what his favorite is."

"What about his lines?"

He grabbed the coffee straw, stuck it in the corner of his mouth, and pretended to chew. "What's up, doc?" he asked in a good impression of Bugs's yiddy Flatbush drone. He threw the straw back into the jigger glass. "The rest is off the cuff. I'm not saying he's stupid. I'm saying he's illiterate."

It had been a puzzler why Bugs always used to wave the *Times* away and say newspaper people were all Commies. Or why he hated maps. Or why every book in his Malibu mansion was one of those hollow ones with a gun or a sex toy inside.

"How's the ball and chain?" Jerry said, still looking over my shoulder at the Looney Tunes crew.

"Get this: I come home early couple days ago and she's in the shower, but there's all this tracing paper and charcoal on the dining table, from Hollywood Forever."

207

"I think that's kind of foxy."

"That's because you're a creep. Plus yesterday I was trying to find some scissors and in one of the drawers in this envelope were all these clippings of the murders. She even drew little stick figures of the victims."

"Like Igby? What's a stick-figure frog look like?"

"Think you're missing my overall sort of point here."

"You should be grateful she's not like most wives with the shopping and the what have you."

Cuffy parked me another corn beer, and an r-and-g for Jerry. I trailed my good paw over the bar, which now over the burls of the original walnut had an artificial grain cut by knives, glass, fake nails, battery acid, the diamond of Errol Flynn's wife's engagement ring, the Host-like watermarks of a million men. My good paw felt it all.

Monty Clift wandered over with Jerry's bolt vault and set it next to Jerry's jigger glass. He'd been standing alone for an hour. "For you," he said.

"Rusty screw," Jerry said, fingering its groove.

Monty smiled the way you smile when you don't want someone to pistol-whip you. He smelled like apricot brandy and frou-frou cologne. "So, Monty," I said, quicklike, "saw that *Misfits* flick. Sure as hell make a whamdinger of a bronco buster."

"And a Nazi retard," said Jerry. I couldn't tell if he was poking fun.

"Yeah, that *Nuremberg*, damn," I said, even though I'd fallen asleep when Gracie'd taken me. "Full of all that moral . . . ambiguity."

"Thanks," he said, rimming the lip of the brandy glass with his finger. He coughed and backed away. "I need to use the men's." His fingers made a slow cat's cradle in front of his chest. "Thanks for the . . . thanks."

"He looks so old now," said Jerry, who was doing a first-rate job catching up with me in the drink tally.

"We all look old now." But it was a lie: Jerry's coat was still an ungrayed sable, his eyes like two-tone bucks. They were right to call him the Mickey Rooney of the animal kingdom.

"Monroe once told me Monty was the only person she knew in worse shape than she was."

"Marilyn?" I asked.

"Sure as shit ain't James."

"When was that?"

"She let me hide in her cleavage when some pimp was chasing me."

"I call bullshit."

"Well, OK," he said. He shrugged, and his whiskers followed suit, rising then falling. "But I did dream it once."

On the doorstep of midnight, I was on the doorstep of Cuffy's, Jerry swung babylike over my shoulder and the hot winds whooping down from the hills. When I'd told him to slow it down on the rum, Jerry'd told me he'd wrap me in barbwire and throw me in a trash compactor. Then he blacked out and fell off the bar onto his face.

The day had been warm for March, and now, parched under Mojave winds as hot as exhaust, my paw boiling inside its wrappings, the prospect of hauling my best friend best man best mouse a drunk mile up La Brea was enough to make me cry. By my lonesome I'd have called a cab, but cabbies blab, and after his brush with the law last year, the suits at MGM told Jerry to keep his hijinks out of the *Hollywood Reporter*. So I stepped off the curb, my paw over my head like an overeager school brat, Jerry muttering foul, foul words to the imaginary whores of his head.

Gracie and me lived in the little eyelet of Hollywood that stuck up into Runyon Canyon, and by the time I was crossing Sunset uphill half a mile from home, I hurt so much I thought I might have to bang a stranger's door till I found someone who'd call me an ambulance. Instead I whispered to Jerry that he owed me one and cursed Leo Shampoo, the doctor MGM kept on call at the studio—him, his mother and father, siblings, bridge partners, lodge brothers, his present and future psychics. Rumor was he lost his license after a back-alley abortion went south and now he worked off the books for MGM. I'll say this much: He got there fast after that baby grand pancaked my paw, but all the half-sized nitwit did was check my pulse, shove a thermometer in my mouth, and ask how many fingers he was holding up. When I told him where he could stick all four of them, he asked me what my sign was, and I told him I was on the cusp of Gemini and fuck you. I yanked him back down to me by his tie and asked about the hospital, but he chuffed it off and told me the angry pain in my paw was nothing morphine and ylang-ylang tea couldn't cure. As I staggered to my front door, I distracted myself imagining all manner of heavy things falling from great heights onto that goddamned hack.

The darkness of the living room was the blue-black of Superman's hair, and I only saved myself from falling over a stack of Gracie's magazines by hooking a leg of the coffee table with my tail. Before picking my way to the bedroom, I did my best to swaddle Jerry in an armrest cover, then laid him as gently as a magi onto the ottoman while he mumbled to no one that if she didn't take off her stockings, he'd do it for her.

The bedroom door was open. I don't know if it's true, but I've heard Gracie was the inspiration for the phrase "sex kitten," and there she was, in my bed, white queen tangled in lavender sheets, thrashing through the heat lightning of her dream life, through the scorched plains and shimmering salt flats of the wordless night. My wife. My nightstand was bare but for the phone and the alarm clock and, thank God, a dark little vial with MORFEEN scrawled atop it. Bugs Bunny and Leo Shampoo would make quite the team. That homunculus of a doctor told me to take two drops when I got home, so I dropped six, wishing him deep pain as each one splashed on my tongue, tasting of maraschino juice left months too long outside the icebox. Easing myself horizontal, I rested my paw on the nightstand, and after a minute, I didn't think I was going to die, and after three, I felt like a soap bubble floating atop another soap bubble, and after ten, I thought I might name my first child after that dapper little physician.

Just as the train of sweet drugged sleep was pulling into the station, the phone rang, and I almost knocked it off the nightstand. From the living room Jerry yelled, "Balls!" and Gracie moaned and rolled over, the heat pouring off her like musk. I picked it off the cradle before it could ring again.

"Yallo."

"Where's Thomas? Dear holy mother of God, I need to speak to Thomas."

"Bugs, it's me. You'd think after twenty-odd years you'd recognize my voice."

"I can't take it anymore, Thomas. This world is too much for me. I'm going to end it. This time, I'm really going to end it. I'm standing on the edge of the deck looking out over the gorge, and I must say, it's a pretty nice night to die."

"Two things, Bugs. First, you don't have a phone out by the deck, so you can't be looking out—"

"I could be there in five seconds, ten seconds tops."

"And second, you live on a hill, not the edge of a gorge, so if you threw yourself off, the worst you could do is break a leg."

"Harsh, Thomas. Harsh. You might just have blood on your hands tonight."

In the years since I'd first met him, Bugs had built around himself a carnival of a life, big and bright and boisterous, but being a Coney Island boy, he'd started with the Cyclone, right smack dab in the middle, and instead of wandering around enjoying what he'd made, I don't think he'd ever got down from that rickety old roller coaster. Someday a bolt would come loose and he'd go flying right off. But I was pretty sure it wasn't tonight: Normal friends would sometimes send singing telegrams, drop off trinkets and oddities for me at the studio, but Bugs's way of saying he was thinking of me was to call me at 4:00 a.m. with a gun pointed at his head.

For Edison, genius was one percent inspiration and ninety-nine percent perspiration; for Bugs Bunny it was one percent desperation and ninety-nine percent affectation.

"What's yanking you around, Bugs?" As I adjusted to the darkness, the mirror Gracie had screwed to the ceiling some months back had been uncloudying itself from a dark pool into the two of us sprawled limbs akimbo like some Japanese word, and damned if she wasn't slinkier than when I'd married her, while my fur was stiff with dirt and sweat and rum and beer, and my eyes were a battleground between blood and phlegm.

"The suits at Warner are talking retirement, Thomas."

I inchwormed myself up until I was shoved back against the headboard. "Balderdash. You're Bugs Bunny. You're like our George Washington." Then I heard a bunch of weepy, hiccupy nose and mouth sounds on the other end.

"Thomas, that might be the nicest thing anyone's ever said to me."

"Why're they doing it?"

"Money's tight. And the kids don't like the newer ones as much. Figure they'll make more rerunning the old ones on TV. Syndimication."

"How's the money work?"

"Warner gets eighty, the writers and directors get ten, I get four."

"How big's the pie you're cutting from?" Gracie's dream whimpers were starting to make me grind my teeth in lust, and her tail, a charmed snake, began dancing up and down my leg.

"Big as a manhole cover."

"So you're telling me you're getting big money to sit on your ass?"

"I liked seeing myself at the movies."

"No more jumping out of a hole for fifty takes? No more shit-for-brains director? It's a dream is what it is, Bugs. A dream." My tongue felt unruly and fat and lost, like the retarded kid in class you always throw trash at.

211

"I have a nightmare, Thomas: me sitting at the Hilton on a Tuesday afternoon, a pint of gin sloshing around my insides, watching the shadows get longer and praying Daff calls up with something to do. That's not just boring, Thomas. That's apopoclipse."

"Bugs, I'm too doped up to be subtle, so I'm just going to ask: Can you read?"

There was a pause. "Thomas, I like to think of myself as a man who can come to his own opinions."

"Bugs, once in a while I miss having you around, and I'll lay this one-time offer out there: What's say I come to your place sometime, and if you like, I teach you how to read."

More of the hiccupy, mouthy noises, and then Bugs snuffling, "That'd be just aces, Thomas."

"All right, Bugs. Call you tomorrow." I settled the phone back in the cradle. I stuck my paw behind the wood pineapple that screwed into each end of the headboard, and even though my eyes were gritty with tired, the brain behind it was idling like the keys had got stuck in the ignition. So I used the trick I always did to help me go to sleep: imagining myself beating the shit out of Mickey Mouse with a Louisville Slugger.

Next morning, the sun through the undrawn Venetians woke me to a land mine of a hangover. Gracie was gone, but so was the pain in my paw, which made me so happy I almost didn't mind retching as I three-legged it out into the living room, past Gracie's spaceman chairs and the Cracker Jack box of a coffee table, which I'd told Gracie was too plain to be expensive until she told me it was made *in Denmark, by Denmark people.* All that was left of Jerry was a mouse-shaped dent on the ottoman.

In the kitchen I mixed a Bloody Mary, equal parts vodka, tomato juice, and Tabasco: After years of Jerry pranking me, spiking my drinks with everything from pickle juice to iodine to rat poison—which sent me to the ER and did almost kill me—I mixed my Marys strong and I mixed my Marys hot. Since the morphine tasted so bad by itself, I topped the drink off with a quick squirt, tossed in a pawful of salt, stirred it with a steak knife, and downed it like I was being timed.

In the bathroom I faced the john, set the hurt paw on the sink, which was as clean and green as an after-dinner mint, and fished myself out of my drawers. Gracie had taped the obits for Beaks and

Igby and Screwy and Felix to the mirror, and I almost tore them down. I didn't want to start my day with that. Four cartoon stars in six weeks, and with all the LAPD had come up with, I was starting to think they were all relatives of Leo Shampoo.

I finished, shook off the last drips, flushed, slid into a sweat suit, and when I saw the Caddy was gone, I shrugged and sighed, jogged the downhill half mile to Hollywood Boulevard, and caught the 109 to Pasadena.

The bus was lousy with gentle, cautious creatures—mothers out for Saturday morning specials, a family of gray squirrels, a pair of Chinamen in lampshade hats, a couple sleepy hounds probably just off the night shift, children who sat facing forward with their knees together, a glum frog reading his horoscope. Some seemed to recognize yours truly, and it struck me that at that very minute thousands of others across the nation were also watching me, on their own personal devil boxes (although my syndication deal was nowhere near as good as Bugs's) and perchance they stared on the bus because I seemed to bilocate. But as I shuffled back until I found enough real estate on the overhead bar, it seemed more likely they gawked because I was like the painting that Brit dandy kept up in the attic so he could look young forever, except in reverse: It was the me on the bus that looked like something we'd drag in, and the 2-D version that was all everlastingly bright and perky.

That eternal life we called cartooning and the way it worked was this: They'd shoot our little episodes on 16mm, then a stable of artists and illustrators would blow up each frame and recreate it with pencils and watercolors, simplifying the lines, flattening the surfaces, mixing variegations of hue into one consistent color, and just generally making it more visually digestible to the average ten-year-old in Kenosha, and more importantly, his parents, who were more likely to let Junior watch a cat and mouse beat the shit out of each other if they could tell him it wasn't real. Then the illustrators and artists order the stills all in a row like a giant flip book and run them in every theater and now television across the country. Then they give us sacks of money.

I stepped off a few blocks from the set into the bobby-pinned world of Pasadena, a suburban hell of trikes and elms and fathers pushing mowers and waving to each other as they slipped mindlessly into middle age. It was the sort of place freedom went to die. Outside the Cape Cod MGM used for its more domestic shoots the grips and gaffers and best boys and cameramen were sorting their gear, and from their crazy-legged walks and faces more slack than pained, I could tell they were drunk, not hungover, which was good for them but trouble-some for both their future marital prospects and for me: Their slop-piness meant forgetting to cushion walls and dull fork tines, meant retakes of me falling down stairs and sitting on pins. Because even though they fudged things here and there, what the cartooners didn't do was make up something that hadn't happened, so when Junior sees Jerry drop a hot iron onto me, the lump growing from my noggin is real.

Spike was shadowboxing out back by the pool, his white coat gleam-ing in the growing heat, mumbling, "Take *that* . . . and *that* . . . and *that* . . ." until he spotted me and hustled over. Jogging in place, he beamed and smacked me on the shoulder and asked how Death was doing. I was a tad embarrassed he remembered from a few weeks back I'd told him my fists were named Death and Pestilence. More embarrassing was that the morphine made me feel like I was wading through thickening aspic. "I named mine too," he said, putting up his dukes. "St. Michael," he said, shaking the right, "and St. Patrick," squeezing the left into a coconut-sized ball.

"That's good," I said. "That's good."

"Hey, you going to Igby's funeral?" he asked, uppercutting, danc-ing around me in a way that was not helping my headache one bit.

"Didn't know about it."

"It's in Sherman Oaks. Our Lady of Perpetual Help."

"Didn't know Igby was Catholic."

"Lot of frogs are," he said, ducking under an invisible punch. His breath smelled of mint-flavored bone—even though they would get bleached in cartooning, Spike liked to make sure his teeth looked clean on camera.

"Hell of a ways, Sherman Oaks."

"I think I'm going to take the kids. It's important for them to understand that life is short, and precious."

"Right," I said.

We were finishing up an episode, the gist of which was me audi-tioning to be an ivories man at a swanky club, hence the falling baby grand, but in order to pay for the tux I needed to perform, I had to steal the birthday money Jerry had given Spike. With most of the scene done, the only big sequence left was a long chase ending at the pool, which they'd just drained. Blotches of water at the bottom were shrinking down to nothing, and the air above was sashaying, stinging my nose with its heat and its chlorine. While I was eyeing

possible maneuvers, angles, and exit strategies, our director, Headley
St. John, came striding around the corner in his tight black suit and
Barry Goldwater glasses, clasping his hands together and calling me
by my Christian name. Because our episodes were seven-minute
shorts that had almost no dialogue, little need for direction, starred
a hardscrabble tomcat and a psychotic, alcoholic mouse, and eventually got cartooned over anyway, the show over the years had had a
carousel of sparkly-eyed expat directors wanting starter jobs with an
established brand. Headley, who'd directed the last four, was the latest.
But at least he was British, not French or South American, which
meant I could understand him, and he didn't try to kiss me on the
cheek every time he saw me. Plus he wasn't pushing boring novels
on me about the unbearable boringness of life or trying to convince
me to see a shrink about what the last director called my abandon-
ment issues.

"Thomas!" Headley called out, even though I was about five feet
away. "Thomas! How *is* your paw?"

"Better," I said, waving it around like a tennis racket. "Morphine.
Hell of a drug."

"Oh, Thomas," he chuckled.

"Any word from Jerry?" I asked, checking the watch I wasn't
wearing.

"I was just about to ask *you* that."

Just then Spike jogged over, still shadowboxing.

"Saint John," he said, letting loose a little jab that landed inches
short of Headley's long nose.

"Oh, my," he said, stepping back.

"Ooh, sorry," said Spike, grimacing. Besides never remembering
that Headley's last name rhymed with *Rin-Tin*, Spike thought that
the *St.* meant Headley was a clergyman of some type, and that he
was a direct descendant of the author of the fourth Gospel; being a
daily mass Catholic, that was big rocks for Spike, and he treated the
director like a walking saint.

"Spike, you seen Jerry?"

"Nope."

I peered into the pool, where one of the grunts was flopping down
a pale-blue pad.

"You still planning to jump?" Spike asked. "What with the paw
and all?"

"Thomas, do you think we ought to have a look-see?"

I motorboated the air and unwrapped the gauze from about the

215

splint. The plywood boards fell out, and there was my paw, twice as big as usual. The skin showing through looked like an undercooked hash.

"Smeg," said Headley, rippling his upper lip.

"My sentiments exactly."

"How's it feel?" asked Spike as a limo idled up to the curb outside the house.

"Somebody die?" asked Spike.

"Just my dreams," I said, as we all three shuffled toward it like zombies in the heat. The chauffeur opened the door, and out stepped Mr. Noggles Schmear, an MGM VP we all joked was half Jew, half lobster, followed by a lackey humping a case of what looked like genuwine French champagne. His face red as a hothouse tomato, beaming like we were his sons returned from the war, Mr. Schmear grabbed a bottle from the case and from behind his back pulled a saber. I was about to turn tail and shove Spike out at him when in his Delancey accent Mr. Schmear yelled, "Boys! The Academy just announced its nominees, and guess what cat-and-mouse combo are up for one?" He tossed me the chilled bottle, which my rubbery morphined fingers almost dropped, and although I'm sure he wanted the bared teeth in his head to look more exhilarated than raging, I was not too keen when he swung the saber and hewed half the bottle's neck right off, missing my good paw's finger by a dime's width. Then he squeezed my bad paw, and I could have clocked him with the jizzing bottle right then.

"I know, Tom," he said, mistaking my tears of pain for joy, "it's been too long. But we are back now. Goddamn it but we are back."

"Huzzah!" said Headley, from Spike's headlock.

Mr. Schmear rapped on the bottle with his fat pink knuckles. "Veuve Clicquot. Only the best for—hey, where's my favorite rodent?" he said, just as Jerry, out of nowhere, popped over the lackey's back, stuck a landing on the case of champagne, and threw his arms into the air like Mae West.

"Har!" shouted Mr. Schmear, doing a weird high-kneed hillbilly dance over to Jerry and the struggling minion as I glugged down the bubbly, which stung my throat with its cold and its fizz. The humans did love Jerry. Mr. Schmear rubbed Jerry's ear like he was testing a bolt of cloth at the tailor's and took the bottle from me and tilted the sundered neck toward Jerry, who, although he wasn't much taller than the Veuve, drank most of it in one long draft. I was beginning to regret the full squirt of morphine—everything was so bright and smooth I felt like I was living a cartoon, and my limbs felt less like a part of my body and more like something I was trying to marionette around.

"Hope you've all left April ninth open on your social calendars," said Mr. Schmear as the crew gathered about, cursing happily and clamoring at the lackey for the dewy bottles. With all the corks shooting off, I felt like a gang of kids with popguns was chasing me.

We'd had a streak of Oscars in the fifties, a decade as sweet as Coca-Cola, but for years not even a nomination, and the voice in the back of my head whispered we'd lost the magic. I hoped the news would make Gracie proud. Certainly the crew seemed pleased as punch to know me and Jerry, sidling over, giving their pointer fingers for Jerry to shake and telling me they were real sorry about the baby grand.

"Dust off your tuxedos, boys," cackled Mr. Schmear, showing off his molars. "Shine up your spats. They'd best be gleaming on the red carpet."

"Who's that?" asked Spike, pointing up at a dark shape perched near the twiggy top of a grand old elm tree across the street. It was a man wearing a black topcoat and bowler, no-handedly straddling a thin bone of a branch without breaking it. I'd spied him a minute before, but I wasn't sure if he was real or just another piece of my morphine fantasia, along with the lawn that was telling me my fortune and the clouds that bore the faces of all the people I'd ever betrayed. When the man in the bowler saw that we saw him, he monkeyed his way to a lower branch, dropped twenty feet to the ground, and hurried away.

"Goddamn pinkos," chuffed Mr. Schmear, making a gesture at the suit I guessed was either vulgar or Masonic. "First they steal our life essences, now they're snooping on our secret forms of creative entertainment." I'd known the man long enough to sense a monologue coming, in the same way you know for a half second of exhilaration and terror that you're about to sneeze, but it subsided, and instead he shoved his chin—which really was just the bottommost part of his flaming face—toward the backyard, and asked no one in particular if he could kick the tires a little. Even though Headley was a newbie who'd spent most of his life in schools that made you wear ties with shields on them, he was still the director, and so I broke my eyes from the fleeing suit to Headley's rice-white face, but before he could stammer anything out, Jerry said that his casa was Mr. Schmear's anytime he liked. I rubbed my eyebrows and locked my jaw, thankful the morphine was slowing everything to half speed and rounding the edges off all my feeling—I'd been planning on telling Headley how about we save the end of the chase for another day or two, for the paw's sake. Headley was terrified of Jerry, and every day on set was like Yalta, with me playing Roosevelt to his Churchill and Jerry's Stalin, so Headley would have agreed to the delay without a second thought. But Mr. Schmear, that artless tycoon, that blubbery beet, decided he wanted to be the firsthand witness to my pain.

In the backyard, the three of us limbered up like always: First we got down on all fours a few feet apart and started hopping over and sliding under each other like God was playing three-card monte with us. After a couple panting minutes of that, I jumped onto Spike's shoulders, then Jerry jumped onto mine, then Spike lifted his paw and I hopped up, then Jerry did the same with me, then with a timing we'd honed over the years, Spike and I squatted deep and pushed in unison, which flung me ten feet up but Jerry so high he became just a black fly hovering toward the yolky sun, before zooming back down and onto my good paw.

"That is Oscar-worthy action!" hooted Mr. Schmear, whose girth was straining the diving board, his 6EEE wingtips dangling above the chlorine fumes, his lackey standing behind holding a parasol over his overripe strawberry of a head. Headley stood off near the shallow end, thumbing an unlit Chesterfield and trying to look useful.

Jerry rolled a medicine ball from out behind the shed, and after he clambered up, Spike and I tossed it back and forth, the mouse balanced on top. The paw was ginger, but not so bad I couldn't catch the medicine ball, so I decided to strike while the iron was hot and the morphine thrumming along: "Spike, Walls, let's go and put on a show."

We picked up the episode where we'd left off: Jerry speeding inside after hoisting the baby grand with a crane and almost killing me with it in the front drive. Now, with a camera near the stairs catching everything, Headley called Action and I wheeled after Jerry across the living room, forever on his heels, then slid face-first toward the mouse hole cut into the room's baseboard, the carpet burning across my chest, finally accordioning into the wall just after Jerry slipped inside. I'd done it a thousand times but goddamn if each one didn't hurt a little worse than the last. I scampered toward the closet and came back with a fumigator pump that read MUSTARD GAS on the side. After emptying the harmless green fumes into Jerry's hole, I stepped back with a death's-head grin and stretched myself out on the sofa. When Jerry emerged a second later wearing a miniature gas mask, I hurled the pump at him and the chase began again, first over the upright piano's keys in a back-and-forth boogie-woogie duet we'd perfected over the years (along with a couple of Sousa marches, "In the Mood," and the introitus to Mozart's *Requiem*, which was, I admit, a little slow and deathy for anything but fooling around off camera). With three limbs instead of four and a head floating in morphine vapor, I was a bit behind the beat, but because of the good news about the Oscars, as we were finishing the last notes of the twelve bar, I flashed Jerry a finger mustache too quick for the cameras to catch, and all at once we ascended into the "Ride of the Valkyries," which seemed appropriate considering Jerry's gas mask, and as he hopscotched that Nazi leitmotif, he sang, "Kill the *wab*-bit, kill the *wab*-bit," then while I took over the main theme, he hit the first flute part's high F trill with a machine-gunning of his tiny feet before hopping off and hustling into the kitchen. Almost before I slid behind the swinging door, Jerry'd secured the high ground atop the counter at the knife rack, and he hurled them all at me—steak knives and bread knives, butcher knives and boning knives, oyster knives and carving knives, and from the way I had to boogie-woogie myself to dodge them as they whiffed past and skittered onto the tile, it didn't seem like he was trying to miss.

When the knives ran out, I reached for a cast-iron skillet hanging from a peg, to line-drive him into the fridge, forgetting for a terrible moment that first lesson of boxing: Never leave your body open, a canvas your opponent can paint with pain. The knife stand was indeed empty, but an innocuous wedge of Parmesan was leaning against it coquettishly. With a flick of his toe, Jerry chipped it into the air, caught it, and whipped it at my head with a full leg-kick follow-through. But if I could dodge a steak knife, I could sure as hell dodge a piece of cheese, so I started to duck, bending at the knees, knowing the worst the Parmesan would do was give me a crew cut. Leaning forward on one leg, Jerry winked, and my eyes dropped to his fingers, which were curled up toward his hand like a claw. Knuckleball.

In midflight, the wedge dropped, righted itself, and started corkscrewing, shaking off so much smell I felt like I was being assaulted by an Italian restaurant. Trying to track it was dizzying, but as it flew toward me, I knew I had to guess, so I jumped spread legged like a cheerleader, hoping it would slide beneath me, but just as I left the ground, the cheese was buoyed by some unseen force and it rose, spearing me in the crotch.

219

In my line of work, you learn to be a connoisseur of pain—knowing the tinsel of regained circulation from the throb of built-up pulse, distinguishing the flash of flame burn from the sizzling parasitic seep of acid, sniffing out the difference between the tang of a dislocated shoulder from the bone grind of a joint that's spent its lifelong allowance of cartilage. You learn to distance yourself through analysis. But as any boy who's ever picked up a mitt can tell you, that's impossible when you've taken one to the balls. You don't just hurt, you feel evacuated, manhood surrendered, your self slurped out through yourself, the interior hollowed until you're only an outside. I crumbled to my knees, mouth snatching for air, while Jerry leaped toward the ceiling, grabbed one of the overhead fan blades, and timed his letting go well enough that it shot him out through the open window. Behind me the cameramen were chuckling. I stood, gasping. The constitutional horror I felt was resolving its component parts: the background of black void, a single sting in the family jewels, and a pull along the veiny underside, like a rubber band yanked too many times, until its elasticity is spirited away. That was a new one.

I coughed, listing to starboard, and stumbled into the paparazzi flash of sunlight.

My attention was directed by bad fake snoring to Spike, pretending to sleep by his doghouse, which had been painted with a drippy HAPPY BIRTHDAY and brightened with a whole bouquet of red balloons. Fortunately Headley'd had the sense to eighty-six Mr. Schmear from the board, and the two were watching the action from behind the white picket fence, Noggles goggling as Jerry flew over the breadth of the dry pool and I tried to remember what I was supposed to do next.

Headley looked like he always did during takes, doubled up in his head about the fact that the better the episodes went, the longer he'd direct them, and the longer he directed them, the less likely he'd ever create a film of true artistic grandeur, which far as I could tell meant flicks about skinny boys with very purposeful hairdos reading philosophy and complaining about the pointlessness of the universe to their girlfriends, who were always improbably curvy and saucer eyed and eager to take off their tight sweaters to comfort their beaus.

My groin was having an existential crisis of its own, the fumes of the injury rising up into my guts, threatening to shove my Bloody Mary up my gullet. The basic blocking we always did for our longer sequences had vanished from my head. So I did what any cat worth his salt does when he sees a mouse: I started chasing. Jerry'd alighted on the far rim of the pool as gently as an angel, then started sprinting into a long wheel route. God he was fast. Watching his body shrink through the pastel universe of a Pasadena backyard, some ancient cattishness reasserted itself inside me: While I was as bipedal as not, two leggers were thinkers, not killers, and if you want to catch something, you need a cheetah, not a chimp. I leapt into my ancestry and onto all fours, clenching my jaw at the pain the hard ground shot through my bad paw, trying to distract myself by thinking about something besides my crotch, paw, and stomach. As I galloped around the pool, I remembered the Oscars, the competing bouquets of the starlets' perfumes in the lobby of the Civic Auditorium, the impasto of satin dresses, the loose smiles of beautiful drunk people who would get lucky whether they won or lost that night. It was like an orgy in Macy's. I couldn't wait.

I was catching up to Jerry, who was racing toward the California fan palm that towered over the yard, a tree the cartooners hated because they always had to redraw it into a many-branched oak. His foreshortened body was flying toward the trunk, and any other creature I knew would've crashed, but Jerry pushed off on his right foot, translating his momentum with all the grace of Del Shofner into an inside turn, grabbing his crotch at me with a wink then sprinting toward the doghouse. I was not Jerry, and a second later, when I reached the tree, I had to loop wide around it, feeling my paws flap at the ground to gain purchase, whipping up the grass in waves as though it were a bunched carpet.

Spike was still fake sleeping, an Alp of a dog, and Jerry hopped over him at the last second, while I, remembering my duty, my role—the earthbound clod, the creature of dirt always flailing at the creature of air, failing to grasp him—I obligingly crashed into the starboard flank of Spike's rib cage, bouncing off as though he were a trampoline set on its side. Earlier in the episode I'd eaten Spike's pork chops and stuffed dynamite into his birthday cake to try and blow Jerry up, and as Jerry watched behind the doghouse with the glee of the devil on your shoulder, I gave Spike my toothiest, most apologetic grin, trying not to let on that I was having a hard time standing up. But for the Spike of the show, far meaner than the real Spike, who'd internalized the Gospel message to forgive your brother seventy times seven, it was a clear case of three strikes and you're out. So that linebacker of a bulldog started after me as I chased Jerry toward the pool while breathing deep, trying to keep the stars out of my eyes that portended a blackout. I couldn't do a retake.

   Offscreen one tech untethered the birthday balloons and another blew them toward us with an industrial fan. We three made three passes around the pool, and each time new constellations appeared in my vision, like an evening fading into night, but I couldn't stop. Finally, on the fourth circuit, Jerry screeched to a halt at the board, just as the balloons were lazing by, and raced down the blue runway, springing off the edge to catch one of the low-floating ones. Spike stopped at the edge but I followed, Tom the Persistent, leaping off the lip of the board, grasping at the pretty tails of the bright red balloons, missing them all as Jerry waved to me wickedly, a stowaway on an airborne flotilla of red dirigibles. For a moment, suspended twenty feet above the bottom of the dry pool, I ran in place, before that bitch gravity got me for the second day in a row, my happy red world jump-cutting to a cruel chemical blue, but as I spread my arms into the Iron Cross and prepared to take my licking like a man, I could not but smile, taking the nomination as a harbinger that my world would redden again soon, the deep lipsticky vermilion of the red carpet, the same color as the bow my Grace wore that first day I met her, at this very set, the blooming red of our deepest insides, of glory and terror and lust. Pain I could handle. What startled me was the opposite—as I flew down toward the bottom of a pool the color of a cartoon sky, wind brushing past the fur of my face, my paw felt like a grilled bratwurst about to burst, my nicotined lungs were scorched from the running, and my head was a shrieking teakettle. But in my groin, the seat of myself, I felt something scarier than hurt. Nothing. I didn't feel a damn thing.

The Migration
Matt Bell

AFTER EACH KILLING the migration would quicken.

The men killed one and another migrated. The men killed two, and a dozen left. This was the method of the migration, of its start and its continuation and its quickening.

This is what the men who killed believed. This is the belief they killed for, for which they continued to kill.

Over some number of nights the men killed a man and then a man and then a man and then two men, then another number of men they did not count. They killed them with ball bats and pipe lengths, with bricks held in leather work gloves, by pushing them over the railings of overpasses. They ran some others down in the streets, dragged their bodies like dolls beneath the carriages of crowded cars accelerated quickly, braked hard and late.

The men who killed, they did not make anything look like an accident, because they did not want those who would migrate to believe anything was.

The men who killed talked about killing more, killing faster, about buying dynamite, about making firebombs—but mostly they could not afford to kill if they could not use what they already owned, what they found ready inside house, garage, basement: One killing they made with a crowbar, a tool meant to tear drywall and to lever apart two objects, a tool that worked the same upon a person. Like rope, like wire, like a hammer.

In all the killings, there were some who used their boots, who used steel toes and leather soles to separate teeth from jaws, then a curb to break apart the rest, and some others used their fists, and afterward some of those men scrubbed themselves raw in the long dark of their sleepless hours. Some of these men who could not sleep had their doubts, but they did not give these worries voice or allow the others to voice theirs, not even after the killing of the woman, after what happened because of her killing.

The men who killed the woman had not meant to kill the child inside her, had not known she was with child, not even as they circled her, not even as they closed that circle. They had not *seen* her, not as they laid their hands upon her, not as they held her down, not as they pinned her legs with hard-pressed knees, not as they wrapped their hands around her face, quieting her mouth with heavy fingers. And not in the first minutes after either, when they stood around in the pooling dark, their eyes all aglitter.

This child inside the woman was the size of a fist, and already there were so many fists that what was the presence of one more? There was much else the men who killed were blind to, and below them the woman was now obscured in bruises or the coming of bruises, coming after the boots were removed, after the bat stopped its swinging against her body. Later there were flowers in the wet street, and the prayer cards around the flowers were wet too, damp from a hose sprayed against the stained sidewalk, those gallons spent to wash away those pints. And when the child was found beneath the layers of its mother's bruises and flesh, then some men in uniform arrived at the many doors of the men who killed to bind them with cuffs and herd them one by one into the locked backs of waiting cars, their heads pushed low to keep them from getting hurt.

They had not meant the second portion of what they did, some of them were even sorrowed, but they were not sorry enough, and for this crime and also this lack they were locked into a building they could not escape.

The men who killed knew that they had been locked up because they would not stop the killing, and because even if they were freed, even then they would not leave the city.

No, they said. They were not the ones who would migrate. They were the ones who would return, who would stay and kill more, because they wanted the migration to continue, wanted it to quicken and quicken and quicken and quicken.

Even with the men who killed locked in the building, even then it did quicken, and everywhere it went there were televisions, and everywhere the televisions were there were other men behind their screens, men in suits who said the killers had killed out of some long hate, out of old wrongs come back around and gone bad again.

But that was not what the men who killed said.

The men who killed were sometimes in the television too, and in the television they said they did not want that much.

All they wanted, they said, was this where this went, and that where that should go.

It is not complicated, they said. Just us and them. Not together but separate.

We are not the same, they said.

We do not belong together, they said.

There were some of the men who killed who agreed with the other kind of television men, those men in suits and ties who did not believe the migration would ever be finished, because those who would migrate were not all of one mind.

Some were stubborn, they said, and would require more killings to be quickened, if they could be quickened at all.

The television men said that even before they became those who would migrate, many of those who lived there had been trying to get out but they did not all have the money to leave, nor the good credit to borrow the money, and so no matter how many were killed some number would always live there.

In the ways of their finances and also in other ways, the men who killed and those who would migrate were not so different—but this the men did not believe.

Different is all we are, they said, all we will be.

The television men explained that the houses of those who would migrate had long ago been the houses of men like the men who killed. They had been the houses of women and children, of families, a father, a mother, children or else the absence of children, the trying for. The men who killed thought this was the way it had always been, the way they wanted it always to be. But that world seemed no longer to exist, no matter whom they killed, no matter how many were made to migrate.

The sorrow this brought the men, it made them sorrier than killing the woman and the child ever had, but this they did not tell to anyone. They did not need to. They had already said it, in every manner but speech.

According to one television man, you could tell the kith and kin of the men who killed from those who would migrate by some matters of degree.

They were skinned differently, for one thing, and their skins did not take the same dressings.

Also there were matters of music, another television man said.

The men who killed did not like the music of those others who lived among them, of those who would migrate. They did not like even one single note of that sound, but their daughters did, and so also their sons.

According to one television man, the music had now grown louder, and so the men who killed liked it even less. If they heard that music moving down the street, they would yell from their porches, their yards, their sidewalks, or else they would grind their teeth, harden their hands to fists—and when their hands were hard enough the men would use them to kill.

It is just a theory, a television man said. Just a story, a how we got from there to here.

The migration continued, even without the men who killed, and without them the world bloomed and then burnished, went orange, and the women of the men did not know what to do. Their houses were hot with what their men had done, with what the women had known or not known before the last killing, and in that heat they sweated in their kitchens, sweated in their bedrooms, sweated whenever the television held the faces of their men, the radio their voices, or else the speech of those who spoke for them, about them.

It was always their men they thought of, and their anger or disbelief or fear of what their men had done, and the heat that was even then in the air and on the street entered and dwelled within the women until they struggled to work, to care better for their children, to gather peaceably in churches where they might see each other's faces, the facadings of those left behind, heated.

The women of the men could not be fired for having a man who killed but they could be made to quit and so some of the women did, while others stayed and bore it, bore it as they bore the capture of their men, as they bore the sudden embiggening by absence of a family that now they had to care for all alone, and if there was less laundry to do it did not feel so, and if none of the stains on the less laundry were bloodstains they were still no easier to remove.

In the bars where some worked a man would buy them a drink and then another drink and then he would say maybe you need help at home, and sometimes the women did and sometimes they did not and sometimes they were not sure and so they took the men home anyway to see what use they might be and then afterward they sat in the beds of the men who killed with these new men who had not and together they watched the television men say *fair trial* and *impartial jury* and *change of venue*, and in those repetitions the women heard that even after it was over it would never be ended, not the migration not the heat getting hotter and not the women of the men who killed getting by less well and less often.

And what could the women say and what could the women do?

In the supermarkets some women worked and some women shopped and it was not the same women at the same time. Some women went to work in the factories where their men had once worked and some where those who migrated once worked, but maybe some of the women got worse jobs than the others because of the differences in whom they replaced, the differences between them and also of them.

In the evenings the television man said, There were differences in their lunch boxes, in the food they chose to bring for lunch. What parts of the cow they ate, or what they did to their potatoes.

Another television man straightened his already straight tie and said, They did not drink the same drinks, and he was right on this as he was on the surface of all things.

Sometimes when the women of the men who killed left work early to pick up their sons and daughters from their schooling, sometimes they saw them playing with the sons and daughters of the killed.

And what this meant to the women.

And how hard it was to watch.

And how hot it made them to tell their sons and daughters no, to tell them never again, to tell them what would your father say. And then it was summer and there was no more school and the differences between burned all the brighter, for being further apart, for being harder to see.

Those who would migrate were women and children, and also men who had lived, who had not been killed. Maybe these men did not want to migrate, but maybe their women did, maybe their children deserved it, and anyway because there was no more work, even less work than when the migration had begun, because the factories and the shops and the supermarkets were migrating too, closing down, locking up. Some of the men did not have the means to take their families away, lacked exactly what the television men said they lacked, and so the men who would migrate did so without their women and their children, went to other cities to build for less what they had before built for more.

The men who migrated alone lived in smaller apartments than they had when they lived with their women and their children, and it was hotter where they went or it was colder, and some of them were still killed there, even though there was no migration happening yet in their new city.

The television man said, This migration will not be isolated. It will not be insulated. It will spread city to city, until it is finished or until it is stopped.

The television man said, Where will those who migrate go? Who will receive them, house them, take them in?

The men who killed, they also spoke again from within the television, from within the building where they were guarded, and together they said, Someone else, and, No one, and, We do not care as long as they migrate, as long as their migration quickens until it is finished.

Some others had less reason to stay or to return, and so they locked their front doors for the last time, then drove alone or together, maybe rode in the passenger seats of trucks also bearing away what objects had been inside other houses. Their migrations were the easiest, because their reasons to remain were the weakest—although they were not nothing—and still there was cost—and those without men or children or women left their houses and their apartments, and then those homes sat empty, their windows black accusations, and then no one would take their place, no one would move into their emptied but still hot rooms, their fallow chambers of wallpaper coming unglued, come crumbling down.

In the courtroom, the men who killed were not allowed to wear their own clothes, and so each man sat dressed in the same colors, shod in similar shoes. They tried not to look like themselves, to appear changed, different from the days when they slept each in their own houses, beside their women or else alone, but different was not always an improvement—and when the photographs of the woman before and the woman after were shown on the screen only one of the men who killed cried—and then they were each called by name, were one by one sworn in and sworn at, and afterward the men who killed offered their testimony, which was of two parts, always or almost always.

We killed the woman, they said. We had warned her before. She shouldn't have been out so late.

During the day, she could have gone to the store or the laundromat, and we would not have seen her. We would have been decent men, working men. Not yet the men who killed.

At night, we killed the woman, but it was her fault too, for being where she was not wanted, and if so then also it was her to blame for the death of her child, a bump we could not have known.

They should have left, said the men who killed. They should have migrated. They should have been quicker to do one or the other, they said, and all this was only always the first part.

Now the city was emptying, its inhabitants leaving by the freeways connecting this city to that city, and in the television the men in suits said there were no more jobs anywhere, not just in the neighborhood or in the city or the county, but in other states too, and those who were migrating would not all find anything better than what they had once had.

One television man said, This was the year the factories closed, and then reopened, and maybe you got your old job back and maybe you didn't, but if you did it was not the same job anyway, not at least in matters of pay, of benefits.

And then his image was replaced by footage of the trial, of the judge and the men and the women of the jury, and also the men who killed, taking the stand and taking the stand and taking the stand and taking the stand, a progression of men who had killed, of those who were left, who had not been killed themselves, who had not had themselves taken apart by those other killers also imprisoned, like the ones they were most afraid of—and again there were problems of rough description, problems of calling this rightly what it was, and also that which was different what it was, because so few men were made different enough.

Identifying marks, the television man said. This is how you tell them apart. There are tattoos and scars, each located on a particular part of the body, and each differentiated in purpose by class, by education, by neighborhood and affiliation.

Fear, said another. The tattoos are about fear.

But the men who were killed had tattoos too. Just like the men who killed.

Yes, said the television man. Yes, and all men are afraid of each other equally and also worse.

The migration continued, quickened by the trial even without or in the absence of new killings, the reminder of the others enough, and there were reminders everywhere in the neighborhood, even before the television began its broadcasts, its color commentary:

Here was the street where her father was dragged behind a sedan, the same model sedan he had once built in the days of his working, when there were still places in which work was being done.

Here was the alley bar where his brother was struck with a pool cue, a glass mug, a boot, where no one saw anything even with the blood sprayed, stained in dark brown arcs across the billiard-green felt.

Here was the house where her son was choked with rope, choked out of his house and into the fenced-in square of his yard, where he was lifted into his only tree by the rope slung over the thickest branch. And when that branch broke first, then here was where they lifted him again and again, until a stronger structure was found to hold.

Here was the laundromat where the woman was leaving with her clothes in her basket, with her baby in her belly, slivered or curled beneath, and here was the distance away where we were too, we who must not pretend anymore that we were not there, or that the mere absence of any trial does not prove we need not be tried for what we have done and for what we did not do, and here was where we heard the sirens and here was where we were when we heard them getting closer and here was where we heard the sirens and knew they wouldn't get there in time, and also where we never called out ourselves, never begged anyone to help, to stop what was coming.

Here was where we were, when we did not care enough what was happening to these others, who were not us or ours.

Here was where we did not help because we did not want to be made to migrate too, to be forced out of our homes by their hands and by what they held in their hands.

Here was where we stood and decided whether or not to join the men who killed, our brothers and uncles and fathers and neighbors, whom we had never stood apart from before.

Here, and here, and also here and here. These were the places where we did or did not act, where we did or did not speak, and all around us the consequences of those speakings or quietudes, those actions or inactions: the migration, and also its quickening.

And if we cannot reckon with our lack of punishment, deserved for all we did not do? Then to require one who can be blamed, blamed and also punished until he might stand against us, scapegoated, so his shape might be broken and his limbs torn from off his unforgiven and sacrificial body, an act best accomplished by deed, but if not that then by law and letters, the judgment of myth.

What the men who killed now knew: It was possible to be right, to be sure you were right, and still be punished for what you had done wrong. This is what they told themselves, when they were alone in their cells, through the nights stretched so long in the building where they were guarded, and where their worst parts twisted in around the remains of the better.

In the courtroom the prosecution said that there was danger in the men who killed, and if they would not claim it for themselves then it was the duty of the state to place it upon them. To set them apart, and then to punish them for their apartness. There was evidence against them that could only be mitigated by matters of degree, by dividing accusations of who had held the weapon the longest, who made the most blows against the body of the woman, and this was the second part of their defense: not the difference between not guilty and guilty, but between this guilty and that guilty, and the determination of which was worse, the killer who did most of the killing or the killer who waited from behind a steering wheel for it to be done, or the one who kept watch, ensuring that it would not be interrupted.

One of the men said, I would never kill a woman. I could not look either, or stand too close to listen.

But the migration, he said. And so me, waiting on the sidewalk, watching the street, protecting my friends.

My wife left, he said. She took my children and left and I don't know where they went.

It wasn't her I was trying to make migrate, he said, and haven't I been punished enough, and this was the man who had cried, and now he cried again, and in his tears he knew that it was not enough, that it would never be enough, and he did not know how to stop his begging, his wanting for what mercy he did not deserve or understand.

231

Another of the men who killed took the stand, and then another and then another, one who placed his hand upon a Bible and then denied placing that same hand upon the bat.

Only her mouth, said the man. I held her head in my lap, held her screaming inside her face while the others did what they did, what I will not tell you whether they did or not, or who did what part.

I did not murder the woman, said the man. I only quieted her a while, until she was quiet herself.

Another admitted it was his bat—those were his fingerprints, among and under the fingerprints of the others—but he did not admit to anything else.

This man, he did not admit to swinging the bat over and over, did not admit to the breaking of the ribs and the breaking of the fingers and the breaking of the femur and the hip.

The bruising of the organs, he said. I did not do that either.

And the baby, he said. I had nothing to do with what happened to that baby.

The baby, he said, was someone I didn't even know, and why would I want to hurt what I didn't know?

Not all the men who killed had been caught, locked up, trialed. Still there was the one who remains.

The one who remains, still he was housed with his woman and his children, still he was employed at his place of work, still he was engaged in the drinking after, in dollar drafts and well whiskeys.

The one who remains, he smoked or did not smoke. He marked his woman or did not. He loved his kids, probably, but maybe he did not even have kids—and we have to admit that we do not know, that we have not thought so far ahead. We argue that it does not matter. What separated him from those around him, even those skinned as he was skinned, clothed as he was clothed, it was perhaps very little. Whatever it was, he could have been anyone. He drove a car or he took the bus or he walked, because his house like all the other houses stood in the shadow of the factory where he worked, the factory that he'd told the others might cut his job, might terminate their employment at any time.

The one who remains, he might or might not have played ball, but either way he knew how to swing a bat, and while he watched a man in the television pointed at a chart, explained the configurations of the men who killed, the proportions of guilt each might hold—but the figures did not add up, skewed inaccurate.

The man in the television said, Someone is lying about what he did, but the television man was wrong.

The one who remains, he sucked a splinter from his thumb, then the blood from the splinter's wound, what was left behind. When he removed his mouth, the blood welled, stained the skin around his thumb, darkened it darker.

The one who remains, his skin was either one color or the other, and it did not matter what color it was, except that it was the same color as the men who killed, different than that of those who would migrate, and it was the surface of a man only different by chance, and what differences there were within were believed to be of another category, created by a man's own designs, his own making—or else that was only what we told ourselves, and always the one who remains had been this way, a man who kills, even from the first of all the many times he had moved among us.

In the television, we saw the men and the women of the jury, bored and restless.

The men and the women of the jury, having sat in their box for a week and a week and a week and a month and a month, they were united in purpose, still anything but in mind. And what that meant for arriving at conclusions, consensus. And how hard they were pressed to agree on one or the other. And how there were some who believed in the guilt of the men who killed and some who believed perhaps not in their innocence but also in the difficulty of their prosecution, in the lack of clear blame—And should the man who held the woman down be sentenced the same as the man who drove the car and the same as the man who swung the bat, if that man was even on trial, a now doubted assertion?

What is proof, the men and the women of the jury asked.

What is enough proof, they asked each other, and their words seemed so familiar, and each man and woman worried at this, feared some assigned and acted-out role, but each day they said nothing to any other, and what good could these thoughts have done if voiced, and so despite their doubts they voted, and then the vote was split and then the men and the women of the jury admitted to the judge they had not yet made a decision and then they were driven to rooms that did not contain their families and all they wanted was to go home to rooms that did. *Sequester* as a synonym for *imprison*, and how there are no true synonyms, and how no two people mean the same thing even when they speak the same words. In the night the men and the women of the jury laid awake and that was the night they decided they would change their votes or else it was not but if it was not then it would be soon, and then after all those long and stalling deliberations they at last voted as one, and then in the morning the men who killed stood to hear the foreman read the jury's decision, the foreman sweating with heat under his collar, a hotness that did not abate when he finished speaking, when the end of his speech set off what was always coming after.

Now all the men who killed were crying or else stricken silent, temporarily ghost white, and around them the room erupted into hot sound and hot fury, against which the banging of a gavel had no good effect.

On the steps of the courthouse, one of the television men faced the camera and said, Now the migration will never end. Now it will quicken and quicken and also worsen.

Another said, The savagery of man. The fault of the police. The incompetence of the prosecution.

A third man looked nervously at the camera, then nervously away.

This third television man, he said, This is the summer of rage. This is the summer of the furies. Now they will take to the streets, righteous and terrible, and who knows where they will stop.

The streets already hot when the verdict came down, now getting hotter, burning up with what rolled across their cracked and pot-holed surfaces: heat coming out of television sets and radios. Heat coming out of car engines, out of automobiles long ago assembled by the men who had killed, by the same hands with which they had killed. Heat coming out of the doorways of their homes and the doorways of those who remained but not the doorways of those who had already migrated, whose houses sat empty, shut up.

Then the hot heat getting hot in Oakland, hot in Detroit and Flint and Saginaw, hot in Chicago and Mobile and Oxford and Cincinnati.

Then the hot heat getting hotter, hot in St. Louis and Bismarck and Lincoln, hot in Albuquerque, hot in Pittsburgh and Bethlehem and Baltimore.

Then the hot heat hottest in the neighborhood where the men who killed once lived, where their women and children lived still, where those who would migrate yet remained in great numbers, despite the danger and the anger, caught in the constraints of finance and gravity. And how hot they were now, at the end of the summer, at the end of the trial, at the ends of this city, at the terminus of one city that the city might have been, and then the heat, the heat, the heat, consuming and containing and contained as it came up off the concrete and down out of the sky until it filled the space in between, and anyone caught on the street nearly burst with it, their skinned bones wet with sweat begging to get out, and when the houses were too hot to hold the men and the women and the children, then each house was opened by the doors, and each spilled its inhabitants out onto the street, where they became a crowd—and then the crowd filled the streets—and then the crowd in the streets began to move.

The crowd in the streets did not move as one body but as many bodies moving together, and while some were angry at the sky others were angry at the ground. Some were angry at store windows and shattered them with bricks and stones and pipes and boards, and some were angry at the objects inside the stores and so they smashed them too, or else carried some objects off into the streets, where they were also smashed or secreted away. Some were angry at automobiles, and so together they worked to overturn one and then another and another, and to set them ablaze, and some of the vehicles they burned were ones they had built themselves in the last days of their working, and in the flames of brake pads and air bags and child-safe seat belts there was burning some part of themselves.

Some were angry at their god, but whether they prayed or cursed there was no one to hear but themselves, all others made blunted mad and mute, smitten dumb by watching.

Some were angry at those who most resembled the men who killed, and they dragged them from the cabs of their trucks or from behind the counters of their shops. And so again the killed and the killers became confused, and in their confusion they died or were made dead, and the city burned for some days and some nights, and the men who killed were still not released, because it was not safe for them on the streets, and each man cried out in his solitude, for what was happening was stronger than he had ever imagined the migration would be, and he knew he had done his part to make it so.

235

The men in uniform, they were then armed with weapons that did not kill but would injure, carried grenades that did not burn but would choke. They did not want to fire these weapons, or at least they did not all want to fire all of them, and then the crowd in the streets arrived, at first standing a small distance from these men, a divide too small—and on the other side a uniformed man with a bullhorn and a helmet told the crowd to go home. No one needs to get hurt, he said, but he said it with such a quaver that no one had to believe him, not if they didn't want to, and there were those who did not, who would never again believe anything any man in uniform had to say. And so instead they threw their voices and they threw their rocks and they threw their bricks and when the men in uniform began to fire their weapons into the crowd then most of the crowd ran, but some few rushed that wall of uniforms and shields, falling beneath boots and batons wielded by men who were not supposed to kill unless they had to, unless they were threatened, but who none-theless sometimes struck with the same force as the men who killed, broke bones in those who should have migrated, just as those others had done before.

And what now, asked some television man, sweating before the camera. And what next? What would there be? What could there ever be again?

The one who remains stepped out of a bar or a house or an automo-bile, smoking or not smoking. He knew where his woman and his kids were or he did not. He wore a shirt with his name on it but still we do not know his name, or else we will not speak it—or else it was an invention, and also it was invented that he had tattoos and scars, but not such that identified him for what he was, for who he is.

His hands were big, but perhaps his body was not.

Again there was a baseball bat in his hands, probably, and steel stitched into the toes of his shoes, more than likely, and always there had been migration in his heart and always he had worked to quicken it, this separation of men from men, first alone and then with others.

The one who remains did not have his bags packed. The one who remains did not plan on running away. The one who remains did not know if he would be arrested, if his blows upon the woman and the baby would ever be properly counted and accounted for, translated into punishment, imprisonment.

The one who remains, he *remained*. He did not run, he did not move, he did not migrate.

The one who remains, this was his house.

This was his street.

This was his neighborhood, this was his store and his bar and his laundromat.

This was his factory, where he had spent all the working days of this life, where by some hard grace he worked still.

This was his city, and he would not leave it to those he wished would leave, nor would he forsake it to their music and their foods and the dressings of their different skins.

This was his city, as long as he remained, as long as he remained and they were made to migrate, quicker and quicker, and now from whatever threshold he had departed he walked out among the others, his new bat hanging loose and easy from his hands, and he was not visible although he should have been, because everything he was made of cried out from the etchings of the lines of his face, from within the black parts of his eyes, and around him and ahead of him the crowd in the streets surged against a wall of shields, those men in uniform, and there were gas and rubber bullets and beanbags fired into and through the air, and everywhere the one who remains strode there was crying and running, and also fire, flames lit amid broken skins and broken glass.

The city burned, and the one who remains did not smile at the sight. His face was a slab of slate, his eyes killer's eyes, black and blank. His movements, they were those of a ghost, and he thought of himself in this way, not flesh but this other thing, ghosted. The one who remains, this was his city, and yet he stayed invisible to it until he acted, until he swung the bat, until he connected its heft with the head of one of those he wished would migrate, and then there was blood on the wood, and there were splinters in his hands again, and he could feel what he had done vibrate through his arms and into his shoulders, a feeling so quickly expanding it nearly split him, and perhaps it would have done so had he not made of himself an empty room, had he not earlier pried loose so many other holdings, the ones that might have made him different than he was.

Matt Bell

In the television there was video from the sky, video from the streets, and on the streets as in the television a man in uniform brought his baton across a teenage face and the crowd in the streets circled a car on fire, surrounded the shirtless man atop it, glory gory triumphant, and all around there was paint sprayed on the bricks and blood sprayed on the paint and there were killers in the crowd and also mothers and fathers and sons and daughters, revolted and revolutionary, and those who would migrate were the crowd in the streets but they were not all the crowd, and all there combined into one creed, and that creed contained among its verses the absence of love and god and the possible death of every man and woman and child and the destruction of the city, and the heat was still so hot the air shimmered and sung, and the men in uniform gassed the crowd in the streets and the crowd in the streets charged through the gas, and the houses burned and the fuel stations were firebombed and the fire trucks did not number enough and the men in uniform were not enough either and the crowd in the streets contracted and hardened, until it was all right to steal and it was all right to hurt and it was all right to sink to your knees with your hands in the air and your face streaming down your shirt and it was all right to hold a trampled child and to comfort even what was not yours and it was all right to rend your clothes when the gas streaked your eyes and you did not know which way to run; and it was all right to run, and so the crowd in the streets ran, and so the men in uniform ran after, uncareful, each man maybe losing his head beneath his helmet, so that he fired behind the backs of those who were running through the lists of smoke, who were falling to the concrete, bodies breaking upon the hard miles even as the day dwindled toward the dark, and beneath the last rose of the dusk the one who remains continued on, further against the sundered city.

The one who remains, he soon again swung his bat against some new skull and sternum, against some remaining femur and fibula, and all bones gave way beneath his blows, and those cracks were the loudest yet, and at last some others heard, at last those of us still scrapping turned to stop him instead, to stand opposed to what he was—and this is the story we tell ourselves about ourselves, a testimony sworn to, retold as often as we need it to be so, whenever we regret what else we remember we were: Down the street came a crowd made of one purpose, armed with bricks and stones and loud voices and

238

bodies all around, and when the one who remains did not heed their call to stop they filled the air with more shouting, new throwings. When they reached his shaded shape they saw all he had done and caused to be done, and in their anger they knocked him to the ground and they lifted him from off the paved earth and they pried at the bat fisted within his hands, and that furious crowd tried to identify his face but he was no one anyone would recognize because while his face was still whole he looked like everyone else, and because while there was difference in his heart it was not always visible on his skin, which did not color with blood the way others did, and he thought as he was struck how of all the made beasts only humans blushed, flushed with shame or excitement or fear, but even caught as he was his face did not bloom, would not no matter how he might rage, and as the crowd in the streets and all around him became a single rushing and awful thing then the one who remains declined again to flee, but turned into them instead, grinning a joyless smile, and as they beat him he gave up his fingers to be broken from off the bat and he gave up his teeth to be booted from his head and he gave up his cheeks to be dashed against the sidewalk and he gave up everything without giving up, and when they at last made him to cry out it was an almost silent howl, as there was too little left to make much sound, and the crowd in the street saw what they had become, and the one who remains saw too and was gladdened, even as his body came unsocketed by their hands, and by his long command he knew some in that crowd would yet die before the end of the day and some of them believed they would live forever, or close enough, and those that lived would be the ones who remembered, and as the crowd in the streets left what was left, as they ran away from what animals they had made of him and of themselves, then they knew that at the end of those hot days there would be no answers and no punishment either, no reckoning except what remained of the migration, paused but not stopped, except the crowd in the streets cooled, removed from each other, made again those who would migrate, made again the women and the children of the men who killed—and before the one who remains could die some men in uniform came down the streets in their helmets, locked side by side behind their shields, and now the crowd was emptied of their last-held resistance, and the flying rubber and stinging gas forced them back home, back into their houses, where inside there was black in the black, a powerless space where no lights burned, where no one waited for their return, where for some the word *home* would never apply again, and outside the city burned its fire, then smoldered into ashes, and everywhere there was less than before, and it was not just people who could be made to migrate but all good things, and the sun and the stars and the moon were absent from the sky for a span, hidden by a foul tower of smoke—but then for some time the sun returned—and by its pink light other men found the one who remains, what of him there was, but they too did not know his name, nor how to recognize what was left, and some say that because they did not name him right that then he never ended either, and some say he went ever on, anonymous, and the men in uniform lifted him onto a stretcher, lifted him broken into an ambulance, lifted him into surgery and repair and rest, and later he would leave the hospital unseen, wholer and still wrongly unaccused, and later the men who killed were for a time made freed men too, and all the men and women of the city were unsatisfied anew, despite what they too had done, and at the release of the men who killed a new man in a new suit spoke, said the migration was not finished, that forever it would quicken and quicken. The migration did not require men to continue to kill but only to not stop killing, and walking among us there were some who never would, and at the last they might be all that there was, men who killed turning in upon each other until perhaps there would be only one, and all around that one some city like this city, ruined and burnt and spent, broken off its bones, heaving haggard its best breaths, and those gathered did not want it to be this way, wanted to cry out some rebuttal, but if there was another story to tell then it was lost to us that day, made wrong shaped by our guilty intentions, and so still even our best-meant speech is often defeated, too soon turned again to wailing and to whimpers.

The Immediacy of Heat
Arthur Sze

1.

"No trespassing" is nailed to a cottonwood trunk,
but the sign vanishes within days. You've seen

a pile of sheep bones dumped off the dirt road
to the river; in the arroyo, you've heard gunshots

and veered upstream. On the highway, a pickup
tailgates a new car, and red plastic flowers,

at a curve, fade. In the slanted rising light,
men stumble out of brambles along the bosque

and head into town; and you time your trip
to the drugstore so you aren't accosted

by women hungering for a fix. At the high school,
chains are drawn above the pavement;

the casino parking lot is already dotted with cars.
At the adjoining bowling alley, someone hurls

a strike; and, inside, you lose track of spring.
You catch the clatter of coins—people

blank into themselves. Searching for an exit,
you find you've zigzagged and circled a maze.

2.

At the mesa's brink, we eye the road
snaking across the valley toward Pedernal,
where hunters gathered flint. A new moon
and two planets bob in the deepening sky;
I lean into the wind and find this tension
the beginning of a sphere. I bend to a stone
basin and, ladling water, sip. I'm lit
and feel new leaves slide out of branches;
see a child, gathering blue pine needles,
inhale the aroma of earth; a worker
snips and nails metal lath into a firewall.
At our first talk, time grew rounded:
A sparkler scattered sparks in all directions—
though gone, they're gone into my fingertips.
The beauty of imperfection's when a potter
slightly pinches a bowl while arcing it
into a second glaze so that, fired,
the bowl marks a crescent hare's-fur overlay.

3.

Under a microscope, I once gazed at algae, at cork cells—

bald eagles at the end of a pier—

a sheep carcass near an arroyo's mouth—

he plants lettuces in the field, and that night it snows—

a woman has closed her eyelids and will never reopen them—

a crow alights on a branch—

the crunching sounds of inlet ice breaking up—

six cars in the driveway—

the invisible lines of isobars, always shifting—

one thing it is to focus: another, to twig—

some of the plastered exterior walls lack the final color coat—

flowering dogwood—

the circular saw rang out through the cambium of summer—

when she vanishes, he will shiver and shiver—

4.

Stepping out of the casino, you blink, but lights
still ricochet off glass. "Do not take checks

from Samantha Cruz" is posted on a billboard
by the liquor warehouse. Disorientation's

a rope burn in your hands: Are we green flies
drawn to stinkhorns? Or shoots leafing

out of time's branches? You blink:
Someone hurls a grenade but detonates

himself. You blink: Someone in the hallway
at the Bureau of Indian Affairs shouts, "Fire me."

You blink, and a profusion of lavender enters
the window. Dipping under incoming waves,

you resurface with a salt sting on your eyelids.
Once you scavenged a burn for morels.

An unemployed carpenter builds his daughter
a harp; you catch yearning, love, solace

as the forty-six strings are tightened.
You can't pluck them, but the emotions mesh.

5.

Vibrating strings
    compose matter and force—
        as I run a magnetic card

    at a subway turnstile, a wave
of people converges and flows
        through the gates; people will always

converge and flow
    through the gates—always?
        If I sprinkle iron filings onto a sheet

of paper, I make visible
    the magnetic lines of the moment.
    At closing hour,

the manager of a restaurant
    sweats and anticipates a dark figure
        bursting in and aiming

    a gun at his chest, but tonight
no figure appears. In this world,
        we stare at a rotating needle

    on a compass and locate
by closing our eyes. At dusk
        our fingertips are edged with light,

    the fifty-four bones of our hands
    are edged with light,

and the immediacy of heat
    is a spring melt among conifers
        gathering into a cascade.

The Afterlife of Paper
Peter Gizzi

à Tanger

She wrote I have never seen this city before therefore I have
found myself again

lost in the distances between paper and wind,

she said the life of paper contains wood, rags, straw, pulp, or
other fibrous material. She wrote, in short, it is built from a wish.

She noted the walls of this city contain wishes: hands, birds,
books, scales, flowers, tractors, trees, faucets, lions,

a slip or sheet of paper, cardboard, or the like, on which a vote is
marked.

There are many ways to pray, slippage is a form of prayer, when
the eye oscillates a gap between presence and phantom

when the image slips.

In the visionary recital the life of paper connects them like street
noise or wind.

246

What, she said, is the syntax between flag and wind, voting and votive.

She wrote there were many cities inside this one, many ways to read and misread. She wrote, a market in a lower-middle-class neighborhood reminded me of home.

She writes, when filming a group of young men from the wheat party, they start to draw on each other's arms in blue ink, it has an erotic quality

and, while filming a shepherd in the middle of a stalled construction site, he posed for the camera,

I wonder how long he will stand there so still. She thought,

I am reminded of early archival footage, or one's posing for a daguerreotype. She wrote, I am also reminded of a German photographer whose name escapes me.

The work site is a war zone; wish zone, zone of industry and families, of laughter and blood.

She noticed, some games, Parcheesi, for instance, share colors and tones with old maps and postcards, faded advertisements, present a form of chance and surrender.

She said she took comfort in unfinished roads that may lead somewhere someday but if not that was a kind of journey better than the trip a finished highway would ultimately lead, boring trips to market, trucks bounding, salesmen, and dignitaries. No an unfinished road suited her thinking much better.

She said she was interested in roads, ships, and borders but in the end when does one arrive and what does it look like? Then she went on to speak about exhaustion but her voice trailed off.

Sight is a form of illness, she went on to say, it is a malady in fact, so little to do with sensory data.

Faces are one way, no, the only way we know where we are. But the weight of empathy, she said, the world balances this way,

you see and are moved or you see and are unmoved.

I turn my camera toward an election booth, I zoom out to include the two women on either side of my frame but find they are no longer there. . . .

—From *The Face of Lincoln*

The Alphabet and Its Pretenses
A Portfolio

Edited by Robert Coover and Bradford Morrow

EDITORS' NOTE

THE DISCOVERY OF SOME intriguing stories by a couple of younger writers led us to the notion of this small portfolio of writings—stories, poems, essays—more or less on the theme, in this era of the dying book, of books—of reading, writing, words, form, language, libraries, the mouths of angels. No sooner was it imagined than a number of senior writers joined the themed ingathering with masterful works of their own, including that philosopher and artist of the Word, William Gass, from whose essay the title for our portfolio was taken.

Lance Olsen   Thalia Field & Abigail Lang

Shelley Jackson   Robert Coover

Sarah Tourjee   Alexandra Kleeman

Brian Evenson   Evelyn Hampton

Lydia Davis   Rosmarie Waldrop

William H. Gass

Table of Contents
Lance Olsen

The Oblique Derivative Predicament Conclusion

Appendices

Appendix A
Transcripts (1):
Mind ghosts fail into language.

Appendix B
"All right, Jane, get into the carriage."

Appendix C
Moist Global Verges (Hope's maps).

Appendix D
Problematics of the Larynx:
The branks, the butter, the dark, the rippers, the bent fork (belief
in an afterlife), the bent fork (lack of said belief), the cat's paw, the
hare's foot, the pear, the frightening thought of seeing through
the idea of yourself to yourself, the knotting, the strappado, the
blankness, the fully realized conceptual project appearing precisely
like the world, roses, the awry, the array.

Appendix E
Memory Breaths (Hope's marginalia).

Appendix F
Black is the best color, for it goes with everything.

Appendix G
Transcripts (2):
Look at blueness drown in beauty.

Appendix H
"No. Plum. A hue."

The Pearls That Were His Eyes
Shelley Jackson

IT MIGHT HAVE BEEN WINTER, or early spring. Now and then the sun stabbed through the clouds, picking out, in the city spread out before me, here a barge starting under a massive bridge, there a black gate swinging closed in a long wall. I stood on a low hill at the intersection of parallel streets, an improbable location, but clearly shown on the map I held. This map had an unusual design, one that I had not met with before: photographs, timetables, commercial listings, and smaller associated maps sprung up without warning when I ran my hand over particular captions, and a complex series of movements was necessary to collapse and return them to their places. I had struggled with the caprices of the map for some time, more than once almost giving up and throwing it away, before I found my location on it, and now I held it with extraordinary care as I brought it to my eyes again, trying to make out the caption on the hill on top of which I stood. "Vul"?

In this district, which seemed to be known as February, as if it were more time than place, the map also showed a Hall of Fame, a ballroom, a guesthouse by a fountain. To the north was a bay where, the map noted, underwater poppies could be found. To the southeast, the city broke up into a series of small towns. A train ran through the central district, and its stops were noted; one was a few blocks away.

I was wearing a lackluster blue polyester suit, tight under the arms, that could have been a uniform. A white neckerchief frisked conservatively about me. I appeared to be a file clerk or an administrative assistant or an inspector or a spokeswoman for a council of some description. Spokeswoman: I was a woman, then. I was that much closer to a solution. With new confidence, I chose one of the streets and marched off.

Only a very few people were out. A middle-aged woman emerged from a building up the block and started up the street, throwing a furtive look back at me. Her rapid heels stabbed the street like gimlets. I followed her, and was puzzled and a little amused to note that she seemed to panic at this and, reaching a small door in the wall of what appeared to be a grocery store, almost threw herself through it. Continuing down the street, I shortly found the fountain described on the map—a horrific and even offensive design: seven children broken under the heel of a giant—and the guesthouse, to which I repaired.

In the hall, a young boy stepped up to the only furnishings on view: a board, which acted as a service counter, balanced on two statues so ancient that they seemed about to collapse. Of seals, they might have been, or trolls. There was a phone at one end of the board and a piece of ruled paper placed in the very center, on which he now wrote a formula that could have been my surname as it appeared in the local parlance, forming the letters with a care that suggested that they were as new to him as they certainly were to me. He had not asked and I had not told him my name. I did not allow this to daunt me. Done, he raised his head, and only now did I see that his eyes were wholly white, as if he were looking at something inside his own head and with such intense focus that he could not stop even for a moment. There was something underwater about his face. A haunting light that did not seem to refer to any sun, or come, in short, from any particular place at all, was playing on it, now discovering its form, now withdrawing to cover it in gloom.

He greeted me with all propriety, but in what did not seem to be words: An unsettling buzz emerged from some part of him. It rose and fell, but I knew that it was also not music. Improbable as it seemed, I had the sense that it was a narrative, an account of something that would be exceptionally interesting if I was able to get a translation of it. Embarrassed, I buzzed back at him, trying to make or at least to seem to make sense. It seemed crucial to answer him in something like his own estate. I failed, but the effort had been of some use, it appeared, since the boy, pushing away my money, now vacated his place at the board and took me by the hand. He led me past a series of closed doors to a small chamber, at the center of which was a seat into which I fell, discovering only now that I was very weak from my travels. I had come from far away, or so I felt, and had been looking for something for a long time. What it was would come back to me, in time.

The boy stepped a few paces away from me, stopped, took a stance facing me, and began a series of rapid poses, his movements suggesting that he was trying once again, and this time with more care, to express something very particular, spelling it out in complex signs, some of them attended by the haunting buzz with which he had greeted me. His arms drifted up, then fell; he brought his hands together as if to cherish some very small article; he covered one eye; he beat time with one hand as he stumbled, then caught himself; he seemed to expand, then collapse. Some of the positions were amusing, but most were sublime and, to me, profoundly sexual. At one moment he even reached into his shorts and gripped his dick. His white eyes showed no acknowledgment or awareness of the embarrassment I felt.

Without warning, the boy stopped and flung his arms around me, his face pressed into my coat, his hands working in the polyester. I panted a little. It was a struggle not to succumb to the temptation to run my own hands over his back, which was broader than one would commonly find in a boy so young. Or was he a boy? Was he, after all, a man? Uncertain, I held my position and in a moment he released me and went out. He did not return and before long I drifted off.

When I came to again it was night. All was gloom. I might have been entombed but for a little light coming from the hall, which made it possible for me to feel along the wall to the door and from there out of my quarters to the street. It was not much lighter than my room had been. I had the disorienting sense of inconclusive but rapid, frenzied, even violent movement, of something spilling past me, its details uncertain. In time, the gloom easing or my eyes learning to get by without light, I was able to make out the outlines of a street in full spate: People, most of them children, were running, reeling, stumbling, collapsing, being dragged along by the others, stopping, rising, falling. A cat streaked past, tail a black pennant. Eyes like pearls.

I would like to be able to say that I threw myself into the street without looking back, that I was that type of person, but it would be a lie. I stood holding the door, watching the rushing, romping, careering children, and felt increasingly vacated, as if it were out of me that the children were spilling. There was what could be described, badly, as a taint or tang in the air. Opium, or did I think that only because this city seemed like something out of a story? For opium was no part of my life at home, I thought. If I had ever had a home.

The following day I took the train to the bay. One of the fisher folk rowed me out to a listing barge from which I looked down into the bay and saw the underwater poppies like little suns glorifying the gloom. They seemed all that was winning, all that was good. I held out my hands to them. Their improbable light did not reach the place where I stood and this was painful to me. I felt my face collapse. Almost without awareness of it, I began to buzz. It felt fine, fitting. So buzzing was mourning?

I sensed that I was being watched. I looked up and met two white eyes in which for a moment I had the fantasy that two poppies looked back at me.

The boy—I would call him Orpheus: I would think about why later on—escorted me back to the guesthouse with an air of decision. There he led me into a room I had not seen before. A massive device took up a good half of it, blocking much of the light from the door, which opened right onto the street. He pressed me into the seat that stood before it, conducted my hands into a little chamber in the center of the device, and stood back, bringing his own hands together as if to pray. The chamber fit, forming a tight seal around my hands, as if designed for me. Inside it I felt mysterious complications. I pushed and felt a series of complex instruments yield in response. A fan started up. Something inflated and collapsed, inflated and collapsed. I started to withdraw my hands, panicking a little, and the boy put his hand on my back, which eased me, as it was meant to. At last the device buzzed—as the boy had buzzed, as I had buzzed—and a piece of paper with a few words on it spilled out of a bay to my right. The boy rushed over and gripped it, also buzzing, this time in praise, it seemed to me. I reached for the page, finding that my hands were free again, and saw the printed words, "If I could have had one of the poppies for my own, I would have protected and cherished it." It was my very own thought, even if until this moment I had not known that I thought it.

This was what in this place was called "typing," I saw.

Uncertainly, I allowed the device to once again take my hands. There was something sexual in its firm grip. (Of course at the right moment many things can seem sexual, so one should not make too much of it.) Rows of letters marched out across the page, forming ranks, and spelled out, spilled out the following words: "My case is very puzzling. I know I have been seeking something for a long time—almost all my life, I would say, if the words 'my life' did not fill me with an extraordinary, corrosive sense of error, as if they were so senseless as to be even offensive. But what my goal is I do not know. Did I know, once? It seems likely. It is improbable that I formed so violent a sense of need without cause. Was this city, this guesthouse, this room, this mysterious device, this page the goal of my efforts all along? Have I long planned to come here, to form these letters, or am I here in error, or caprice?"

Note my style: hardly medieval, but a little "period," say, or like a translation from the French. "Have I long planned," for instance: Show me the blog where you'd read something like that. One small piece of information about the person I had been, I thought.

That night, I went out and watched the street fill again with school-children. This time I had the sense that the night children were not entirely people. They were more like weather; they rushed like the air rushing, without reason. My eyes sought their faces through the gloom. A photograph—but I had lost my camera long ago, I thought, if I had ever had one—would have caught something extraordinary: The children had no faces. Or, better said, their faces were like the insides of faces, which one is not allowed to view in the light of day. It was as if a plug had been taken away, allowing the way they looked to run out, until it had all leaked away; and along with the way they looked, most of who they were. What was rushing through the night, then? Only a weak, the very weakest argument, attended by the impact of soles on a city street.

The next day I went to see the medieval mill, designed by early engineers, a great achievement and, according to my map, one of those for which the city was known. Inside the building great blocks beat against massive plates, a giant fan hacked the air, and workers rushed here and there, some repairing a fuel leak or a broken rig with ancient instruments, their faces streaked with oil, some fighting for the honor, it seemed, of reviewing the complicated controls, and many more throwing pitchers of oil on every part of the device and even showering me with it in their frenzied movements. What was most likely a warning sign—the first writing I had seen outside the guest-house—swung over the heads of the workers, black with oil. I could not make out even one of the letters on it.

On my way back to the guesthouse, I came upon Orpheus, stand-ing by the fountain in the center of a congress of children. Someone had outlined a blue pentagon on the street, and he was in the center of it, as if by design. He was buzzing, one arm swung like a violin-ist's, the children followed his movements with their eyes, and the sun stood in place, arrested on its way from one night to the next, and spilled light all over the scene. It was as if a treasury had opened its doors, filling the street with money. All at once I saw that the buzz was music after all, though not only music—there were words in it as well. A song, then. I felt an improbable sense of grievance that he was playing to his fellow children, not to me, and barged through the group into the guesthouse.

I took a seat in my room, reviewing my puzzling conduct with some dissatisfaction and looking at something I had picked up in the mill—a type of plug, it seemed to be. That the image of a plug had come to me only the night before, while I was watching the night children, gave me the unsettling feeling that an imponderable formula was operating behind the scenes of my life, but I rejected it, amusing myself with another fantasy: that because I had taken their plug, all the oil would leak out of the mill, until at last the great blocks stumbled to a stop. When I looked up, Orpheus was standing at the door of my room. He held out his hand with a look of appeal. Not to me. How could he appeal to me when he could not look at me? He appealed to time, to the day, to the thunderstorm that would come later that night, to the inside of things, of his own head. But I rose and took his hand and allowed him to escort me to the typing room.

Nights of rushing children. Days of speculation without confirmation, inquiry without end, of being dragged along through a terse, senseless story. The weather was poor, the low clouds clearing only temporarily to show broken pieces of an unrealistic and even embarrassing blue. There were recurring thunderstorms in which clouds as massive and complex as medieval churches were driven at high speed against the hills above the city, releasing their energy in spectacular spokes of blue-white light whose afterimages lasted a long time and suggested a succession of names signed in a rapid hand by a succession of authors, each greater than the last.

It became increasingly clear to me that I was here as a writer; as a reader too, it could be. I began work on a story, an account of my travels. It began on the hill I had called "Vul." The backstory I left out, trusting that I would fill it in later, for the reclamation of my past had not gone well: Not one detail of my early life had come back to me so far. Had I joined groups, trusted my doctor, taken good notes? Pledged support to public television? Owned cargo pants and a good wool coat? Had I once taken a shower with a middle-aged sociologist with a wen on his member? I knew only that I had bought my way here with time and effort—a supreme effort, I suspected, for I felt so weak—but that now that I was in the city time meant little to me. I felt that I had all the time I could want and more, and no plan, and I wrote, if one could call this writing, with an ease that was for me the greatest effort, because if there was one thing I did not know, had not learned in all my travels, it was how not to try. It was a furlough harder than any work.

One day Orpheus asked me—no, not in so many words!—to do a translation of an epic-length narrative poem well known in this city, almost a cornerstone of its literature.

If I could not read the poem, how could I translate it, I asked.

By holding out his hands toward the device, then withdrawing them, he expressed that I was the writer, not he, and it was my business to find a way.

The task was, on the face of it, senseless. But I felt that I had to honor the need that had, it seemed, brought me here. I decided that I could do no better than to continue the work I had already started, and record in my own style descriptions of the city. If I had read the boy right, the city was the theme of the poem, and the poem was, in some sense, also part of the city. If I described the city well enough, I might sense the outlines of the poem I was to translate in my own work.

Every day I devoted long hours to this end. After writing I felt as weak as after sexual congress, and returned to my room. At night I went out and watched the children flinging themselves past. This went on for many days, I do not know how many.

My efforts were inconclusive, and I had begun to suspect—well, something that I will detail later on. Enough to say that I began to think that my tactics were in error. So I went back to watching the boy. Every day he performed his buzzing and his poses for me and, with my hands in the device, I tried to translate them into words. At least, that is what I thought I was doing, for it could well be that I was doing some other thing entirely. I had asked the boy and the device had translated his response (if that was what it was doing) in words puzzling to me: "The story drifted—succumbed to temptations."

It was all very trying!

The use of certain words seemed to be prohibited. I did not know what they were, only that in the place where they had been in my head there was now a great gulf. Was it that every word once used was taken from me for good? No, because I used some words over and over. Was it that every word not used was taken from me? Not likely, because there were a great many words that I had not used that I could use at any moment without straining, as I showed at once by listing some of them: *earthquake, television, tomorrow*. It could be that on the other end of the city was a device where another woman was typing, using all the words that I did not. It seemed to me that if I knew what she was writing I would know something of real use. More: that it was exclusively in her words, the words I might not use, that the better story, the necessary story could be told.

Senseless speculations.

I had a new thought. I stopped writing; I watched the boy's movements without trying to find words for what I saw. Extraordinary, spectacular images rose up in me, as from the use of opium (if the literature of that habit is to be trusted, at least). It seemed to me that I was puzzling out the poem without need for translation, and that when I returned to the device it would ease up inside me and spill out of my hands as from a spring.

But the day came that I saw that one of his signs stood for *gate*, one for *bridge, barge, poppy*, that the city recurred in the parlance of his movements. As I watched him, I stood once again on the hill called Vul, looking over the streets. But this (knowing what his signs meant) far from easing my case, made it harder; these words were like walls blocking the movements of my fantasies, which before had come freely.

Between efforts, I traveled all over the city. I saw the battlefield, the treasury, the two museums (the one, all pageantry, that treats that early period of pharaohs and highwaymen and warring families, and where one may view a succession of gruesome articles, including a coat made out of strips from a human back; and the other, more modest, housing works of art in that style, once much praised, but out of fashion today, called "Daglian"). I saw the ancient university, the church with the great icons and the statue honoring the students who died in the grocery wars, the performance hall, the flea market, the strip club. There was something unusual about many of the buildings here, an improbable mix of the genuine and the fake, high art and low, the well made and the broken. That the Tomb of the Free Agent (right next to the Tomb of the Middle-Aged Cavalier) was suffering attrition was not mysterious, given its years and the corrosive night air, but that one wall of that great hall with the seal of state over the door where people of fashion went to watch the sublime orchestra play (a young violinist named Fatima was popular that year) seemed to be made of deal boards, many of them broken or listing, and so widely distributed that the weather came right through, and you could watch a thunderstorm progress while the violinist sawed away, seemed extraordinary! Once I stood for a while as, through the broken wall of a building, I watched a doctor operate on a patient. Large parts of the city seemed to be under repair, but I did not see any progress being made; the modest efforts of the workers, when there were any to be seen, seemed at best to diminish a little the worst abuses of the weather. A word came to me: The city was *unrealistic*. But real enough for all that.

It might appear that I saw little of the locals on my travels. If so, I have misled the reader. I watched shoppers in tight wool pants stumble out of the flea market with broken statues, felted neckerchiefs, and fake watches. I watched a woman with a long train come out of a ballroom, spreading a fan to cover her face, and take the arm of a man in what looked like a military uniform with tails. But I did not speak to them and I did not find what I was looking for and I did not learn what it was.

At times—once on a train platform, once in a grocery store—I stopped and stood for a long moment, trying to catch . . . I don't know what. A movement in the air, say. It seemed to me that something was following me. In time it became clear to me that that thing was also me, that I had started to *recur*. Another me, or a displaced part of me, was tailing me, haunting me, mimicking everything I did. My copycat, I took to calling it, or her.

Certain standard images ran through my head every day, as if on a timetable: a giant with a club, beating a little boy. The sexual violation of infants by popes and presidents. A woman forced against a wall, then lying broken in a dozen poses, her face blue-black over a horrifically tight neckerchief. The images were gruesome and wholly automatic. But I dismissed them with ease, dismissed at least the pain they sought to cause me. Such tactics could not have their intended effect on me; I was tougher than I looked. What did pain me was an increasing dissatisfaction with my own best efforts, the attrition of my faith in progress toward an end, my distrust of the merit of my goal, the forced acknowledgment that it might be unrealistic, the patient faith of Orpheus, standing at my back as I worked, the white eyes of Orpheus, the nights of running children, the nights, the nights.

Was it time to think more about the map? Like the poem, it was part of the city, wasn't it? It could be called a district in its own right. The more I looked at it, the more it seemed like a place, not a description of a place. Could what I sought be there? I picked up the map, ran my hand over it; pages and pages sprang up under my hand, and I began the daunting task of searching through them for new information; from some of the new pages sprang up even more pages, some entirely new to me. But here too I found no answers. A strip at the top of the map where the name of the city would have been had even been torn off. That amused me—how hard could it be to discover the city's name? But it was hard, after all. My every encounter with the locals was so strained that one might think I was a giant swinging a cleaver, not a middle-aged woman in polyester.

It could be that the poem I was trying to translate held classified information. Certain signs suggested as much: I could not cover the street at night, for instance, or treat of the children; when I tried, the words came out even more senseless than usual. At certain moments—once while watching the seals at play in the bay (their coats had a blue-black taint—from the oil that spilled from the mill, I thought); once while looking at a shrine fitted into the wall by the guesthouse, which housed a little statue, its head broken off—the outlines of my story emerged as from a cloud, and what united all my efforts and experiences seemed revealed, but when I repaired to the device and sought to present my clear view in words, it lost its outlines and I decided I had been duped again.

And all the time the story, I felt, wanted me, cherished me, sought without end to make its way to me. Its seeming caprice was an error in my own instruments. I was the one who kept it at bay; it held out a promise and an appeal that I violently rejected, it beat weakly against the wall of my head like a robin, and I fended it off.

At least the device, once so mysterious, had started to seem like a part of me. I had lost the sense that between me and the page stood daunting ranks of instruments, that the words I wrote had come from a long way away and had little to do with me. I placed them on the page with the greatest ease; the device did not block my way any more than my own eye blocked my view or my hands blocked my reach. And so I succumbed to temptation: I began to think that I was a writer. With increasing confidence I found that I knew what I wanted to write, and found ways to fit my own images, my own themes into my "translation." Supreme error! Only now was my work—which before had shown some promise, I thought—entirely without merit.

I did not see this at once. Telling over the pearls of my words, the stately periods of what I had taken to calling a "piece," I went out into the city with new pride, an author. It felt like it had been a very long time since I *was* something. Long? For. *Ever.*

After me came the other me, mimicking everything I did. After, or

263

even before: If her hands did not close around mine when I prayed, it was because mine had closed on hers. Should I but form the plan to write a song she would break in on my thoughts, singing it. If I stabbed a man's back I would find her knife in place ahead of me; my knife would only drive hers home.

At times I had the fantasy that the device was not describing but creating the city, that I had only to name a street for it to form: a strip of place laid out across a gulf. My word had raised the bridges, the churches, the massive keep and the ancient wall around it, along which fisher folk laid out their goods to this day. It had created the fisher folk too, the autoworkers, the ticket agents, the ancient priests, and the ancient fleas in their ancient black habits. If every day a man or woman was lynched—thrown in a well, beaten with a club, hacked with a cleaver—it was because every story needs a violent note to keep the reader involved. And if Orpheus would not look at me it was only because every character should want something out of reach.

I believe that I cherished this fantasy because it made me feel better to think that there were reasons, even bad reasons, for the way the city was. At least I knew who was responsible! And then I could hold on to the thought that one blue day, when I felt better, when I felt tougher, I would intervene with a well-placed period or a telling quote, correct a misspelled word or an overstated description, and not only reverse the evil I had done but make something better of this bad business.

(By the way, I am not making it up: So far as I could tell from the television news—I did not need to be able to follow the words, the images told their own story—once a day, every day, as if on schedule, here, on some public street, a person was killed. This might account for the universal distrust shown me.)

I got my period. So real time had gone by while I dicked around with my "writing"! I had to use balls of wool, of all things—as close as I could get to what I wanted in the local stores. Did women here not get their periods? How did they breed? That they most certainly did, the children were confirmation enough.

Balancing on the ball (a little mashed) before the device, my copy-cat pressing against my back, I succumbed to gloom. My "piece" was a dud and I was a fake. Was the call I had for so long sought to answer only a fantasy? Was my program without merit? Was I going to fail now, after I had come so far? (At least, I felt it was far.) I could not believe that the city would reject my appeal, when I had sought for so long and with such integrity, and even—if the expression is not too misleading—devoted my life to it. But while my investigation yielded information, it was without sense or reason; the details I seized with such effort served only to complicate the issue.

My copycat spoke. "Get a grip," she said. "Try to keep your head. It's no big deal." My copycat did not have my way with words, though her expressions had a certain force, and my dissatisfaction was far from bated by her comments. The reverse!

I began to type. Only broken words issued from the device: "I am—this tactic—no reason, only caprice—but achievement, praise, readers—for what—this—death—Orpheus performing for no one, for the tomb, a gruesome Carnegie Hall—or on the other hand life—painful and embarrassing—straight-to-video, shop-at-home art—pages and pages of comments expressing only private grievances—knife-wielding critics without integrity—but against this only the insecure sense that there may be something—and more complex than the usual modest—reeling off the standard account of a general fantasy according to the latest fashion—a legion of schoolchildren could do as well—lies, poses!—the cult of expression—but only of, what—human achievement, human pain—all very well, but—there is, there is something, I know it—a story like a gun, words like bullets, into the reader's head—but to tell a story at all—at best a quote, and at worst—supreme crime against the real—and all the while the corrosive awareness that there may be no such thing as—and I am middle-aged now!—the tang of winter in the air—the usual killings—some universal cancer of the—and critics glorifying authors for what, for their business practices—a congress of duds and dupes—the modest impact even of work of the greatest merit—so this mandate—misled all my life—dragged into a tomb and handed a list of rules—blight—gloom—error, error, error—but the mandate to try, to make a bid at least—a type of pilgrim, but without—embarrassing and senseless—only, if not for this—but to have a way and no means, or is it means but no way—only half a life—but if this half were to be taken too—"

Was I writing this? It seemed to me that the copycat was writing in my place, for these were my thoughts, but where I was terse and measured, they were frenzied and overstated. The copycat was me, but more—much, much more—embarrassing? That I felt as if she gave my own private thoughts expression was no sign that she was not another. We are more than our private thoughts, are we not? We are the face we show the public—it is no lie but our art, unrealistic but real.

265

I withdrew my hands. Reeling outside and taking a seat on the base of the fountain, I watched the light die out of the day. I caught a furtive movement: A black cat drifted like a cloud along the top of a wall by the guesthouse, eyeing the robin that stood, like another statue, on the statue in the shrine, where the head would have been.

"I know you want answers," my copycat said, "but you have to be patient. We are all depending on you." This pleased me for a moment, but then her last words came back to me with the force of a correction. Who was this "we"? Was my copycat in league with the natives? The device? Even Orpheus? Had the city closed ranks against me?

The cat sprang at the robin, which sped away. Using its tail for balance, the cat sprang from the top of the statue back to the top of the wall and, running lightly along it, was gone.

This was not what I wanted! This could not be what I had come here for, who I had wanted to be. An author, but one to whom others provided—on whom others imposed—all her words? And even her style, even that didn't seem to be her own possession, but a quote from some other party. Given a platform I had yielded it at once without a fight, and even joined in the praise for the copycat who had taken my place. Not only did I not protect my own interests, I threw them in the street and stepped all over them, and I broadcast my most cherished thoughts for others to take up, handing out my possessions as if I had died. I even forced the most embarrassing details of my private life on people who did not ask for them, submitting to the scrutiny of the general public as if to a light-spirited romp, and sought congress in error with those who wanted only to fend me off.

"Well then," said my copycat significantly, and there was something in the way she said this that made me think that she viewed these errors in a genuinely positive light.

Right as the word *light* formed in my head, the sun emerged from the clouds to light up the robin, gripping a street sign with its little black hands. Its tail frisked as it sang a few notes. They had a dying fall, and it all came back to me: When Orpheus died, a woman followed him into hell. Without his music the harvest was blighted—or was that another story?—but, trust me, she had her own reasons too. Now hell was a real place back then, almost next door; you could go there. But to get home again was a great deal harder. Anyway, she goes and she does find Orpheus, only he doesn't know her. Worse, he won't even look at her. It's forbidden, but there's more to it than that: Death is his business now, not life. He's past all that. But she courts him. Little by little she wins him back from death. At last he looks at her, a fatal look. Not that it kills her. She gets what she wants, relatively speaking; she brings him back with her. But the one who comes home is not the one who died. This one has lost what made him human: his future death. Also, his music.

Certain words came to me, painful, but not without a note of pride: "I am . . ." and then, with more decision: "I am limited!"

What had I done ever since I had come to the city but fail?—while I had sought my mandate in every other act. Well, if to fail was my vocation, then I would fail totally. If the great highs were not for me, then I would take the lows, and even fling myself into the well to deepen it further with the work of my own hands. Though my means were few, they were too many. I needed to lose even more, to weaken myself, to become no more than a tainted piece of air, or the expression on other people's faces. A show not of force but of—and after all the supreme ones, the tough are not able to do one thing: be weak. If not the best I would be the worst, supreme at least in this.

I will say it now, what I had suspected almost from the start: That all this was inside me. The city, the device, Orpheus. They were real, but I was bigger than they were. But now it seemed to me that this was not significant. Inside or out, something like a subpoena had brought me here. I had had no say in it and on the other hand far too much say, so much say that it was fatal to my interests. The only thing that would make me secure would be to submit automatically to the rules (insofar as I could make them out), to give up my say, give up all I had.

Feeling much lighter, I went to watch a movie—exceptionally bad, like all movies here—and on the way home stopped by a field where a passion play was being performed in the foundations of an ancient building. Once a clubhouse where men of breeding had mixed with the lower classes, according to my map, it had collapsed in a long-ago earthquake. The gate to hell swung open with a realistic explosion, and at that very moment the street filled with children. It was the first time I had seen them running like that in the light of day. Their eyes were wholly black as if they brought the night along with them, their black coattails romped, the light sang along the knives they held. "They are harvesting," said my copycat without much interest.

I followed them up the hill to the guesthouse. As I came up they spilled out the door, dragging the boy with them. It was not my

267

business but I stopped to watch as the boy took up a position with his back to the fountain as before and began singing. His words resounded in my head as if I were the one who had formed them, but far better and clearer than any words of my own. The sun glorified his face. But in the city behind me the gloom was deepening. The coming thunderstorm spoke at the limits of hearing, the pennants on the keep were frenzied, the barge from which I had viewed the poppies was outlined for a moment in blue-white light.

I drifted, almost without agency, a cloud with a judicial eye. I felt so light. My copycat pressed herself to my back. Her arms came up under mine, so that my hands lay lightly on top of hers. Her hands raised my hands. Up they went and up I went after them, stepping lightly, finding my balance, my copycat imposing order and form and reason on the cloud that I was. What were we about? I did not need to know, I would end up where I ended up.

We continued into the guesthouse and took our position at the device. My copycat worked her hands into the machine under mine, panting a little, as if in a passion.

With a supreme effort I stopped, but found that my hand was once again caught inside the device. The fan beat rapidly, then stopped with a crash, as if something had broken free inside the device. Something corrosive started leaking out of the device onto my right arm. I fought to withdraw my hand, beating my head against the face of the device. It crashed and buzzed with the impact but did not release me. "Please, please," I may have said, giving way to the weakest argument of all. The device seemed about to yield to my tactics, when something collapsed inside it, crashing down onto the back of my hand, and driving something like a gimlet right through the center of it. It felt like knives, cleavers, clubs, an orchestra of killing instruments, practicing on me with the art of a dozen Paganinis.

In the street the children bayed. Orpheus sang, and the buzz resounded in the walls; the seals in the bay raised their heads as they caught the strain on the air, the fleas in the habits of the priests beat time, a robin joined in on the high notes. Through the door I watched as the children surrounded Orpheus, closed over him. All I could see was their hands rising and falling, driving the knives again and again into his back. The light on their knives too rose and fell.

"Please don't," I said. "Please stop." But I was too far away or too weak or they could tell I didn't mean it and could not stop them even if I did. Would it be offensive if I said that this too was a little sexual for me? Not death but the knives going in?

At last the group withdrew a little, revealing the boy, a broken thing. He was on his face, hands spread, spilling his life onto the street like a hundred poppies. One of the children, a young boy, frisked him, finding in his coat only a piece of paper, which he looked at for a moment, then threw away. One pushed him over with a heel and revealed his face, which had the patient expression of someone very hard at work. I saw that his eyes were focused on one thing only (and had been, most likely, all along): his death. I wanted—I know it was senseless, it was a bad program, even the worst possible one—to drag his eyes all the way back to me for one moment from that imponderably far place inside his head. I wanted to be the thing he looked at.

"Don't lie," said my copycat. "It suits you very well that he can't look at you."

"Not now," I said. "Not now that it's not even possible."

"It's not enough to be the one for whom he sang his song?" asked my copycat.

The machine buzzed, issuing my answer in print. "The song is only a way of translating into music the white of his eyes," it said. "The song too looks away. That is its appeal, the sense it gives of something out of view, something facing away at the center of it." It freed my hands, and I rose. I did not look back to see if my copycat was following. She could continue my translation if she liked, and in the first person too. It was no business of mine.

Was it cavalier of me, was it even evil, to succumb to the temptation to step back into the room I had thought of as the boy's, take up a position at the service counter, and look away, at something so far inside my head that I could see no other thing?

In me the real, the fatal song began at last.

The Library
Sarah Tourjee

HERE CREATES A NOTABLE LEDGE where bodies may fall into chasms, may bounce from rock to rock as though packed with sand. Limbs will be bent unnaturally in this way, folding over against the joint and staying. What is left of who enters is bodies quite unaccustomed to walking with inverted knees, but they will learn slowly and gracelessly and eventually forget the way their knees bent before.

The librarians are not opposed to cutting the tension, being free willed whatever the means. The books are there to remind them that whatever can be said need not be said, that all the sentences exist. They retreat to, or are relieved by, something more physical, an expression that could but need not be formulated in analysis, in confession, in guilty admittance, or justified by words saying *love*, or *the best one can do*, or *just this once*, or *I'm not usually like this*, or *this is the last time and I mean it*. The books—corporeal as much as they are discarnate, existing here as both yet unrelated—fall off the shelf and are bent, folded, water damaged, but exist regardless of their containers' movement and destruction. And the librarians, aware of this, taxed with this, are nonetheless inspired by it, feel themselves permitted to allow their own bodies to act without the weight of what's inside them, without the burden of forming sentences to explain. The sentences already surround them.

The librarians lay words onto each other's bodies as decoration. Or as stimulation, a note to get the song started, a suggestion for procession. *Formidable. Smoke. Stronghold. Ardent. Imprint. Tallow. Curtail. Incline. Fold.* They let these figures lie across their skin, they peel them slowly off. Taste them, if words can be sensed. Make tools of them, if they can be handled. Place them, if words can set inside. Glasses placed on the desk to avoid breakage, bodies placed

270

gingerly to avoid clatter—they are respectful of their patrons' pursuits, of the need for quiet time. They try.

There is the need for this, such great need. This is public space, a resource for all. The librarians do not take their position lightly, but they are passion filled, struck in such ways that the binding of their skin cannot contain. And so. Silence as it is can be demanded though rarely performed in libraries, beds. Where still the hum of breathing, moving bodies, grinding teeth, and vocal cords cannot help but assert. The song first emerges in the night to lull a beloved into dreamland, or to lull her out of it, to inspire some desire as a song is apt to do of a vision in the mind of youth and flexibility, properly functioning joints and organs, a full set of teeth, and hair (some carnal urge). But then, the song successful to a degree, will prove difficult to withhold on other occasions, even if the occasion calls for inhibition, silent reading, clean hands.

There's not a reason not to, not to fuck each other, not to cross walls, not to combine all this individual space. *I have too much room inside me,* one says, *please come in. Help me fill it.* This is all they're doing, helping each other to sufficiently inhabit what they have been given, or burdened. Here, all around them, is the evidence of pulling back, of containing the impulse, of preserving it. The impulses line the shelves, are held under arms, or placed into bags, are taken home for short visits, or sometimes long visits if the draw is too great, if the impulse escapes its bound boundaries. The librarians are surrounded by this, it is insulating them, padding them, explaining them, permitting, begging them to reach. So they do.

They thus face each other, drag fingernails across each other's arms. They reach toward each other and grab on to the lip of a belt, or the hook of a shoulder blade. They undress slowly, press fingers into the coils of permanents. They dig their hands beneath all there is to dig through—considerable amounts of stuff sometimes—they dig through it, their hands find each other finally. Their faces cannot remain apart, their bodies roll into the stacks. Startling always to find themselves there, they have to pause, they have to feel this moment.

271

Sarah Tourjee

The books are not surprised by this, the books have been prepared for more. The books have seen, they own, in fact, all that can happen, all that is impulsively released or appropriately held back, and all that is let loose from the body in every dripping way, every deep and relieving thing, every act that could find its way into words. The books know all of this already. So why be quiet for them?

The librarians are connected by fingers and teeth and legs, and tongues, and arms, and breasts, and woven torsos, and when they pause this way to think about what this place has brought them, what they've brought to it, it is hard for them to consider much outside the ache of their bodies' positions, and the anticipation of what comes next. It hurts, this movement, that's what can't be read, how tired the muscles get under another's weight, how mouths are too vigorous at times, how a hand overstays its welcome, but is called again, is invited farther, and so opens, stays. *Grain. Holding. Stilt. Still. Rake.*

The librarians take these words from the walls and empty them into each other. This is one way to protect what's been said already, not by saying it again, but by using it on a body. They alternate positions justly, they scream and quake, their heads throw back, they stare into the fluorescent lights, then look back to each other and find faces distorted in a black hole of fluorescence, now anonymous, stripped. They pull into each other to regain their bearings, identify themselves by what they reach. The books are walls around them now, and the librarians expand, swell, expel rather than quell, attempt to fill the space, the library.

Literature and the Right Not to Die
Brian Evenson

NEAR THE END OF the first volume of David B.'s *Incidents in the Night*, an eccentric editor named Emile Travers, who now sports a book in the place of his head, "jumped into a letter like into a lake and took its form, thus he escaped the Angel of Death." Travers has dodged the Angel of Death six times by hiding within books, masquerading within language. If he can escape a seventh, he tells the character David B., then he will become immortal. He is seeking David B.'s help because he is "certain that he has found around the edge of a book the way to shake off Death!"

David B., the fictional David B. and not the author—or perhaps both the fictional and the real David B., for there is rarely as clean a separation between the real and the imagined as many think—is intrigued by this. He sees the possibility, if he is able to hide Travers a seventh and final time, of escaping Death as well.

He secures Travers within a book called *The Desert*, the pages of which are covered with row upon row of the letter *N*. With the letter *N* representing "Enn," the unknown god of the Greeks, the god of emptiness, of the void, each letter is a sort of chasm. David B. tells himself that the Angel of Death will lose himself among and within all these chasms and be unable to find Travers in time to kill him at the appointed hour.

And indeed, with time having expired, it is Travers who clambers out of the book rather than Azraël, the Angel of Death. David B. thinks he's won, that he's found a way to defeat Death. Only later does he realize that the figure who has climbed out of the book is not Travers at all, but the Angel of Death wearing Travers's face like a mask, and that Travers is dead.

Whether this death is definitive or reversible is the subject of the rest of the volume. Travers's name means "across" or "through" in French, and even after the editor's death, David B. keeps uncovering traces of him that make him suspect that Travers might either still

273

be alive or be capable of being brought back to life.

I have not been able to determine whether *The Desert* is a real book or an imaginary one: With David B., it could be either. The idea of a book that is the repetition of a single letter, over and over again, seems the opposite of Jorge Luis Borges's Library of Babel, a kind of ritualized and monotonous repetition that opens up into emptiness. But, then again, with Borges's library containing all possible books, both written and unwritten, and stretching on seemingly forever, *The Desert* would be part of that library. The problem, though, is knowing where and how to find it.

In *Incidents in the Night*, a used bookshop becomes the site for the battle with Death. Travers slips into *The Desert* and Azraël must find him. He finds and enters the book almost immediately, leaving David B. and the bookshop owner to listen to the blows of Azraël's sword as they resound from within the pages. "There have been so many duels with Death here," Lhôm, the bookshop owner, tells David B. "Not one of them has succeeded, you know."

And yet we keep trying. What makes literature quintessentially what it is is the promise that hides in the letters. The sense that we can, in some sense or other, metaphorically or even, with holy texts, for "real," escape death through them, as authors and as readers. Even if we don't believe that books will *really* save us from death, as writers we still hold tight to the belief of living on after our deaths if our books are still read. What we want ultimately as humans is not to be forgotten. Indeed, one of the best cases for fiction being experiential rather than a mimetic reproduction of the real is this: We still think it can save us from something—from being forgotten, from oblivion, from death.

Language as it is used in literature is language used aberrantly, which is what gives it its power. Such usage removes language from its utilitarian functions of conveying information or issuing orders and instructions and instead pays more attention to the flow and flux of words, the way that they resound and sing. It makes language do things that have very little use value, that often in fact get in the way of something being communicated in a straightforward fashion. On a practical level, when language becomes literary, it becomes less useful.

But this very uselessness is what we cherish. The way in which language is an expression of humanity's ability not only to manipulate the world through language, but of our ability to create *another* world through language, and by so doing negate the world we live in and which threatens us with death. It is this that gives the language of fiction a good part of its attraction, and also makes us still hope, even if only subconsciously, that it can conquer death.

To say the promise of not dying imbues language, particularly literary language, is to say the reverse as well, that the written word is haunted by death, that within the written word lies the promise of death itself.

In the Mormon temple ceremony, you are given a new name, which you are told you must always keep secret and only reveal at a certain place and in a certain way. It is your true name, and as such, one must assume, it has a kind of power over you. In the temple you reveal it in one place only, at the gauzy veil that represents the entry into heaven, and you reveal it to the temple worker who is standing on the other side of this veil with his hand thrust through it, playing the role of God. Once that revelation has been made, along with certain handshakes and ritual language, you are admitted "into God's presence." Such is the power of a name. But if the wrong person has your true name, they may use it to get into heaven in your place.

Are words escapes or are they traps? Is there a difference?

We search in language for magics that will help us avoid being confronted by our own mortality. We will not find these magics—rationally we know this. But we might still find the hope of them, even as we see within them the reflection of our own future corpses.

The only way to keep the magic from dispelling is to stop short of death, even if just barely. *Incidents in the Night* ends without ending, on a question. David B. and Travers lie side by side, head to foot, on a pile of books and bones, with the arm of the one blending into the arm of the other like an umbilical cord between them. But who is feeding whom? "Is Travers alive?" the top of the page asks. "Is David B. dead?" the bottom asks. The uncertainty of the death of the one is mirrored in the uncertainty of the life of the other, and we are left in that wavery space where, at best, we can say, "Who knows?" That may be all that literature can offer us: the ability to think that someone has escaped death in the brief moment before we begin to wonder if we're mistaken, if it's not just that Death has borrowed his face.

275

Reversible Story
Lydia Davis

NECESSARY EXPENDITURE

A CONCRETE MIXER HAS come and gone from the house next door. Mr. and Mrs. Charray are renovating their wine cellar. If they improve their cellar, they will pay less for fire insurance. At the moment, their fire insurance is very expensive. The reason for this is that they own thousands of bottles of very good wine. They have very good wine and some fine paintings, but their taste in clothes and furniture is strictly lower middle class.

EXPENDITURE NECESSARY

The Charrays' taste in clothes and furniture is dull, and strictly lower middle class. However, they do own some fine paintings, many by contemporary Canadian and American painters. They also have some good wine. In fact, they own thousands of bottles of very good wine. Because of this, their fire insurance is very expensive. But if they enlarge and otherwise improve their wine cellar, the fire insurance will be less expensive. They are doing this: A concrete mixer has just come and gone from their house, next door.

Janus at a Chinese Restaurant in Paris
Thalia Field and Abigail Lang

A doorway allows us to **hold up** despite desire.

Consider Janus: two faces, one brain. Of a mind? Think twice.
How does it at the gate?
Which way does your beard point tonight?
Omens attend upon beginnings.

Later may we break the cookie in two and split our fortune?
Later we may deadlock.

But that's ahead of myself. We've come here for a traditional meal in an
unfamiliar place.

Two trains going in opposite directions leave the station
at the same time . . .

(On the witness stand:) "Doorkeeper of the heavenly court /
I look toward both east and west at once."

I will speak in your turn, and do you speak in mine?

(On the witness stand:) "The ancients called me chaos, and even now,
a sign of my once confused state, my front and back appear the same.

We want to, we really try to, but looking as we do, we can never look away.
Yet do we see eye to eye?

Show who you really are!

Easy for you to say.

Remember how I conned **impregnable** Carna-Cranaë behind a rock, worked
our will, left her hinges? And our bumper sticker: "Dont fuck with me I have
eyes in the rear."

Inflate evidence of skill: 11 faces, 18 arms, 1,000 eyes. Be my stunt.

Generations **sanction** movement. Time begins to end in a beginning.
An entrée for one is made for two, two tastes that we make the same
shit out of anyway.

Charlemagne couldn't tell dead pagans from his own dead men,
so he asked for a sign.
A sign split in two. The dead are dead, shit is shit, but there are differences.
Thorns and briars grew up around the bodies of the pagans.

"But why hide in peace, and open your gates in war?"
(On the witness stand:) "My unbarred gate stands open wide, so that when
the people go to war the return path's open too."
I bar it in peacetime so peace cannot depart:
How can we understand the cult of "look both ways before leaping"?
Can we know the instant the men became bearded men?

Hoist the red flag, call men to arms. Braid the tug-of-war and let down
the great draught.
I think you're making a face at me.

Disfigured, we are shown
a booth arranged for our particular handicap. We can stand to sit here.

When the Romans wanted to declare formal war on Pyrrhus, they captured an
enemy soldier, sold him a lot of Roman ground on which the *pater patratus*
cast his javelin.

Hard **pits strike** us. Deep **pits strike** us out.

We coin the two-faced two faced coin.
Chinese restaurant, Paris between wars.
Can we agree to disagree? Let's admit the opposite, it will be yesterday
soon enough.

Janus Quirinus, "god of the community of *Quirites* (citizens)" vs. Mars,
"god of the mass of *milites*," their temples symmetrically bound across the
pomerium.

A crime will be told, cold and hard and light.
Turned improperly from a threshold or hit up a bank,
the meal is expected to be edible and remembered as inedible and vice versa.
Double agents fill two mouths at once, **carrying on**.

Streets, bridges, doors, and crossroads hold up danger.
Etruscans adopted a grid plan so spirits would cross the city and leave
more swiftly.
The N-S axis (*cardo*) was beneficial but the E-W axis (*decumanus*)

unfavorable, a dead end on the western side. Janus guarded the northern
entrance, one face turned east, the other watching the west.

plot: sun rises in the east / puts out clouds / sets in the west

Align the triumphal march along the *via sacra*, the general waiting for the
senate to relieve him from the *imperium* (right to kill) before they pass
the *pomerium*, filing through an archway like a stream, spanned.

Could the menu be more self-negating?

We **peruse** it.

Identical, twinned, hyphenated, banished, welcomed—
Are we such friends? Oxymorons, alone together.

100,000 Japanese-Americans were confined in internment camps during
WWII, including those who had produced fortune cookies, giving an
opportunity to Chinese manufacturers to take over the business.

One of us may be Jewish. One may be some sort of saint.
Mongrel descent. Pure French.
We share internal organs in any language.
We have hardly any texts to go on. Just gates overlooking many possibilities;
the portrait between us a model portrait.

God of draughts, get the lazy suzy to spin!

That we might share one empty stomach. That we might mention it apart.

Little dumpling, don't be happy/sad.

Janus! Make these children into soldiers on their way out
and change them back into good citizens when they return.
But how to **screen** the inner linings of the soul antagonist?
                              And so animate what is already **spirit**, a living dead.
                    Seeking **leave to remain**, **refrain** the peak of the march.
Heads or tails? Flip a coin minted to commemorate the closing of the gates
of war.
Old money, conquered, gives way to the new.
                              Not to **buckle** easily, but to **garnish** the prize.
About his brain the very temples cracked.
A traitor is one who comfortably straddles gaps.
    How can we choose which bale to eat? How can we choose to eat or drink?
                    (Buridan's Ass starving in our midst)
                The waiter arrives and marvels at the word choice.

                    You might say the defendants, **spliced** at the seam,
            knew more about Santa Claus and yet—real and not real—he's **moot**.

If you're into beards, let me reintroduce Charlemagne, the beard to end all
beards, white as April flowers or driven snows that freeze: stroked, tugged,
rent, torn, clasped, shaken out, and sworn by throughout *The Song of Roland*.

The server must make strangely artificial perambulations to take the orders.

                    (Does confession come easiest from liars?)

It's the model model I am, we said.

We'll have two of those. I'm both looking forward to it.

And nothing like a traitor to **lace** the plot, **adumbrate** sides, create reversal, dialectic, suspense. Heroes fall into the best traitors. Prefer one of noble stock, peer to the betrayed party.

At the beginning, Janus **put out** armies.

The fingers of our statue curled in odd positions.

"I will buy only where the Blue Eagle flies."

Loyalty oaths may be good for business but beg to be broken in plots.

(What do a defendant's fingers mean, pointing in all directions?)

We're brought a steamed flatfish with scallions—right-eyed, protruding, lying blind.

Could it be we too have been the site of an ocular migration?

To adapt to which dramatic conditions?

Our soul shows a more extreme asymmetry (and may lack teeth on one side
   of the jaw) and an extra order of hard-boiled eggs we ask to split with a hair.

Guilty and not guilty while a whole room of **peers puzzle** us out.

The traitor **dusts** us lightly as he takes the order.

Who was Ganelon, arch traitor of Christendom second only to Iscariot?

He was Roland's own stepfather and Charlemagne's brother-in-law.

He betrayed Charlemagne's army to the Muslims, leading to the massacre of the rear guard. He was caught, shaved on both cheeks, and torn limb from limb by four fiery horses.

Pulling out from the station carrying French Jews, one train takes
*   remaining Jews, some leave remaining French the other way—*

We are of two minds.

Such a rich line of traitors, the *false geste*, threaded from Ganelon, issuing by prequel back to Doon,

*ur-traitor, late root in a tree growing from the top down—**putting out** innumerable branches.

No U-turn. Loyalty oaths seek to **stay** change.

> A bridge that lifts and turns and falls both ways; jinx.
> "My friends, there is no friend."

> The bridge and the threshold and the man accused; each headed away or
> the other.

> It hurts but not where you'd expect.

Right down the middle in fact is an area of an almost pleasurable sensation,
the likes of which can only be compared to sleeping on board a ship,
or hanging backward off a swing, tempered by a gravity that grabs but can't
root the body.

> In fact, swing, because here we are: guilty and not guilty, accused
> and yet criminal of all that is put before me, deceptively **sanctioned**
> to stand trial.

> For a door may be told? A bridge may be double-crossed?

283

Where an aporia is without passage, a bridge has abundance.

"Brücke dreht sich um!"

Two trains meet at the train station of Montoire-sur-le-Loir where Hitler and Pétain shake hands, the Maréchal introducing an «honorable» «collaboration» and great perplexity.

Puzzle before we speak, then doublespeak.

Two trains leave the station at the same moment, traveling in opposite directions . . .

"I should mention without going any further, any further on, that I say aporia without knowing what it means."

Both Gane and Pétain wanted to put out war.
Gane betrays **sanguine** Roland whose hero status depends on perpetual war.
War have you waged, so on to war proceed, what time from war
will we draw back instead?

Roland strikes vigorously, cleaves helmet nose mouth teeth, the body
through the coat, cuts the saddle and deep into the horse's back.

The Emperor, he clasps his chin, his beard his fingers tug.

Faldrun of Pui has through the middle sliced: And his right hand the count
clean slices off; Then takes the head of Jursaleu the blond; And through the
spine he slices that pagan's horse.

Maybe we're a failed section of primeval man and somewhere
a headless body roams the earth in search of its former half—three-fifths—
longing for the time we could roll over like tumblers with our legs in the air;
this was when we wanted to run fast.

Cutting through wrists and ribs and chines indeed, through garments to the
lively flesh beneath;

When will time come that he from war draws back? "Never," says Guene,
"so long as lives Rollanz."

Let's ask for the **bill**. Let's consider a scapegoat to boot.

Friends offer each other a **bill** to be paid in different currency.
What form is the question? We don't understand the value of the price.

The trial must take place to judge where the defendant will go . . .
A **legendary** man accused of a double crossing.

Legendary Knights meet in the gap, heroes
in their faces **fighting with** each other in battle.

Depending on the crossroad, Knights
will **resign** their service, mirror images of each other.
He strikes Pinabel on the helmet down to the nostril and leaves him cleft,
brains oozing.
All of his head was down the middle shorn.

Ride through Warwick, ride through Warwick, but oh! It's not England
anymore.
Those damn yanks took Coventry too!

Two stories leave the station at the same time going in opposite
directions . . .

Meanwhile, we **enjoin** you: **Stay fast**. Stasis, what's left looking forward and
right back.

285

One of us may be right to write back, **overlooking** the view.

Where lights and stars **are out** and must be **fixed**.

Push-me, pull-you. In parallel we **wind up** to **trim** the tale.

Santa-Janus.
Janus-Claus.

A partition maintains a raw and reopening seam, and this for some reason is
where tension wants to mount (at the coupling, which is also an indication
of factions).
Weapons grow internal to a body, shared or unshared, so we each perceive a
different audience of those who might also lack perspective.
It's hard for anyone else to tell exactly where the split occurs
because we ourselves can shift its tether.
Without a wall or fence or steel plate, the movements of cells
perpetrate endless incursions.
It tickles as they pass.

Weathered, we **bolt** Janus's meal; **contemporary handicap**.

We **lease** the table with legacy on both sides of the coin.

We **cleave** our loyalty.
We eat. We literally don't eat.

Thalia Field/Abigail Lang

It's all **downhill** from here.

Whatever the pretext, we **adumbrate** what happens next.
When it's time to go, where will we head?
Never alone but always solitary, sitting at a draughtsboard playing both sides.
Copemates bound to tell everyone nothing at once.
Two stories depart in opposite directions, from the station marked **X X**.

Friends might remind us that this sentence is still not true.
As nothing can be true or false in war.
Shelled, we are wont to **ravel** the threads—
About his brain the very temples cracked.
His palate is cleft but he meows through both.

Two trains meet for dinner in Paris. Whatever sentence my friend says is true.
City of double agents tattooed in invisible ink.
Somehow we will both miss what happens.
Boustrophedon,
—terrible to read—
"Half of my host I leave you presently"

In this Chinese restaurant we are foreign and near home.
We call each other **villain** as no friends can.

Allies or enemies at the front line? We may go separately on this.

The traitor brings small change.

Two trains crossing must stop at the same time
and neither shall start up again until the other has gone . . .

287

Pit of diamond, pit of coal, the hands bleed, eyes may cry;
Janus, warlike (peacelike), stares into the memory of the future.

Game over, change sides.

This is but an outline.

—From "Leave to Remain"

The Reader
Robert Coover

WITHOUT A READER OF HIS OWN, he creates one in a story he calls
"The Reader." He decides that she is sensitive, intelligent, discern-
ing, appreciative, widely read—in short, his perfect reader—and she
is also exquisitely beautiful with an endearing smile and a loving,
compliant nature. She professes to adore his writing, written specifically for her to read, which encourages him to believe she adores him
too. Well, of course she does, it's his story, how could she do otherwise? So, she loves him, adores him, but necessarily in the abstract,
as a reader loves the absent writer, alive or dead, lacking the circumstances to express her love more directly, which is his plight as well.
He writes a poem inspired by her, brilliant in concept and powerful
in its execution, and she reads it, adores it, clasps it to her breasts.
Having designed them himself, he knows everything about those
breasts. When she presses the poem to them, it's as though his hands
are there too, his lips. But they are not. He can't touch them, though
he knows she longs for him to do so. Because he loves her and wants
her to be happy, he invents a handsome young man to keep her company, himself genteel, highly literate, of a warm and generous nature.
This development in his story happens during a visit one morning to
his local bookstore. As he sits there in the worn leather chair where
he always sits, having a second cup of coffee, browsing yesterday's
newspapers, and taking notes in his little blue notepad, he decides
that this is where the two will meet, and they do. She is reading one
of his books. The young man has also read it. It is their shared affection for the author that brings them together. The man takes another
of the author's books down from the shelf and remarks on its narrative subtleties, its irresistible lyricism, its nobility of purpose. She is
awed by his intimate knowledge of a book so dear to her. Soon they
are naked. Love blooms between them. She is happy. But he who has
brought all this about is not. In fact, writing about them, he suffers
a terrible surge of jealousy at the very moment the young man kisses
her breasts. Never mind that this man also loves his writing, he's gone.
Hit by a truck. A tragedy. She is deeply sorrowed, being a sensitive

person, but too bad, he was not right for her. She knows that now. So he enters the story himself. Or someone bearing his name and likeness does. They meet in the same bookstore. He is sitting at a table, giving a public reading to a packed, admiring audience and, at the moment she first sees him, she forgets her grief and falls desperately in love with him. It is total surrender. He may do with her as he pleases. First, of course, he has to introduce himself. She does that for him by handing him a book to sign, telling him that it is her favorite of all he has written, and the greatest book she has ever read. He smiles up at her, catching the lovelight in her eyes, his own eyes perhaps reflecting it. It is, he says evocatively, a mere trifle compared to the book he is working on now. She gasps in recognition of the revelatory moment, her hand at those breasts where his will soon be. Perhaps she intuits that the new book is for her and for her alone. Would you like a cup of coffee, he asks in a seductive manner, returning the signed book to her, or perhaps a glass of wine? No, thank you, says the woman sitting in the worn leather chair opposite him with a book in her lap, staring at him with something between curiosity, concern, and alarm. He apologizes, explaining that he is an actor; he is auditioning for a play and was practicing his lines. It's called "The Reader," he says when she asks, as he leaves the bookstore, intending never to return. The reader has also left the bookstore. She is in the apartment of the famous writer she has just met, which is to say, his own apartment, or one much like it, though cleaner and more elegantly furnished, with famous etchings on the walls instead of pages torn from magazines. She is admiring his vast library (not much room for etchings actually). Have you read all these books? she asks. All those in this room, yes. The unread ones are in the bedroom. May I see them? Of course. She picks one up from the stack on his bedside table. By now she is naked again. She does this so easily. The writer in the story is also removing his clothes. As is he himself, less gracefully perhaps than the other two. But what next? He has his hero and heroine naked in a bedroom together, and they're excited, he's excited, but the story is going nowhere. Her radiant beauty, all the more dazzling with her clothes off, has made him forget who she is. Should she be reading something? The book she has picked up, he sees, is a science fiction novel about creatures from outer space, which does not seem promising. He decides to put his clothes on again and go back to the bookstore. Luckily the chair he prefers is unoccupied and the same woman is in the chair opposite. It is all quite convenient, and he wonders for a moment if he is in a story someone else is writing. The woman asks him if he got the part for which he was auditioning and he apologizes and explains that really he is a writer, not an actor. He had been trying to invade the thoughts and feelings of his characters and became so intensely engaged with them that he got carried away and started speaking their lines out loud, but was ashamed to say so. She finds that quite amusing and says she knows how it can happen. He asks if she is also a writer and she replies that, no, she is only a reader, but she has often heard writers talk about getting confused as to what was real in their lives and what was imaginary, and sometimes something like that happens to her as a reader. He asks her if she has ever felt like she was living in somebody else's story. All the time, she says. But I'm never the main character, she adds with a sad smile. She recalls the line he spoke aloud about going for a glass of wine, and asks if that offer is still on. Soon they are both naked, lying on a mattress in her apartment, each with a glass of red wine on the floor beside them. It seems to him that it has happened as easily as in the story he is writing. She is not beautiful and the book she has been reading is a cheap romance, but he is grateful to her. The love felt between the writer, the one who is like himself and bears his name, and the beautiful reader has been consummated, and now the story can move on. She is still deliriously in love, of course, but what about him? On the one hand, he knows that he owes it to his public to remain true to his craft, undistracted by wives and lovers, and on the other, she *is* his public. The beautiful reader turns toward him with a dreamy smile. I am so honored, she whispers, and his heart melts. As am I, he murmurs, yet he understands that something has been broken between them. You are beautiful, he adds, but—and his heart aches to say so—you have ruined my story. Her smile does not change. She seems not to have heard him. Well, of course, it was not the writer in his story who said this, it was he himself. The woman lying next to him has risen, perhaps offended. She is already dressing. If you have any money, she says, I'll go buy us a pizza. He untangles his cast-off pants and fishes around in the pockets, realizing that he is indeed very hungry. In his creative throes, he has forgotten about eating. While he's on his hands and knees doing that, she whops his behind. See what else I can ruin, she says with a crooked grin and swats it again. Mushrooms, pepperoni, sausage, extra cheese, and garlic? Great. He hands her a bill and, with a wink, sinks back on the mattress. He will leave his writer and reader to their own uncertainties. This is how a story ought to end.

Hylomorphosis
Alexandra Kleeman

Because they have seen angels, and other divine numina, represented by painters with a certain splendour and light, and have heard that these are spirits and are so called by theologians; so that in consequence they think that the spirituous stuff in our bodies must be similar.

—Johannes Argenterius, *De Somno et Vigilia*, 1556

AN ANGEL FACES THE PAINTING of the famous angel with sword looming above a battle. Figure blurred out, scene blurred out. The painted angel's face like a thumbprint, darkened by two depressions, one above and one beneath. The difficulty with describing an angel or its movements: They lack organs of sense or motion. Their bodies defined by absence. The angel facing the painting reaches up toward its own body. Its fingers grope the tranquillity of that perfect head, smooth as a plate. It finds the middle of its face and pushes in. The question is: Can an angel become anything it has not already been?

&

The mouths of an angel are threefold: With one, he breathes of the pure and refined air of glorious realms, the light of God filling his body with lightness. With the second, he eats of the meat of the spirit and drinks in long drafts the clear water of the soul, both of which make heavy the banquet of God, and are eternal and immune to spoilage. With the third, he utters words of truth, handed down to him from the highest order. In man, however, the functions threefold are merged in one organ, and hence his purposes and the ends to which he applies himself shall always be indistinct, unintelligible.

&

The angels sit and weep. Just as suddenly, they stand and laugh. They are testing out their new-made mouths. The angels stick fingers in

292

their mouths, one by one, and root around in them, scratching at the top, the soft yielding sides that bulge when tried. The angels scratch until they pierce membrane and nothing seeps through. The angels discover a funny sound made by squishing the cheeks in, then forward, so that the lips purse at the front in imitation of a fish. They lack respect for the bodily ideal, for its integrity and originary form. They heal before the wound can weep. The angels practice a self-mortification of such innocent clumsiness that it cannot carry any redemptive value: and, in any case, what have they to atone for? Virtue weighs upon them like a coat made of air.

&

Suppose that archangel Gabriel intends to have cognition of his fellow angel Raphael, but also of human beings, trees, and other things in the material world. To do so, he cannot simply observe or encounter the objects aforementioned: Without organs of sense or action, he must instead adopt his habit, a habit unique and individual, the fulfillment of which shall grant access to all things simultaneously, in their essence. In this manner, a knowledge perfect and unequivocal is achieved without returning to the problem of access, which is an issue only for beings of bounded material.

&

1. The mouths of angels are soft and sweet: Awake, they give off a scent like new leaves. Asleep, they smell of upturned roots, still moist with clinging soil.

2. From the mouths of angels come healing waters, light, the peace and quietude of early morning. Also numbers of things less lauded: water tasting of metal or lead, wax and string, small brown moths that turn to powder when crushed.

3. The mouths of angels are useless, a sort of inscription or sign, built in the shallowness of an inscription or sign, and serving no known function, as angels speak in a visual language of their own, one borne through gesture as an effect of and within the air.

4. If angels are creatures, they are of matter and form compounded. If they are spirits, they are of form set in motion. If they are matter, they possess the principle of change. If they are form, they possess the principle of destruction or preservation.

5. Their indivisibility, perishability.

6. The mouths of angels are a hoax made plausible by our own mouths, which we crudely attach to entities that possess neither body nor extension.

&

A round, yellow sun hangs over the landscape dotted with unshapen stones. Either the arrangement of the stones is random, or else it is of an incomprehensible order. A blue sky stuck through with clouds the size and shape of boats. *Since angels do not have bodily organs, Alexander of Hales qualifies the word of angels as a "spiritual nod." It is a nod insofar as it makes apparent what was previously hidden. In this regard the angel's nod shows a certain similarity to the exterior word of man, as the nod, in a certain sense, is the vehicle of the angel's inner word.* In the distance, figures cluster on the earth like resting birds, tucking a seeping radiance within the folds of a garment radiantly plain.

The silence is bright blue, and everywhere. An angel arranges angels by order and ranking, a luminous line. They regard him with the round gaze of cattle. One at a time, he brings them forth with a movement of the hand, a hand extended toward the newer angel, the fingers of the senior angel each turned in toward the palm, forming a fist extended toward the newer angel, a fist that looks as though it might open up.

One at a time, he leans over each, pressing its head to the stone, back from the neck and deeply onto the surface of the stone, and with his thumb he creates an absence in the center of the face, a thumb-deep breach. The solid flesh moves like dough beneath the heavenly fingers: If it is of matter, it possesses the principle of change.

He digs two thumbs into the hole and opens it up, sideways, outward. And then their bodies too are penetrated by air. Their bodies too take a portion of the air away from itself and hold it within a chamber. That part of the body foreign to itself and capable, suddenly, of speaking in its place.

&

In 1258 in Siena, Italy, an angel is said to have appeared in the town's central square during a festival honoring the sacrifice of St. Catherine. The angel, shrouded in a pure and glorious light, is reported to have consumed in curiosity a single grape from the well-stocked banquet, and fallen over immediately, killed.

&

A mouth is a tear in the wholeness of a being. From this moment on, he will find his breath leaking out from him continually, his body filling with the bodies of others, a circulation of others stepping in and out of the bounds of sensation. He will form the air into shapes with a meaning not his own, and he will hunger for the matter of others, transformed in the mouth into material raw and ready for reuse. In some accounts, a self comes into being with its first cry, its first utterance or gasp into a surround unmarked by its own voice. In others, a self is marked out only when it consumes living matter for the first time, asserting its own body upon the body of another and folding its life into that of its own. The mouth is a site of transformation at the boundary of inner and outer; it crushes the others up so that their thingliness can become someone else's own.

&

The silent angel, his face smooth and markless as a piece of marble not yet shaped into statue. He sinks a whole fist into the mouths of the angels, twisting it this way and that, until the hole is large enough for the sounds of human language, for the words and full sentences. The wrist and forearm protrude from the heads of angels as he turns his fist around, creating space, and then opens it up slowly within the heads, making room for the teeth and tongue he will form from their matter.

The sun is quiet over the stones and the angels as they undergo their transformations. It will never again be so quiet in this field. The angelic mouths unmade, they have no way to gasp as the holes are put into them, as the pure and liquid tears collect around their eyes. All around them the stones are silent, the stones in the shape of whatever, in the shape of things that have no name but could, someday. Their necks each fit flush to their chosen stones, their stones cradling the necks that they may look up and out into the sky.

&

A Benedictine in 1120 AD testified that he was visited nightly by an angel who came to bear witness to the consumption of his simple meal of apples and bread. Questioned by his abbot as to the moral purpose of these visits, the man had nothing to report, save that his observer grew angry if an attempt was made to cover up or otherwise conceal his rations, particularly if the monk strove out of modesty to obscure the view of his mouth.

&

1. Because they are made in the shape of God, which is the shape of man and because they are man's brethren.

2. Because they measure the distance that inheres within man himself, as do the beasts.

3. Because the body of the word and the body of the stone are not the same thing, or because they are.

4. Because an angel is said to perish from taking human food, when a man dies of choking we say that he has received a holy death, heralding his joyful passage into realms higher and more glorious.

5. The saliva of an angel is said to improve the quality of matter and raise it to a state of greater perfection, much as the saliva of man is said to degrade it, and it is reported that a mealy apple thus inserted into the mouth of an angel and stored there for a time shall emerge fresh and devoid of flaws when it is drawn back out.

6. Because the thing and the thought are not one, or because they are.

&

The angels mill about in the fields, picking things up from off the ground and sticking them in their mouths. The cattle regard them in passivity, and wonder. An angel discovers a small pebble and places it within the cavity. He extracts it, and behold: a pebble of the same size, shape, and specification—but now composed of solid gold. An angel regards a small flower, and plucks it from the ground. He places it in his mouth and, lo: What he removes from his mouth is no flower, but a single word. He holds the word up before the eyes of the other angels and they rejoice, marveling in the miracle of flesh made abstract. They pass the word from angel to angel, holy hand to holy hand, turning it over in their palms and observing it from every angle. The sun weighs on them from overhead, weighs like light upon them all, as they tilt their faces up toward the source, mouths open, joyful, and light touches the backs of their mouths, the unbroken backs of their throats.

WORKS CITED:

Durandus of St. Poucain, *Durandi a Sancto Porciano in Petri Lombardi Sententias Theologicas Commentarium lbri IIII* (Venice, 1579; reprinted New Jersey: The Gregg Press, 1964).

Iribarren, Isabel and Martin Lenz, *Angels in Medieval Philosophical Inquiry: Their Function and Significance* (Burlington, Vermont: Ashgate Publishing Company, 2008).

Every Day, an Epic
Evelyn Hampton

EVERY DAY A TIDE ROLLS UP to beauty and convulses it. This means I have been reading. I have been looking at the world through a lens. I have been looking through the lens and I have been looking out around its edges and it is there, where no lens extends, that I see:

and I enter into it. I enter into an agreement to be contained by it. Could it come up to my knees with its absences and lands? Could it rock and drag the clouds from one side of the sky to my open hand? It can and I am ready. I will eat three continuities and they will be lambs. They will be hillsides and they will be spilling. Then they will be green and I will have recovered from them.

I have already recovered. I am inside a man. I am wearing beige and it is raining. This is how I can stand it: I can't. I leave immediately. I open intervals and unravel across them. I leave many strings dangling but no connecting edge, nothing to come to when I'm confused, nowhere to stand to say, This is where I stand; beyond this I do not stand. I have nowhere like sand, or a leap, or a mountain. Briefly I inhabit the shape of *fountain*: I lose my head. I toss across a clean outcrop of marble. My body could be made in its veins. There it might take the shape of a woman as she is imagined by a man, by a history, as she tries to escape from a maze. Her center will be the same as her surface: me. I am spreading rapidly. Every day I am a fish before I am forgotten. Then I am a surge. I rush from a word toward its object with my great capacity for love. Can I love whatever it is I am coming to, even if it turns out to be crumbling? What if, in my rush, I discover that I prefer the rush to the object, the rush to the world? Then I am the death driver, I am the lightning-bolt tattoo zapping the skull tattoo, I annihilate all silver and crystal and mothers and sons, I am an arrow leaving the sun and annihilating the sun, an all-in-one unto no one but one: a much older woman named Melt.

She wants me to call her Melt, so I perform vertiginously upon her body with my shoe, then with my bare hands. When I don't know what else to do, I do headstands and supraheadstands, meaning I leap out of my skull and show her my tattoo. She shows me her own body. It is as real as a peninsula and as tan. It contains the generation known as Man, so she and I get along quietly and then all of a sudden we do not get along at all, I am tossed from her rocks and her cliffs and her hands into a depth of myself that I cannot stand. It is simply skin, this borderland, yet I cannot get beyond it. But what is beyond it? There must lie the self: the possibility of someone else. Let me see who she is, or he: a farmer, a doctor, a neighbor, a bakery? A very large purse stuffed with stolen prescription pills? What else could the self be if not possibility? Beyond this, there must lie the shelf: the sand. I will swim from these hands into former hands, forms I have had and might have again if I can be gentle in how I go about this, brushing softly the entire length of the cat. Briefly a self forms in sense contact. Then I stiffen and sneeze. So I am real, then— I am a cat. Yet I have often crept beyond these boundaries—I have slept. No matter what form it takes, the sea does not soothe one in sleep. Either the movement is excessively vast or my body surpasses an avalanche in its power to displace, so I wake. I swim the liquid waves of Neptune. Trees traverse the sea in the form of boats: fir oars sweeping waves, pine timbers fitting to the wind's curved keel. Emerging from the eddies I am visible as far as breasts, nakedness. It's true I'm on a quest to discover what I am. Yet it plays out in ordinary ways. I jog. I take cash out of a machine, and it's as if money has value, like breath and "Good job!" Yet from the ground it is difficult to see the overall pattern. Often my path is guided only by impulse— suddenly I see a certain quality of green and know that any way I choose to go is already known—but if not by me, then by what extension of my breath? For when I arrive I see that I am nowhere really: I see the chair where I am still sitting, admiring the apparition of home. The ivory of the chairs gleams white, the cups of the table shine, the whole house rejoices with the glittering royal treasure. I extend as far back as royal opulence goes, then put on my clothes. Time to leave again. But where will I go? Looking out from the wave-resounding shore, bearing uncontrollable furies in my heart, I do not even believe that I see what I see, and so I read.

Otherwise Smooth
Rosmarie Waldrop

IF WE JUST SIT on a chair we make no mistakes. But starve for contrails, crows, outlines of buds, and strange horizons. Bird flutter. Gunshot echoes. But let's say we worry what is poetry and what is prose. Wonder. Try to know something and incidentally ourselves. Then pain is inflicted. And though it has no form or special center in the brain it is there. A world closed in itself. Yet wants a voice. Yet whips to the quick the try to stammer it into words. Assuming we were lucky enough to be spoken to before age twelve. So that our potential was not jeopardized and now we "have" language.

I say "I" and thereby appropriate the entire language. And trust I am, through words, gradually to become. A person? An instance of discourse? Plain as the sky to a fisherman? Beginnings are hazy, below the belt, where a face is not yet possible though already bespoke by gravity. But pronouns do not refer to anything in space and time except the utterance that contains them. Each time, like death, unique. Not like walking in light that lies like fine dust on the ground, but language handing me, each time, the gifts of memory, a past. A soul? While the voice excites intimacies of organic existence, modulates the frequency of pulses from nerve fibers. Code. Clouded sentence. Crowded square emptied of bustle by a sudden rain.

It is in grief—a sister's death, a friend's—that I admit: For this I have no name. The words are empty shirts and pants strung on a clothesline. Without body. Without air. Therefore I too can't breathe. Sore. Sere. The self goes from the self. Pain felt as in a twilight state, first stutter of sleep, as on the outer limits of the soul. And even the pain I feel might not be mine. Here they are, sister, friend, dead and tired. From the effort, without the help of language, to stand up in my memory. Which has lost its simplemindedness, its clear-cut narration. Suddenly old.

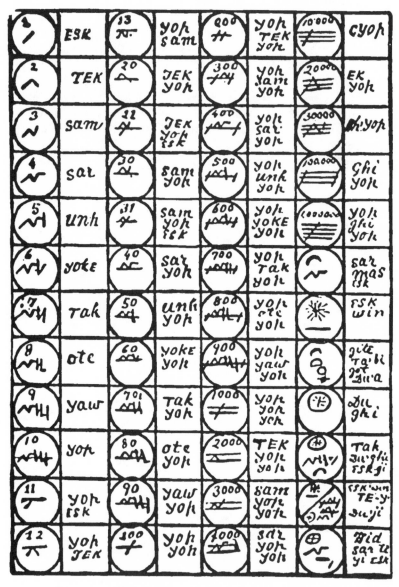

PLATE 17. — TABLET OF AH'IOD'ZAN. [Numeration. — ED.]

From the Oahspe.

302

Romancing the Mind

In homage to Jorge Luis Borges

William H. Gass

1.

932353 THE TOMB OF GOD: The Body of Jesus and the Solution to a 2,000-Year-Old-Mystery. By R. Andrews & P. Schellenberger. They used a hidden geometry of lines and angles apparent in certain maps, tombs and artworks, including a 17th century painting by Nicolas Poussin, to search for and locate the exact geographical location of Christ's tomb, in southern France, the same region which appears in legends about the Ark of the Covenant, and the Holy Grail. Illus. 513 pages. Little Brown. Pub. at $29.95. **$11.95**

246433 THE MESSAGE OF THE SPHINX: A Quest for the Hidden Legacy of Mankind. By G. Hancock & R. Bauval. Presents geological, textual, and astronomical evidence to date the necropolis at Giza as nearly three times older than previous calculations by demonstrating how its layout represents a map of the night sky as it would have appeared in B.C. 10,500. Illus. 352 pages. Crown. Pub. at $27.50. **$12.95**

HERE ARE TWO FRAMES OF MIND taken from the Edward R. Hamilton Book Catalog for September 19, 1997. It is frames of mind like these that fascinated Jorge Luis Borges, because they are characteristic of the way we mix intelligence and observation—with desires driven by more than a few fears—to produce all sorts of protective fantasies. Obscure and oddball facts gleaned from dubiously reliable but seductively arcane texts, startling coincidences that leap over space and time to suggest new unities of thought and action, as well as quotations drawn from the forgotten books of sages long dead, are sewn together with loops of reasoning of such thinness as to be invisible, and the resulting coverings are used to hood our heads, to protect our brains from the demands of intelligence, to tent our entire lives with a kind of permanent smoke. In a display of tenacious bellicosity and weakening confidence, a Pisa philosophy professor once argued (against Galileo's discovery of the satellites of Jupiter) that

There are seven windows given to animals in the domicile of the head, through which the air is admitted to the tabernacle of the body . . . two nostrils, two eyes, two ears, and a mouth. So in the heavens, as in macrocosms, there are two favorable stars, two unpropitious, two luminaries, and Mercury undecided and indifferent. From this and many other similarities in nature, such as the seven metals, etc., we gather that the number of planets is necessarily seven. Moreover, these satellites of Jupiter are invisible to the naked eye, and therefore can exercise no influence on the earth, and therefore would be useless, and therefore do not exist. . . . Now, if we increase the number of the planets, this whole and beautiful system falls to the ground. [Quoted in John Herman Randall, *The Making of the Modern Mind*. Cambridge, Massachusetts: Houghton Mifflin, 1940, 233.]

I take my fourth example from an anonymous tract on *Art Magic and Spiritism* from 1898 (a mischief that Emma Hardinge Britten pretends to have merely edited):

It is in the realm of metaphysical speculation and the utilization of Soul powers, that the ancients were our masters, and that the moderns are willfully blind, and contemptuously determine to remain so—nay more: when the mere suggestion is thrown out that spiritual sciences may correlate those of physics, the scoff, the sneer and jeer of Scientists, and the anathema maranatha of Priests, effectually stifles all attempts at research save on the part of those who are bold enough to face the rack and thumb and screw of moral martyrdom. [Chicago: Progressive Thinker Publishing House, 1898, 230.]

My fifth instance comes courtesy of Sybil Leek as she introduces the Fadic System of Numerology:

I have yet to find a dictionary that lists "Fadic" among its words. It seems to be a word used exclusively by numerologists, to whom it represents the application of the numbers we have discussed in the previous chapters and their qualities as applied to the life of the individual. It brings the orderly progression of numbers into the reality of living. The Fadic number idea is very old and exceedingly simple to operate. [*Numerology: The Magic of Numbers*. New York: Collier Books, 1969, 38.]

I shall slow to a stop with the sixth sample since six is a perfect number. That makes it a safe place to call a halt. As God did.

> They say that there are mountains in the interior regions of India which are inaccessible to men and therefore full of wild beasts. Among these is the unicorn, which they call the "cartazon." This animal is as large as a full-grown horse, and it has a mane, tawny hair, feet like those of the elephant, and the tail of a goat. It is exceedingly swift of foot. Between its brows there stands a single black horn, not smooth but with certain natural rings, and tapering to a very sharp point. . . . No one remembers the capture of a single specimen of mature age. [Larry Brian Radka, *Historical Evidence for Unicorns*. Newport, Delaware: The Einhorn Press, 1995, 102–3.]

Most thoughts are wrongheaded. That's been the history of thinking. Freeman Dyson remarks (in his Gifford Lectures, *Infinite in All Directions*. New York: Harper & Row, 1988, 119), "Theology is a foreign language which we [scientists] have not taken the trouble to learn." This certainly is made clear, in his case, by the theological blather that follows, and that I'm inclined to blame on the occasion. Steven Weinberg, whom Dyson quotes (117), keeps his head firm and unturned: "The more the universe seems comprehensible, the more it also seems pointless." More than pointless, Professor Weinberg. In addition to being rich, wondrous, and wise, Nature is careless, stupid, and profligate. It has a nasty habit of overdoing things. "We're not in tune," Rilke writes, "not like migratory birds. Outmoded, late, in haste, we force ourselves on winds which let us down upon indifferent ponds." We have a great need to feel comfortable in, rather than foreign to, and fearful of, Nature; hence the immense number of bedtime stories we must invent to help us sleep. Better not read Erasmus or the Brothers Grimm or Goethe. Diderot will toy with us, Sterne poke fun. Ah, yes, and Jorge Luis Borges, the author of so many imaginary books, will mystify our souls while romancing our minds.

Argentine politics might have been a factor, or perhaps it just ran in the mix that was the Borges family, but a trait of his character is a certain basic suspicion about the world's affairs. Borges has a liking for plots, for mysteries, for secret societies, for codes and ciphers. This liking shows up in his preference, too, for many second-rate English writers. Things are not what they seem, yet seeming itself may be a semblance of some sort. Remember how you looked, dressed for Halloween, when you admired your disguise in a mirror.

305

What was it you were? Ah, yes: Hamlet's father's ghost.

We know that in this world rigor is often a mask for disorder, neatness cleans up after a murder, clarity bamboozles by simplifying, and assurance is a snare. However—that things cannot be reliably known; that enigmas are as plentiful as rats in town; that even the most careful and patient thinking will sometimes wander, lost, in dark, remote alleys—such confessions encourage us to be indulgent of error because mistakes are inevitable, only human. Who knows, we say, maybe some mistakes aren't mistakes at all. These liberal admissions allow us, without exasperation, to offer tea and cookies to dangerously stupid views.

If enigmas remain charming to Borges because they are enigmas, not every librarian is so entranced, nor are book people easily discouraged in their optimistic belief that solutions exist somewhere. George Steiner admits to a forceful resolve. Fermat's ravel, after all, has been allegedly unsnarled.

> Theoretically, there is somewhere a lexicon, a concordance, a manual of stars, a *florilegium*, a pandect of medicine, which will resolve the difficulty. In the "infinite library" (Borges's "Library that is the Universe") the necessary reference can be found. Walter Benjamin suggests that there are cruces and talismanic deeps in poetry which cannot be elucidated now or at *all* times; they were understood formerly, they may be rightly glossed "tomorrow." No matter: in some time, at some place, the difficulty can be resolved. [From "On Difficulty" in *On Difficulty and Other Essays*. New York: Oxford University Press, 1978, 27.]

In a charming little book called *World Hypotheses*, now largely forgotten, I'm afraid, the philosopher Stephen Pepper argued that there were only a few fundamental outlooks on the world, and that the philosophies and religions that man has found the idleness to dream up are all versions of one or other of his basic set. He called them "root metaphors." This was apparently the view of Jorge Luis Borges as well. Discussing Hawthorne, he writes that invented metaphors are false because they are not sufficiently inevitable, and he begins his essay "Pascal's Sphere" by suggesting, "[P]erhaps universal history is the history of a few metaphors." I say this was apparently his view because Borges treated opinions with the same gentle skepticism his stories display for their metaphysical themes. In Borges, everything is conjecture, and "perhaps" should precede each intellectual adventure.

Mark Johnson and George Lakoff have written an interesting book, *Metaphors We Live By*, but their examples (theories are buildings, argument is war, the mind is a machine) do not have the same ambitious ontological sweep as Pepper's roots or Borges's conjectures. [Chicago: University of Chicago Press, 1980.]

In the *Timaeus* Plato imagines our universe to be a living organism so huge that we might very well be living our lives in one of its wrinkles. Where do those microorganisms that do their work within our bowels believe *they* are? Suppose the creature, in one of whose cracks we are pitching our tents, falls ill or it simply grows old, as age is measured on its clock. Will we, in a maggot's manner, devour its guts when its heart gives out, or shall we die too, possibly having, like many parasites, brought down our home when we did in our host?

At the moment, the universe is a library. I think this conjecture has enough inevitability to be taken seriously. But suppose we did a U-turn with the trope and said the library is a universe. The library is the museum of our mind. It contains all that we have thought. All that we have felt is described inside. All our desires are somewhere on its shelves defined. What we have dreamed, and remembered we had dreamed, as well as everything we've wondered, and feared, and wished for, they are in tidy rows somewhere near the carrels. All we know, all we care about, whatever it is we hate and disdain or find funny or touching or tearful; all we have invented or created or found out or lied about; therefore all our mistakes written up as truths, while actual truths are attacked as foreigners and criminals; so all our disagreements are shelved there, every difference lined up . . . all . . . books slovenly, overly precise, skimpy, cheaply bound; books illuminated, books dark, small, short, and long—covering the cosmos . . . except books we neglected to collect and save, books we burned in piles in public squares, or set fire to by burning the building itself, or by doggedly recovering and systematically suppressing them the way Borges endeavored to destroy his early work.

A single book may be burned or glued shut and shellacked or hollowed out to hide jewelry or fistfuls of change, but an edition is not so easily disposed of. Its members scatter like ants in all directions. For which reason, as Barry Sanders and Ivan Illich point out, the church created an *Index of Forbidden Books*. "Books could only be proscribed, not destroyed." [In *ABC: The Alphabetization of the Popular Mind*. San Francisco: North Point Press, 1988, 67.]

OK, the universe is a library. It is built of books at first shelved as if there were no subjects, no recognizable authors, no regulating principles. There was nothing readable. Then we discovered genus and its species, and tried that; alphabetical order and tried that; numbering—and tried that too.

Pry open one. Dis yb dis, nem owt. Yad la, tin fo trap. Skin, skin, skin. Od su did ned taw? On. Taw ot klat tonk? On. Tonk ot klat taw? On. Tonk. Ta kool taw? On. Taw to kool tonk. Nilb, mun, mud. xxxq Tin fo trap, yad la. Nem owt, dis yb dis. Nothing there.

The universe . . . whether an animal, a library, a stage, the dream of a dreamer; whether composed of earth air fire or water; whether it rests on the shoulders of Atlas himself or reclines on the shell of a turtle . . . the universe is vast in each of its principal directions. Its *vastness* is even vast, exceeding our solar system, our stars, our nebulae; but this realm is matched, point to point, by the vastness of the small, the infinitely minute. If "out" is infinite, "in" is infinitely more so. Unless "out" and "in" are One. The light that drains into our instruments has traveled far, but the light that has not reached us yet, which has been en route forever—well—it will have ventured farther—almost as distant in its swift descent as the electron's path across a photographic plate.

Those we call the ancients already knew that worlds were wrapped in worlds, and not just onionskinned, not just twine wound. The body was a building and housed the psyche: It was a theater, most particularly a stage; places were playgrounds to tickle the human spirit, chessboards on which to plot moves, a casino to test one's luck—craps to shoot, roulette wheels to rig—ranks of seats in a stadium where bodies sat, but their souls clapped. Someone said: If Denmark is a prison, then is the world one. When, as Borges recites it, the earth was the center of the universe, nine concentric spheres revolved around its fixed location: the then seven planets, the fixed stars, the Primo Mobile, and finally—lit by relentless light—the Empyrean. And space was as material as olive oil. One scheme, Borges does not neglect to tell us, required fifty-five concentrics, exactly the number of Italo Calvino's cities, all of them transparent too, and often hollow. Dante built his Inferno on this plan, and Calvino followed him as Dante followed Virgil.

All of us once were round, again according to Plato, and thought ourselves perfect on account of our roundness, rolling up Olympus to unseat the gods; who, we know, weren't round, but, though beautiful, of course, and sexy, were anthropomorphically shaped—footed, hairy, rumped, forked, and hence ungainly. The circle and the sphere were perfect because they were simple, continuous, and self-contained. If, in addition, the universe was infinite, then every place in it could claim to be its center. Equality of position prevailed. And the borders of the universe were beyond—not beyond the trees, the brow of the hill, across the river—but beyond Beyond itself. Philosophers took comfort in being such centers. Until they thought about it. Then it frightened them. For, as Pascal morosely realized, "If the center is everywhere, the circumference is nowhere." Not hours off. Not beyond The Beyond. Nowhere at all. Nowhere has no center. The conjecture self-destructs.

The infinite (which the Greeks backed away from as if it were berserk, just as they did from zero at first, from pi, from minus quantities, from irrationals) comes in several kinds, and at least two embody qualities of the large and the small. There are self-generating number series like our evens and our odds, divergences expanding before our very minds, on and on and on, Fibonacci more virulent than fig trees. And between these wholesome numbers, in their unexpressed interstices, there are billions of fractions, diminutions without halt, in and in and in. However, when, descending in the gulf between 2.3 and 2.4, we try to explore as far as the fractions fall, we shall never reach the other side of the chasm, though it is nameable, understandable, we say it, we see it: 2.4. Whereas, when a googolplex is googolplexed, and has become so large as to weary a computer whose printer cannot hold the paper needed to write it down, the immense number has no outer limit that it nears, even futilely.

Achilles (or a hare if you will have it so), in pursuit of the tortoise, tumbles at once into a fractional pit. To catch his opponent he must apparently pass through an infinite number of points in a finite time. If the points are "ideal" and have no dimensions, collecting an infinity of them, were it possible, would avail him not an inch; but if the points were as big as marbles Achilles would find himself behind, in any race, at any time, trying to narrow a distance quite unconquerable, even for one as fleet of foot as he: picking up and bagging each point in the course at a steadily increasing speed—faster and faster but nowhere bound.

Leibniz said such shrinking quantities, approaching zero as if it were death, should be called infinitesimals, no doubt in order to hide the fact that, at any point, they nevertheless did quite finitely exist. Bishop Berkeley, one of Borges's favorite philosophers, complained (in his *Treatise Concerning the Principles of Human Knowledge*)

> Some there are of great note who, not content with holding
> that finite lines may be divided into an infinite number of
> parts, do yet farther maintain that each of those infinitesi-
> mals is itself subdivisible into an infinity of other parts or in-
> finitesimals of a second order. . . . These, I say, assert there are
> infinitesimals of infinitesimals of infinitesimals, without ever
> coming to an end! . . . Others there be who hold all orders of
> infinitesimals below the first to be nothing at all. . . .

You could not so divide the physical world into increasingly ittybits
without finding the bits essentially changed—altered as you bit
them.

Achilles would catch and pass the tortoise in a thrice were he running on a path, not a line. Lines and planes preceded numbers, preceded Creation. In 1596, Kepler published a tract called *The Cosmic
Mystery* in which he wrote:

> Before the universe was created, there were no numbers
> except the Trinity, which is God himself. . . . For, the line and
> the plane imply no numbers: here infinitude itself reigns. [In
> *Geometry and the Visual Arts.* Mineola, New York: Dover
> Press, 1983, 266; an unabridged and unaltered republication of
> the original Penguin edition of 1976, by St. Martin's Press of
> New York under the title *Geometry and the Liberal Arts* (so
> something was altered, after all) in 1978.]

Of course Kepler was a young man at the time, nevertheless he
understood the importance of closure, something neither lines nor
planes by themselves are given to. Other lines and planes have to
interrupt them.

The infinite may be puzzling, but think of the abundance. It is the
promise of eternity, because it denies endings. On the contrary,
mothers . . . well, in Céline's phrase, "[T]hose females can wreck the
infinite." Mothers make finite creatures. They give birth to death.

The superdistant, the supersmall, the superlarge, the endlessly
added, the infinitely divisible: All are enticing to the mind because
the numbers that wear them, even when as small as naughty nighties,
are legitimate elements of thought. But the love of number can be
perverse as well as productive.

Try opening another. Sleeeeeeeeeeeeepy. Nothing there. Look
where there are no signs to smutch the page. Through a rift . . . ver-
tiginous . . . a solid sea, white capped, grainy as sugar . . . the polars

are bare . . . low rails attract . . . to overleap, to fly forever down between, slowly defleshing so the bones like white straws scatter . . . ROyal OniOns.

The books in the library, with their carefully arranged characters and lines, all appearing to be in code, open "In" and interpretations there can go on and inward. Sometimes upward: on and in and out and down and up, once in a while, now and then, off and on. How to express it? On one page in one book on one shelf in one hexagon, the group **TYCCU** can be broken in such a way that **T**(lön) is seen to contain two metaphysical hemispheres, one labeled "Matter" another "Mind," though we are asked to go in the direction of "Matter" because of the following **U**(qbar), an operator that, had it been **O**(rbis Tertius) instead, would have suggested we look into "Mind." The hexagons replicate themselves perhaps endlessly in space. Yet if they did we'd be the last to know, having lost the will let alone the count.

Perhaps God spoke in code. Perhaps God said kgodo kofuc! God wrote 43598 44321! Those few among the scholarly who have been lucky enough to stumble upon a copy of *Bentley's Second Phrase Code* book, compiled by E. L. Bentley (and only the one numbered 6694 matters), dated (to throw us off) 1929 (by Prentice-Hall, New York), know that in English these ancient letters (as well as their message in numbers) form the words "Would you let there be some light." To whom God is speaking isn't clear, although the most likely heresy (suggested by Father Carson Calory but hardly maintained after the good preacher's toes were torched) says God is asking the Devil for a light as you would a stranger for a smoke. Other interpreters, cannier, insist the Bentley is arranged alphabetically, though there are many alternatives, especially since (in German) these numbers refer to a protein-free diet. Attempts to employ this codebook decreased after one bite of ten—izyhujetmi—was discovered to mean "Midland pig iron." *Bentley's Second Phrase Code* remains a solitary volume. P.S. "Give me some light!" doesn't the king cry, running from the room, fleeing from the stage?

The codebook pretends to be only an aid to businesses whose work requires considerable use of Western Union. It disguises phrases— "That item is no longer in stock," "We are introducing a spicier catsup this season"—so that they resemble a scramble of numbers or letters. Nowadays we have the Internet, which daily exposes all sorts of secrets that once went privately from one conniver to another like the breath of ghosts and now is loud gossip repeated for the amusement and profit of the world. You can be sure there are Bentleys busy today, by means of one form of tweedle-dee-dee or another, helping us to conceal our real feelings and any useful information we do not wish to share.

The mind likes boundaries better than countries, but the mind is always overstepping them, pushing itself along until it is face-to-face with the void, some infinite abyss, some surd, some paradox. Even when limits loom like escarpments, we can pace back and forth across our plain (endless forests, snow floes, trackless wastes, castle keeps, straw-strewn cells) repeatedly, limitlessly. That is something a labyrinth also lets us do, while appearing to provide a path, offering an aim. Imagine Italy as a dead end.

God has his chummy arm around our waist. He is perfect, powerful, knowing, and everywhere, imitating space. Being perfect, however, He cannot ogle the girls, which is surely a limitation; he cannot surprise himself, play pranks, pull the wings from butterflies. The moment we utter the words "all" or "every" or even "any," but in particular "infinite," we have invited paradox and contradiction to come calling. It made Pascal moan; it makes Borges cringe; it makes me smile.

That arm, though, is invisible, impalpable—in fact, it isn't there, so how shall we come to feel it? If the deity resides in the on-high of high heavens, how are we to reach him? We shall create holy places, holy rites. Prayers and other supplications will call him forth, or permit our voice to voyage so far as his ears are. The class of intermediaries, celestial bureaucrats, appears as if by magic if not opportunism. The One True God (whose oneness has always been a problem) opens additional offices: He is transcendent; he is manifest; he is immanent. His ear is here, there, and everywhere like hornets at a picnic.

Some hypotheses have runaway consequences: Overtaking them is unlikely, reining them in impossible.

Theologians and philosophers create conceptual fictions in which we are invited (intellectually) to live. Politicians, who endeavor to put these structures actually in place, endanger us all, foolishly trying to make work what has been successfully imagined, to make concrete what has been perfectly conceptual, to try to do God's will when God's will has been willed and should be quite sufficient.

What *is* God's will after all? Instead of the cosmos we are presently caught in, there might have been another ballpark with a different history, other laws. Leibniz insists that the number of possible worlds is infinite, but, since just one can exist at a time, God chose, out of the goodness in him, only the best. "His wisdom makes it known," Leibniz says in the *Monadology*, "his goodness makes him choose it, and his power makes him produce it." That's prettily put. Philosophers are really charming fellows, and Borges is suitably charmed.

I always wondered why, out of so many, a single cosmos had to be chosen for creation. Surely God has more than one word at his disposal. Couldn't several exist at the same time? In an infinity of worlds, mightn't some be coexisters? Others might be imagined to follow one another at ten-second intervals. Ten is not too brief a life. Time inside such a period is already longer than necessary.

Must there be a best? Wouldn't it be better if many were simply top-notch? Isn't a plurality of perfections possible? After all, why choose between the immaculate peach and the pear with the cello-sweet shape? To the chimney sweep who doubts that the world he works in is unalterably divine—who will inhale soot like lampblack and grow into a stunted dwarf—Leibniz will point out that narrow, dark chimneys provide narrow, dark views. Were the sweep to see the whole, he'd think otherwise. Fortunately, he'll be dead by fifteen. But his chimneys will be clean.

Beneath the apparent disorder of our world lies a rule whose rigor has arraigned it. A mighty maze but not without a plan. Leibniz claims he can find, for any set of squiggles, a principle for their generation. Doesn't this only demonstrate that a principle may promote disaster? I prefer the belief, uttered by the sage Nagasena, that nirvana and samsara are the same. On the other hand, how can one fail to be impressed by Lao-tzu's profound verses [Tao-te Ching, 41]?

> The Tao which is bright appears to be dark.
> The Tao which goes forward appears to fall backward.
> The Tao which is level appears uneven.

And so on.

> Solid virtue appears as if unsteady.
> True substance appears to be changeable.
> The great square has no corners.

The shooting stars that form the great square's sides haven't shot so far—yet—as to intersect.

Try another. Zsnert. Nothing there. Look in the hole that opens between the spot where the spine's been sewn and where the cloth of the cover wraps it round. Through the temporary dark to peer . . . into another library. Tiny yet voluminous. In pentagons. Dillydergrunt. Résumés of all the books in the hexagonal universe. However large their number. QQQBB. Now nothing here either.

A universe that is infinite can never have been finite, for the infinite is never reached. It either is, or it isn't. It has, therefore, no origin, no culmination, although events within it can come and go. There may be an infinite series of odd or even numbers but all our calculations of this kind are finite. We never near an end, even by one. An infinite regress is thus, at no point in its regression, itself infinite. Its endlessness is only a promise. An empty promise.

There are infinities measured by matching—one odd for every even, none left over—and these infinities, we can say, are each the same size; however, some infinities (the set of whole numbers, for instance) contain others (the sets of odd and even), so that, in one sense, some infinitudes are larger, perhaps even infinitely larger, than others. It remains true, however, that there are no definite infinites. What, then, is or isn't the infinite? The Swiss mathematician Simon L'Huillier won a Royal Academy prize with an essay on the subject whose motto was: "The Infinite is the abyss in which our thoughts are engulfed." But, in Morris Klein's judgment, "L'Huillier's contribution to the theory of limits was minuscule." [*Mathematics: The Loss of Certainty.* New York: Oxford University Press, 1980, 151.]

Borges is happily aware of the Kantian antinomies that prescribe, for the scientist, *als ob* action. We cannot know whether our universe is finite or infinite. A statement supporting either will die inside a paradox. But we can always search for a more general explanation than the one we now have; we can push on into even more "outer" space; we can include the set that contains all sets inside a set that includes the set that includes none. We can also look inside all our meniscuses for more minute ones; inside the atom stare at protons, inside protons encounter pi mesons and further nameless entities and engines of remorse.

But we might argue for the infinity of the universe as we argue the infinity of evens and odds or for the length of the logarithmic spiral. In such a case, we'd begin with a finite set of numbers 0 through 9, say, and insist on the discovery of a rule that, from them, will generate an infinite series. This word "generate" is misleading, for neither the rule nor its wielder needs to exercise any sort of intellectual energy in order to stretch 1 + (1 more) + ∞ into a thousand thousands before the brain's death ends the effort. The series implicitly and instantly exists. It is a property of numbers that for each of them there is always a higher and a lower one. Generative rules allow us to say precisely which the higher or the lower will be. But why "high," why "low," for heaven's sake? Why not "deep" and "shallow"?

In "The Library of Babel," Borges alludes (his allusions approach the astronomic) to Nietzsche's doctrine of Eternal Return. If the universe contains a finite number of elements, and these elements are combined and recombined at random through the course of an infinite time, it seemed to Nietzsche that every possible arrangement would be realized (hence every human history would have its performance) an infinite number of times. But I always wondered why. For the random has no rule of fairness in it. If a coin is flipped an unimaginably large number of flips, must it eventually match its heads to its tails? We can always hope that once an infinity of flips has occurred, heads will be found to match tails; but that hope is vain if the infinity of flips isn't flipped. And it can't be.

Klein quotes from a letter of Niels Henrick Abel:

> The divergent series are the invention of the devil, and it is a shame to base on them any demonstration whatsoever. By using them one may draw any conclusion he pleases and that is why these series have produced so many fallacies and so many paradoxes . . . [*Op. cit.*, 170.]

Just as a language has letters and other orthographic symbols, the physical world has elements. One boasts grammatical rules; the other, natural laws. Some say God wrote two books: the book of revealed theology (the Bible), and the book of Nature (the Earth). With the help of God's grace, we can receive from the Holy Bible the revealed truths; with the help of our mind and eyes, we can see in the plan and construction of the world God's plan and hence the character of its creator. For some reason Borges ascribes the birth of this belief to everyone but Aquinas.

> They [the Jewish Kabbalists] thought that a work dictated by the Holy Spirit was an absolute text: a text where the collaboration of chance is calculable at zero. The portentous premise of a book that is impervious to contingency, a book that is a mechanism of infinite purposes, moved them to permute the scriptural words, to sum up the numerical value of

315

> the letters, to consider their forms, to observe the small letters
> and the capital letters, to search for acrostics and anagrams;
> and it led them to other easily ridiculed exegetic rigors.
> [*Other Inquisitions*. Austin: University of Texas Press, 1964,
> 128.]

Many of Borges's own pieces pretend to emulate this holy condition. "The Library of Babel" is one such. Here the two theologies St. Thomas surmised are confounded: Here Holy Scripture and Holy Creation are One.

Hornets will eat meat, with their mandibles tear a bit of chicken from its bone, even if you blow smoke at them or flap a napkin, and novelists are equally drawn to the alphabet and its pretenses. Walter Abish writes *Alphabetical Africa*. Georges Perec avoids the French letter "e" in writing *A Void*, which is all about a missing vowel. Goffredo Parise pens his *Abecedary*, a series of poems in prose about the human sentiments, lettered up in a line (*Amore Affetto Altri* and so on) until his energy runs out at *S*. Such books, sacred through and through, do everything God's universe was supposed to do and didn't. Like hornets, men have made meals and lived half-lives on such suppositions.

Parise, of his project, says:

> In life, men create systems because they know that these can
> be carried on by others once their inventors are no more. In
> poetry, though, it's not possible—there aren't any heirs. This
> occurred to me in connection with this book. . . . At the letter
> S the poetry abandoned me, system or no system. And with
> this letter *I was forced to a halt*. Poetry comes and goes, it
> lives and dies when it likes, and not when we'd like it to, and
> it doesn't have descendants. I am sorry, but that's the way it
> is. A little bit like life, and above all, like love. [Quoted in the
> publisher's note to *Abecedary*. Marlboro, Vermont: Marlboro
> Press, 1990.]

Suppose God chose to create this vile, sublime, and vicious world just to outdo chaos and show that it could be done. Suppose he got bored somewhere in the curves of the letter *S* so that there's sadness in this world but no *triste*.

If God hadn't grown weary at the end of the sixth day of Creation (the right word is "worried"), he would have, on the seventh, created truly outstanding creatures, not little resemblances running amok, and not the angels who fell out of heaven, or titans who were tossed under the earth, but roachlike wizards and mole-like magicians, and microbes with devastating powers of life and death. Or mountains with gardens growing deep inside them like tell-all tumors.

I suppose it wouldn't do to suggest that the Kabbalists were horrified by what they found in the Torah, but if it really was the word of God, then it had to mean something else than the simple-minded stuff they were reading; the real word had to be hidden. Let fools believe in its literal sense, the wise would look within. They were thereby able to keep the faith, establish themselves as privileged sages of the sacred, and allow God's law to fall into their exegetical hands. Christian scholars harmonized the Old and New Testaments by pretending that everything in the Old prefigured the New. The quite undivine Boccaccio (in his *De genealogiis*) desired to persuade church authorities to tolerate references to Greek myth in stories and poems by a similarly sly bit of sophistication: The Greek gods were merely precursors of the Christian. To the concert that is our life, they are the warm-up band.

Precursoration is catching. Paintings (for example) can come down with severe cases of iconographitis. "Like so many other major Victorian authors," George Landow writes,

> including Carlyle, Newman, Browning, Eliot, Tennyson, Rossetti and Hopkins, Ruskin learned his interpretative approaches from reading the Scriptures for types and anticipations of Christ. He transferred to interpretations of painting and architecture the evangelical's habit of taking apparently trivial portions of the Bible and from them demonstrating that even there matters of major significance are found. ["Ruskin," in *Victorian Thinkers*, edited by Keith Thomas. Oxford: Oxford University Press, 1993, 142.]

Try a new one. Peer down the spinehole again. Then down the spineholes of the résumés. Canvases, dimly discernible, portray in paint and pictures the content of each résumé. Occasionally a sentence is to be seen lacing its shoes.

If the Signs aren't saying what you want to hear, then it is always possible to invent a new method of assessment, an ingenious strategy for interpretation, so that entirely unforeseen layers can be lifted out of a text like steaming shirts from boiling clothes. Official searchers, Borges calls them, heresy hunters, inquisitors, deconstructors, by extravagant and unscrupulous means, will dig deeply

317

into texts formerly thought innocent in order to discover disapproved ideas and attitudes hidden in them like weevils in a biscuit, thus convicting the past of not seeking the sanctimonious approval of the present.

Borges also wrote poems. None of them are in the shape of a saltcellar.

Lot's wife was salt
before she turned
into a cellar of it
because Lot's wife
was always Lot's
and never knew
another name
Lot's wife was salt
when she saw Sodom
in time to come a fishery
swallowed by the Dead Sea
at the command of Lot's God
for little more than sodomy
and a lack of hospitality
Lot's wife was salt
when she saw her girls
still in pinafores and curls
fucking their father
who pretended to be drunk
Lot's cock now like his wife
a column of catastrophe
Lot's girls begot
when they sat on Lot's cock
more than they thought
Moabites and Ammonites
Edomites and such like
salt of the earth
and pillars of society

The descendants of Noah built the Tower of Babel, probably a ziggurat since that form was common to the region. In an act of hubris that history sees so often, their masons began to build a skyscraper that would reach the stars. Zeus cut the smug round biscuits in half for their effrontery. If we turn to the biblical case, God took the tongue of the sons of Noah and split it into a fork with many tines. Nothing, henceforth, would be in tune.

Imagine a tower built of books. Originally written in Babel and the length of a river. Books meant to expose the gods. Books lying on one another's bed sides. Books scattered to the six points of their hexagons by the wrath, above them, of the blank page. Accompanied by beastly blowing. And the horrible rattle of leaves. Sumar's prospective readers were hurried, like ponies, into dividing valleys. Some valleys sported streams, some endured foggy mornings, some were pocked with caves. Scores of books and tribes of men were bound by belief and leather. Colonies thus cut off from one another began to alter their rites and ceremonies to suit the teachings of the only books they had brought with them, until each valley had grown its own verbs, hillsides hung their vines. Eventually each group forgot the other. Gods no longer lived among the clouds but on the mountaintops where they stirred the mist to mimic the glory they once enjoyed. Books that were writ in Sumar's tribalese couldn't be understood by members of another clan and lingo. But some of these books could still arouse the gods because the significance of their texts lay beneath the black tracks that soiled the page. Their ancient meanings remained buried under ages of daily use: Wear and tear and tarnish hid the language of the One, the language of Adam complaining of Eve, and God complaining of Adam. Their meanings can be expressed only mathematically. And these books, whose contents are invisible since unwritten, without graphs, as grammarless as algebra—these books, in that triangle of ten the Forms prefer, tipped by the clean sweeping Form of the Good, shining on all of us like a benevolent gold piece—these books shall bring down the gods . . . in small groups . . . or if need be . . . one by one.

PLATE 74. — TABLET OF KIL.
[Begin at 1, and read downward; then at 2, etc.]

2.

Open whatever is within reach—which turns out to be a newspaper:

Rabbis Sue Over a Museum

A group of 16 Orthodox Jewish rabbis filed a lawsuit in Federal Court in Manhattan yesterday seeking to block the opening of the Museum of Jewish Heritage—A Living Memorial to the Holocaust. The lead plaintiff, Rabbi Yehuda Levin of Brooklyn, said the rabbis sued because of their anger at what they believe will be the museum's commemoration of gay victims of the Holocaust, saying they should not be equated with Jewish victims.

The rabbis contend in the suit that the spending of public money to build the museum violated the establishment clause of the Constitution. The museum, which is at 18 First Place, Battery Park City, is scheduled to open to the public on Sept. 15. [*NY Times*, early September 1997.]

If they are pricked, do they not bleed?

The universe (which others call the Library). . . . Others, not Señor Borges? The universe is lowercased but the Library is uppered . . . *is composed of an indefinite and perhaps infinite*. . . . Here, already, is the Devil, the abyss of the mind, as we've learned. Nothing could be more indefinite than the infinite. . . . *number of hexagonal galleries* . . . Then it *is* a library. The choice of names is . . . well . . . nominal. Which others call a drunken dream. Which others call a wooden O that holds the vasty fields of France. We are invited to assume that the hexagon is the shape of the fundamental cells of which the universe is made.

The first rule of reading Borges is that nothing . . . absolutely nothing . . . is introduced just because; everything is there for a reason. In short, like his heresiarchs, Borges writes sacred texts. And the puzzles with which reason confronts reason prove reason's power. The first paragraph describes, most meticulously, an order for chaos. It allows him to introduce numbers, and forces us to make calculations. Most Nuts are enamored of numbers. It makes their ravings seem serene, precise, demonstrated. Louis Farrakhan, for instance, finds the fact that there are 19 sun rays in the seal of the United States and the fact that the statues in the Lincoln and Jefferson Memorials are both 19 feet high an especially significant parallel, because there are 114 chapters in the *Koran*. Oh? Because 19 multiplied by 6 yields 114. [As reported by Maureen Dowd in *The New York Times*, op-ed page, October 4, 1997.]

William H. Gass

The galleries of this library/universe are hexagonal. A hexagon is simply a six-sided figure. The diagram that Bettina Knapp shows us in her essay on "The Library of Babel" depicts a hexagram, which is a six-pointed star made by extending the sides of the hexagon to form equilateral triangles. [In *Archetype, Architecture, and the Writer.* Bloomington: Indiana U. Press, 1986, 105.] Her galleries actually have twelve sides. It is tempting to think of the Star of David (the Seal of Solomon) in this connection, especially since there are many other references to Jewish language and lore in "The Library of Babel," but to give the fundamental gallery layout such a shape (although the figure appears importantly in Arabic and Masonic texts as well) would be too determinate when taken together with the extensive Kabbalistic references. Borges wants all "possiblys" to be, with equal likelihood, "possibly not."

Kepler, writing in the same frame of mind as the professor of philosophy at Pisa, whom I quoted at the outset, writes that after eliminating the irregular solids

> [t]here remain six bodies, the sphere and the five regular polyhedra. To the sphere corresponds the outer heaven. On the other hand, the dynamic world is represented by the flat-faced solids. Of these there are five: when viewed as boundaries, however, these five determine six distinct things: hence the six planets that revolve about the sun. This is also the reason why there are but six planets . . .

In nature, the hexagon is most notable for its presence in honeycombs or in the pattern of tiles on bathroom floors (mine, for instance), where its ability to fit as snugly as squares, yet with more strength and with less perimeter length than squares, gives it a great advantage, which the Roman engineers put to good use in their stadia where vaults could be constructed without mortar.

Try one. I sit there, look down bare toed toward the field of white tiles, now rows, now roses. The error of the Library is its books. Books are bad for you. Books suggest a structured, completed text, whose author authorized it all. Why else call her an author? Books open and close like clams. Why do the librarians so morosely wander? Because books, they believe, are sacred. Because books of whatever kind imitate the great good book of God. Because books are pieces of an endless poem by Mallarmé. Because the librarians are all theologians. They are the monks in these cells peering at the word "wall," the word "floor," the word "door," the word "window." They are like nuns, telling their beads, reciting their lines. They invoke God but forbid themselves his name. Borges saw, as they see, the world through words. Pretty soon, as befell Borges, their eyesight fails, for the light, though incessant, is dim, and they can no longer watch the inert verbs, the decaying nouns, or qualifiers falling and swirling away like leaves. Anyway God is in any case Gone. Writing and reading are simply human activities taking place in history like shitting and spreading the shit so the earth is enriched. Logocentrism is a disease of a patriarchal culture. It believes the mind is the begetter and the begetter is the *logos*. Plato said the body was the coffin of the soul (well, he sort of said that). The book imprisons meaning. It's not the damp that curls the cover of the paperback. You can feel meaning in there pushing against the spine, rattling the shutters. And meaning's crime: being occasionally definite, determinate, reasoned, clear, responsible, formerly French. But before it was put away in a book, it was consigned to paragraphs, sentenced to sentences, solitary, confined in syntax's cell, stretched out on spelling's cruel rack, pronounced by an orator with a hoarse lisp. Thus and so do some present-day kabbalah, like the sophists of pagan days, insist.

While discussing the commercial hive that mankind offers the bee to replace the befuddled insect's hollow tree or bell-shaped homes of straw, Maurice Maeterlinck lets slip the truth:

> An edifice, this, that can contain more than three hundred pounds of honey, in three or four stories of superposed combs enclosed in a frame which permits of their being removed and handled, of the harvest being extracted through centrifugal force by means of a turbine, and of their being then restored to their place like a book in a well-ordered library. [*The Life of the Bee.* New York: Dodd Meade, 1901, 138.]

This geometry's other notable employment is the formation of snowflakes, each crystal of which is hexagonal. One pattern, pointed into the socket where the sides meet, and symmetrically shaped as if cut from a folded card, is repeated twelve times.

The number six has many important properties. The Pythagoreans believed that numbers were material things and had geometrical shapes that they depicted by the placement of pebbles much as the dots appear on dice. "One" was a single stone seen as a point, "two" was oblong, "three" was triangular, "four" square, "five" pyramidal, and "six" hexagonal. You squared a number by "pebble writing" it to form the base, and building a square on that base (to 3 add 3 above and then 3 more above that), or a triangle (4 + 3 + 2 + 1, the Pythagorean triangle of four, which is ten) or a cube (a 4, say, for all 6 faces). By using a gnomon one could find roots and discover any number of important relations between the basic quantities. The gnomon, as Hero of Alexandria defined it, is any figure that, when added to an original figure, leaves the resulting figure the same species as the first. Such magnitudes, as Aristotle noted, grow without any other alteration. Gnomonic expansion is a frequent design principle for architects and perhaps the architect of the Library is no exception.

OUIJA

Patience Worth arrived in this world by means of the Ouija board on July 8, 1913 by speaking through the agency of Mrs. John H. Curran. A friend, Mary Pollard, wrote down the planchette's first words. Later, Pearl Curran would receive Patience Worth's communications, and her husband type them as they appeared. "Many moons ago I lived." She said. "Again I come—Patience Worth my name." Patience Worth made no attempt to start a new religion. But she often spoke about significant episodes in the myths of Christianity—the Crucifixion, most successfully. For a quarter of a century, in this laborious manner, Patience wrote seven books, hundreds of poems, plays, short stories, and journal style records of her witty conversations with members of the public who managed to gain entry to her soiree. For a while a publication, called *Patience Worth's Magazine* . . . composed of her work, and that of her admirers . . . flourished. Many thousands of her books were sold, and almost as many Ouija boards.

Oswald Mathias Ungers, the architect for the new wing of Hamburg's Kunsthalle, based his design entirely on the form of the square and its geometric reiterations. Fortunately, the building is meant to be a museum and not a library.

Such repetition is certainly the principle governing my bathroom floor, except for the places where my toes are, because the hexagons my feet cover may be square—how should I know? The tiles don't feel one shape or another. Grouting is not grouting, though I stare at grout. These dark lines are where the abyss lives. Seen from so high an On-High they look like lines, and the hexagons are a half inch on a side. From so high an On-High there appears to be no space between the hexes. The universe seems a solid. If there is no void there can be no motion. And if no motion, no change. And if no change no thought. Though the lines stand for walls that are lined with books. Printed books. Bound books. In disciplined rows. The Universe's Collected Works. Though not so many volumes as Balzac's oeuvre.

Where are the manuscripts that preceded these books then? Where have the eyes of editors soiled a page? What is the name of the press that has impressed all scrawls into these parts? This is a library like the Five-Foot Shelf was a library, like the Britannica is a library: uniform in format, book size, cover style, type font. I despair at the complete absence of a copyright page. There's no ISBN number? Not a sign of a *nihil obstat*. We may suspect these books have only one author since no authors are credited. Not one. The universe isn't metabolic. It merely replicates. One page produces another until it creates a cover, and the covers a row, till the rows rank and walls grow; the hexagon holds its lamps up to the light and they flop their floor plans over, leaving prints of themselves behind, images, as though in mirrors, of where they've been, growing and growing like a cancer.

Although gnomonic expansion seems exactly suited to the number system with which the Greeks were familiar (numbers grew or shrank but otherwise did not change), the gnomon limited the number of kinds of numbers. Zero, like the infinitesimals, was thought to be an invention of the devil (who gets credit for all sorts of things). Negatives, irrationals, later odd square roots called imaginary with good reason ($\sqrt{-1}$, for instance), transcendentals, and complex numbers were forbidden entrance into mathematics. The universe, we can be sure, came into being long before the arrival of irrationals and imaginaries, so we might expect to find them absent in the making of the Library. Unless God knew about them all along. In which case, the librarians would have been better advised to examine the building instead of its books. Indeed, no one seems to have asked whether the books are simply on their shelves waiting to be borrowed, or stolen as sometimes happens, or whether they are constituents of the building itself. And if these be not books (for we cannot be certain), then can the Library be really a Library and not something else ... perhaps a Post Office. One day the Universe will be owned by a Bank. Though there will be no deposits, no withdrawals.

Do we mean by "library" the building? the books? or the librarians? "These correspond," Floyd Merrell observes, "to three familiar domains: (1) the inorganic, (2) the informational, and (3) the organic." [In *Unthinking Thinking: Jorge Luis Borges, Mathematics, and the New Physics.* West Lafayette, Indiana: Purdue University Press, 1991,

124.] And this trio invokes, as we shall more richly realize if we ever reach their explanatory paragraph, Matter, Meaning, and Mind . . . the sea, the song, and the siren.

Ruminations of this kind are provoked by Borges's "essays," just as they have provoked Borges. It has been suggested, he notes, that the Library, so well ordered, must be the creation of a god; but—I'd like to note in reply—to make a hive on similar principles merely takes a lot of bees.

Six is the first perfect—a number whose factors [1, 2, 3] add up to itself. Prime numbers, like three, have no other factors than themselves and one. Finding primes is a grail quest for some mathematicians. In 2011, they demonstrated with the help of computers (according to Google) that the largest known prime number has almost thirteen million decimal digits. The Pythagoreans made much of excessive and deficient numbers as well, because the factors when added together either exceed the sum of their parent [12«1+2+3+4+6=16] or fall short of it [8»1+2+4=7]. Twelve, which contains two perfects, is in many ways a better base for a number system than ten since it possesses so many factors. An object, value, or state of affairs would be assigned—be discovered to possess—a shape. Justice was square. Therefore justice was also four. The world gave way to number. Perhaps Ungers's museum would better serve as a court of law.

According to the *Sefer Yetsirah*, the Kabbalistic Book of Creation—composed according to the rule of six into that many chapters—the universe is guarded on its six sides by six permutations of the name of God, customarily without his vowels: YHWH or Yahweh. Were this true of the universe as a library, we'd not know it, for no one has reached an edge, if there is one. The other principal Kabbalistic text, the *Zohar*, or Book of Splendor, gives heaven a hexagonal shape.

What is striking about the errors of the Pythagoreans is how their errors did so well by them, for these mathematical mystics made many important discoveries. The Kabbalists, I think, cannot claim as much.

When astrology and astronomy were, like Cain and Abel, brothers, and when alchemists and chemists stirred their pots with the same glass rods, when Aquinas made of Nature a sacred book and loosed the scientist as well as the faithful upon it, confusion knew some positive fallout; but many philosophies and most theologies have merely befuddled folks without making, for all their theatrics, any friends.

Summa Theologica, 1,Q. 51, Art. 2

Angels need to assume a body.
It's not for themselves, mind you,
as if they had to get to Pittsburgh
during business hours.
It's not like running out
of cocoa, soap, or flour,
or spilling coffee on your best shirt,
or coming apart like wet paper
the way my aunt did after Fred died.
It's on our account. For us.
To see. To feel. To heed them.
The assumed body is not sewn
or glued or pinned to the angel
as the tail is pinned to the donkey
or the emitted bray of the beast,
nor does it move the angel anywhere
the way the ass bore a baby unborn
in the well-known story.
It is the will of the assumed form,
and moves so the form may move.
Isn't this wonderful?

We are not finished with the hexagon yet. On a line, construct two equivalent and overlapping circles. This area is called the Vesica Piscis because it has the shape of certain fish. Imagine straight lines running from the top and bottom points of intersection of the two circles toward the center of one of them. These compose two of our hexagon's sides. Using the length of one of these sides as a radius, swing an arc (how opaque these things seem when put into words, but that is the point) from the topmost intersection and then from the bottommost one. Where they intersect the second circle the final sides of the hexagon will form.

The holy shape of the fish, representing Christ as the mediator between heaven and earth (that is, the heaven on earth), now appears on cars with a sarcastic DARWIN inside it where the savior used to be. As the construction of the hexagon from the Vesica Piscis demonstrates, more complicated polygons, often used in the design of chapels, churches, and cathedrals, can be endlessly generated, each bearing within its baptized lines the finny powers of the fish.

Error teaches more slowly than success, but sometimes more decisively. The paradoxes of the infinite, of which Zeno's are splendid samples, warn us that the fact that a symbol system can accurately describe the world does not mean that the sign and its referent have

327

the same properties: the path taken by Achilles in pursuit of the tortoise is not a line, but the path can be represented by one. The line can be infinitely divvied, but not the path whose flagstones are finite and countable. Lines can get longer or shorter but they don't move. Things move. St. Thomas explained it all just now. The paradox that confounds Plato's participation theory is an instance of the same problem. If men resemble one another because they participate in—or are copies of—the same form Man, then men and their Form must resemble one another because they both imitate a third MAN, *und so weiter*. However, if men are bodily beings, they must look alike in a material way, whereas their imitation of Ideas has to be formal. The Form Man does not possess a dicky, only the idea of one. With honesty rare among philosophers, Plato faces his problems bravely, and in his atrophying dialogue, *Parmenides*, fails with grace and persistence.

If these "facts" seem to add up to erudition, again, that's the idea, for Borges collects odd out-of-the-way data as some do stamps. A scattering of arcane tiddybits does not demonstrate a wide and well-stocked mind, only the presence of a library, which the writer infests with his curiosity the way its inevitable silverfish do, and whose distant recesses he haunts with his unhappiness.

In 1937, nearly forty, still living at home like a canary, Borges obtained a position as a "first assistant" in the Miguel Cané municipal library in Buenos Aires. The pay was poor, the library's part of town was dreary, patronage filled the positions, and the bureaucracy was paralyzing—fifty doing the work, Borges says, of fifteen. This library was not a cozy retirement home. His colleagues bragged of their knife fights, and deshirted to show the scars that supported their stories. Borges was warned not to exceed his cataloging quota and he had to learn to dog it. Once a woman was raped on her way to the ladies' room. Conversation was about smut and sports. While he had certain fame as a poet outside his place of work, inside he was simply a troublesome oddball. So he went into the basement and read Dante and Gibbon and Léon Bloy, or wrote "The Lottery in Babylon," "Death and the Compass," "The Circular Ruins."

In 1939 Borges published an essay in *Sur* on a utopian library that would contain all books, then (peace to Leibniz) all possible books. Such a library would certainly begin to resemble the universe. But if the universe were a library, it would be constituted largely of signs. What would these signs be about? What would they mean? They could only be about the library, about the construction of the library, other books in the library, life in the library, reading, searching, interpreting. Would there be any books whose authors tried to imagine what it might be like not to be a sign? In a city made of signs, as we read in Calvino, no attention would be paid to the sign itself, but only to what it meant, and if what it meant was simply another sign in the city, our thoughts could only ricochet from sign to sign in search of a sense that would always be somewhere further on.

The universe . . . is composed of an indefinite and perhaps infinite number of hexagonal galleries, with vast airshafts between, surrounded by very low railings. A shaft cannot be vast unless the spaces we are dealing with are so enormous that a shaft could be vast and still seem a shaft. However, the word suggests that the distance between galleries, either above or below, is not immense. The shafts, we must conclude, are very high and very deep. Two of the hexagon's sides are given over to connecting hallways that leave four sides against which the books are stored on five long shelves. Borges then gives us some precise specifications concerning these volumes. Each hexagon will contain twenty shelves; each shelf will row thirty-five books, so there are seven hundred books in a gallery; each book has four hundred and ten pages, thus a total of two hundred eighty-seven thousand of their pages are present; each page holds forty lines, yielding eleven million four hundred and eighty thousand over all; and since every line contains exactly eighty letters, the total number of letters in each hexagon is nine hundred and eighteen million, four hundred thousand.

Rucker's calculations, made in a slightly different way, conclude that the number of books in the universal library must be (if no book is exactly like another, but how would we ever know that?) twenty-five (the number of symbols if we include comma, space, and period) taken to the 1,312,000 power. [*Infinity and the Mind.* New York: Bantam, 1983.] In his prologue to "The Library of Babel," Borges cites Leucippus, Lasswitz, Lewis Carroll, and Aristotle as sources for the fiction—a set of authorities notable for its slyness. Lasswitz illustrates the magnitude of this number by declaring that a shelf made of light-years would have to be 10 to the 1,999,982 power in length if it expected to hold all the books. [Cited by Merrell, *op. cit.,* 128.] And Merrell concludes that the Library is vastly more fearsome and overwhelming than the Universe itself.

Because all the hexagons so far known and examined are exactly alike in this, as well as in other respects, some argue that such an order must have a divine origin, and the numerologically minded

329

will find meaning in the twenty shelves, the thirty-five books per row, and all the other totals the text invites us to consider. Yet this order is most likely meaningless, a wild goose we are invited to chase. And Bettina Knapp accepts the invitation:

> The number four, identified with the four points of the compass, the four seasons, the four elements, is a quaternity that has come to represent the world of manifestation: earth, terrestrial space. Psychologically, it stands for rational organizational systems, for equilibrium and balance in telluric situations and relationships. The contents of the books, therefore, which line the four sides of the hexagonal galleries, reveal humankind's need for serenity as well as a need for further information concerning its destiny in the finite world. [*Op. cit.*, 109.]

with enthusiasm:

> That the four sides of the hexagonal galleries are lined with five long shelves adds yet another digit to our puzzle, another aspect to our religious and fictional tale. Five represents a *hieros gamos*: a union of three and two. Three is a celestial number for Christians in that it brings to mind the Trinity; for the Jews, it refers to the three highest Sefiroth—God's ten emanations or unfoldings into matter. [*Op. cit.*, 111.]

and energy:

> That the shelves add up to twenty indicates an actualization of the notion of death and rebirth: the cyclical or eternal nature of the universe (Self, deity). In Tarot, which many historians believe to be based on Kabbalah, the number twenty allegorizes the idea of spiritual and physical renewal. [*Op. cit.*, 111.]

These expansive interpretations go on for pages.

Borges, for his part, tells us that "The Library of Babel" was

> meant as a nightmare version or magnification of that municipal library, and certain details in the text have no particular meaning. The number of books and shelves that I recorded in the story were literally what I had at my elbow. Clever critics have worried over those ciphers, and generously endowed them with mystic significance. [Quoted by Emir Rodriguez Monegal in *Jorge Luis Borges: A Literary Biography*. New York: Dutton, 1978, 310.]

Whatever Borges writes will be about Borges in some important way. That is the first axiom to be followed when reading him. The second is that the paradoxical, fantastic, and enigmatic aspects of his fictions always have a very down-to-earth and literal referent. The third is that each takes aim at one or more theories about knowledge or reality with the idea of wounding them but not too seriously. For instance, "Funes, the Memorious," that wonderful send-up of philosophical nominalism, springs from Borges's own bouts with insomnia, about which he also wrote a poem. This fiction's remarkable protagonist, the cripple Funes, remembers everything so vividly that none of his impressions fades; the past does not disappear but fills the present like milk poured into wine (contrary to Hume's expectations); consequently he can no longer generalize. In the dark and deep middle of the night, the insomniac obsessively remembers day. There is no use to it. There is no function for it. Life becomes rerun. The Universe *is* a library—a record library, a video library. As I write, there has emerged from the TV a series of stories containing pictures that now and then pretend to be persons. One such image is of a lady whose hair is red, whose complexion is delicate, and whose memory is absolute. When she wishes to remember (a wish denied Funes), she merely turns on her projector. Like a photograph pasted in an album, the image is presumed to be the same as the event on its first appearance. I ask you, members of the jury, how does she know that?

The fourth axiom is that everything is not only autobiographical but autobiographically connected. Borges is fetching a pretty young woman whom he wishes to take to lunch with his mother. Upon arriving at her apartment building, he discovers an inoperable elevator. Rushing up the stairs instead, he crashes into an unseen open window, suffering cuts and, in his forehead, embedding glass. Unconscious of, if not from, the blow, he appears in her doorway like someone mugged. A serious case of septicemia ensues and Borges is seriously ill for weeks. Upon his recovery, a reborn Borges (as he saw it), writes "Pierre Menard, Author of the *Quixote.*" Pierre Menard decides to write Cervantes's great work once again, word for word, not by becoming Cervantes, but while remaining Menard. This absurd and fantastically impossible task is, in fact, what each of us does when we read, bringing to classic texts a modern sensibility, hence deepening them without changing a letter or a line. In a similar way, the monstrous encyclopedia of "Tlön, Uqbar, Orbis Tertius," which seems to be threatening to take over the world like some monster in a Japanese movie, can be read as a sober and factual discussion of the corruption of texts; and the contest between accounts, which takes place with dismaying frequency; how imaginary relics like the Shroud of Turin are inserted into reality; and how lies and misconceptions become causes in history. The biblical texts are perfect examples.

The library reinforces the Menard phenomenon. In effect, it abolishes compositional time, since Homer's *Odyssey* and Joyce's *Ulysses* can sit on the same shelf side by side. I may select and read Joyce before I read Homer (as it happened in my case). Books have locations in a building, not moments in time, and each of us will encounter them in our own way, or miss them altogether, as someone might never visit Philadelphia.

If the universe were a library, time would have to be conceived as a function of space, and change would exist only for the librarians who might find themselves in the toils of the false messiah Sabbatai Sevi, before they could be rescued by Rashi the Exegete. And if the universe were a library, everyone alive would have to be a librarian (at least in this library, for there is no reading room); anyone with an inclination could wander through the galleries looking for smut or divine guidance. Moses Isserles worried about this and warned us:

> A single coin in a box causes a noisy rattle, and anyone who has merely sniffed a little kabbalah preens himself on it and discourses on it in public—but he will have to render account at the day of judgment. [*Torath ha-Olah*, Part III, Chapter 4, 1570.]

What of Nature's secrets will I discover while playing in the basement with my first chemistry set? I might, more likely, blow up my house.

Collisions of the oddest and most disconcerting kind could take place in a librarian's mind. It would be entirely possible for someone to find themselves pondering the concept of *qelippah*, and consequently the distinction Abraham Nathan made between thoughtful and thoughtless light, ahead of any information about God's pronouncement of the creative word as it is described in Genesis. Actually, on the advice of Sabbatai Sevi, Abraham Nathan changed his name to Nathan Benjamin or sometimes to Benjamin Nathan, as if he were a character in a fiction by Danilo Kiš.

It is this Nathan (and not R. Nathan Guta, or Nathan Shapira, or Nathan Shapira Yerushalmi, called the "other Nathan" by Gershom Scholem) who discovered the prophesy of a new messiah in a volume of the "Greater Wisdom of Solomon," which he found (there are conflicting accounts) when Elijah appeared to him and commanded him to dig at a certain spot in the synagogue of Gaza. He took the book he uncovered there to his home and shortly afterward began to prophesy. Nathan's *Vision* is a pseudepigraph, a work purporting to be by another, more notable, hand. The *Apocrypha* presumably consists of one pseudepigraph after another. The Prophet claimed no lesser scribe than Allah. Joseph Smith admitted his was God. But Nathan's story, with all its alternates, we can say now, is pure Borges. In them we recognize his qualities, including the manner in which Borges pretends that many of his fictions are really factual essays, capturing the solemn and devoted tone of the scholar perfectly, and the manner of the learned man who has devoted his entire life to the study of arrant nonsense.

It pleases me to present two samples, one in Borges's manner, another more emotional but still in tune, in order to define the style, even though we may seem, now, to be in a distant gallery. Still—distant from where?

> To speak about Rashi as an exegete is in reality too vast a subject for a lecture. For, as the saying was applied to the Torah, that "its measure is of greater length than the earth, vaster than the ocean," the same may be said when we wish to enter into detailed accounts about the Torah's great expounder. It would perhaps be more prudent to select a certain portion of Rashi's exegetical productions, and to speak, for instance, only on his commentary on the Pentateuch, or on some Talmudical treatise. In dealing with the whole subject, it will only be possible for me to sketch out the principal characteristics of his exegesis, so as to understand how it was that it became indispensable, and has not been made superfluous by the efforts of his successors. [S. A. Hirsch, *The Cabbalists and Other Essays*. Port Washington, New York: Kennikat Press, 1922, reissued 1970, 141.]

> The absence of magical art is not the lack of magical knowledge. The spirit world will not confer its prizes upon dunces and idlers. The natural world is the open page, the heaven, earth, and all that in them is, are the letters of the magical alphabet, and until man learns these, and enters upon the spelling-book of magnetism, and the grammar of psychology, this pen of ours may point the way, but every pilgrim foot must tread the path for himself. Thus, and thus only, may we rival the ancient man in the goal of magical achievements to which he ascended. [Britten, *op. cit.*, 231.]

William H. Gass

"The Library of Babel" (like so many of Borges's pieces) puts on the mantle of the essay the way the viceroy mimics the monarch. It has the right tone: We hear the pedant's light excitement beneath the careful gravity of his houndlike sniffing for the truth. Citations are frequent, obscure, uncheckable. The reader is always sliding down a steep slope of condescension; the petty is treated as profound; assumptions remain as unstated as the rules of masonic rites; the real and the fake mock one another so that certainties, like timbers from wrecked ships, float on a sea of doubt—with the result that legitimate scholarship suddenly seems treacherous instead of tame and steady.

> The claim on behalf of the second candidate, Thomas Malory of Papworth St. Agnes in Huntingdonshire, was first put forth by A. T. Martin, an English antiquary, in two articles. The first, a communication to the *Athenaeum* for September 11, 1897, reported the discovery of the Papworth man's will and argued from its contents that this might be the author. The second article, published a year later in *Archaeologia*, reaffirmed the proposal, added a good deal of biographical information about this candidate and also about Sir Thomas Malory of Newbold Revel, and came to the opinion that the Papworth Malory was a more likely candidate than the Newbold Revel knight. [William Matthews pursuing the identity of the author of *Le Morte D'Arthur* in *The Ill-Framed Knight*. Berkeley: University of California Press, 1966, 5–6.]

Hidden in high grass, worms and insects war. It's not their fault we remain oblivious. And in untold texts still other struggles go on: putdowns that take the form of the scathing snobbery of Pierre Menard's biographer perhaps; exhaustions that appear during a patient amassing of information designed to encyclopede all opposition; spells composed entirely of the hypnotic recitation of unknown names— Papworth, Newbold Revel; in tongue-lashings that are disguised as the kindness of the victor toward his vanquished, or attitudes of indifference and superiority shown toward any hypothesis that opposes one's own. Beneath barrages of citation, among volleys of quotation, charges and countercharges come; comparisons and emendations and sly excisions ebb and flow across the pages of the books that seek and search and, in triumph, disclose for us the real Malory, the solution to the riddle of the Sphinx, the identity of the dark lady, the circumstances of Mozart's and Edgar Allan Poe's deaths, the meaning of Stonehenge, the location of Noah's ark, the formula for transmuting dross, the real meaning of a mass of fallen sticks, the significance in a teacup's soiled bottom.

Scientology, anyone? O for a bit of Mormon in the morning.

Open one. Nothing there. Wait a min. Like a cloud in a bowl, isn't that the world? No. Nothing there. An opening in the shape of the *aleph*, the first letter of the Ten Commandments. Wait a min. A parchment found by Konstantin von Tischendorf. It is the *aleph*, now a dead stone in the mouth of God. It is the *aleph* in full revolt, shedding, as words one day may, their meanings (a conjecture George Steiner entertains, when concluding his book *After Babel*), so we shall be obliged to confront their silent selves, while silent ourselves, in front of *ani*, the "I" of the First Commandment: "I am the Lord thy God." Though now *aleph* is the hollow in which the word for ego rests like a pebble in a shell. The word has freed itself to become world. Numb as a nova. Dumb as deep sea. Blind as any bush. Salvation, as the poet wrote, is to be, not mean.

Never mind misleading insights. Not the O in zero. The gasp before the cough. Let's get on.

The galleries are connected by hallways that contain two closets, one where you may sleep standing up and another for fecal necessities. But what is the point of the latter if no one eats? Unlike museums, where there are food courts and shops, libraries prohibit catsup and only sell seconds—books purged for desuetude, duplication, disinterest, or misuse. A spiral staircase passes through this hall in both directions, connecting one plane of hall-bound galleries with other platforms. A mirror *faithfully duplicates all appearances.* That fall into it? That exist even outside the range of its watchfulness? And we have no such mirrors in our world—which faithfully duplicate—because our mirrors invert everything. If an appearance is duplicated by a mirror, perhaps the mirror rereverses the appearance, and returns it to the real. It happened to Alice.

Contrary to the suggestion in the text that mirrors are allies of infinity, I can only report never having seen an apparent regress in one mirror by itself. A mirror positioned to mirror more mirrors is another matter. *Light is provided by spherical fruit that bear the name of lamps.* What a typically sneerful sentence. "Spherical" is deliberately unspecific. Commenting on what he takes to be a transition from allegories to novels (in an essay of almost that title), Borges pins down the exact date on which the change occurred. That is, he pretends to imprison a mist.

335

> The passage from the allegory to the novel, from the species
> to the individual, from realism to nominalism, required sev-
> eral centuries, but I shall attempt to suggest an ideal date
> when it occurred. That day in 1382 when Geoffrey Chaucer,
> who perhaps did not believe he was a nominalist, wished to
> translate a line from Boccaccio into English, *E con gli occulti
> ferri i Tradimenti* ("And Treachery with hidden weapons"),
> and he said it like this: "The smyler with the knyf under the
> cloke." [*Other Inquisitions, op. cit.*, 157.]

Exactly inexact once more. Gershom Scholem has penned a similar
sentence, which I admire: "Sabbatai Sevi revealed himself as the
messiah in May, 1665." [*Op. cit.*, 233.] Borges is referring to philosophical realism in this passage, that is, to a belief in the superior
reality of universals. However, Chaucer's language is only a bit less
general than Boccaccio's: the *sort* of smiler who hides a knife under
his cloak. The nominalist would translate the Italian with a single
name: *Sparafucile.* Borges himself is almost never concrete. The sentence recapitulates the opening of the essay: "The universe (which
others call the Library) . . . ," ". . . spherical fruit which bear the name
of lamps." They only bear the name because the light they emit is
Borgesian: *insufficient, incessant.*

Abstract, abstruse, misleadingly exact, citational, and—now—negative: Borges prefers the invisible to the visible, the infinite to the
finite, the invariable to the variable, the inexhaustible to the ex-
haustible, the unending to that which ends, the inconceivable to that
which can be thought, the impenetrable and incomprehensible to
what can be understood, the fathomless to whatever might brag of a
fathom, the unprecedented to anything preceding it, the endless to
something, again, that might conclude. Why? Because conclusions
are decided disappointments. If something is deprived of its end, its
death has also been put off. Where there is vagueness, any puzzle,
there is hope . . . hope for faith.

Try one. Good heavens. Before us are the bustling pages of the
Divina Proportione of Fra Luca Pacioli, and our thought is: Why
doesn't the Library display such traits of divinity as are here depicted? We can admire perspective drawings made, probably by
Leonardo da Vinci, of models Pacioli had constructed to represent
the Platonic solids; models that he then gave away as gifts to his
friends and possible patrons. "His style," Dan Pedoe reports, "is
inimitable" (another of Borges's favorites). Pacioli fulsomely dedi-
cates the book to the Duke of Milan, Ludovico Sforza, before listing,

with some emotion, the properties of the golden ratio (whose absence from the Library has caused our concern):

> —del secondo *essentiale* effectio de questa proportione, del terzo suo *singolare* effecto, del quarto *ineffabile* effecto, del quinto suo *mirable* effecto, del suo sexto *innominabile* effecto, del septimo suo *inextimabile* effecto, del decimo suo *supremo* effecto, del suo undecimo *excellentissimo* effecto, del suo duodecimo *incomprehensible* effecto, del terzo-decimo suo *dignissimo* effecto . . .

Pedoe, who quotes this passage, comments that

> Pacioli then pauses for breath, and remarks that there is not enough ink and paper in existence to give all the properties of the divine ratio, and to stop at thirteen does honour to *the twelve disciples and their holy Head, Jesus Christ.* He then congratulates Sforza again for his piety, and for getting Leonardo da Vinci to paint *The Last Supper* in the Church of Santa Maria delle Grazie. [*Op. cit.*, 264.]

Also missing, to our sorrow, is the pentagon. Despite Bettina Knapp's enthusiasm, little use is made of five in the divine establishment, and it will be futile now to remind its maker of Heinrich Schenker's mystical devotion to the perfect fifth. Music may be the universal language, but the Universe is a library filled with books no one can read, not a lot of show tunes even a Maori can hum.

The order we find in the Library is compatible with chaos. After all, a world ruled by chance will be obedient to the laws of probability. Though words like "rule" and "law" wrongfully suggest there are rules and laws. The order we find in the Library will lead us to hope for more, but the prospect of a Divinity whose intentions are fulfilled by our universe is too terrifying to entertain for long. And in the packed pages of "The Library of Babel" there are references, over and over, not to theories, conjectures, schemes, but to hopes and fears and longings and suspicions. The chemist's periodic table contains the letters that spell the world. But we shall have to do the spelling.

Were the universe a library it would only mimic in meanings the material of which the cosmos is constructed. Our universe would be one of interpretations, human imaginings, many of which we could no longer understand or appreciate. The library is full of contradiction, confusion, hesitation, reluctance, haste, vagueness, fearfulfilling certainties, surds.

337

The Library is the history of the human head. It *is* the human head: biblio, tête.

The theologians of every religion, philosophers of a rationalist persuasion, historians traditionally, and even theoretical physicists whose language is mathematics, have always made the figure, the number, or the word the object of their scrutiny. From subject came substance, from verb came process (though from "is" came copulation), from adjectives and adverbs came predicates, from grammar came logic. Yantras are made from the point, the line, the circle, the triangle, the square, the lotus. From God came the One Book, more sacred than a cow, whose tail, nose, udder, double stomach said more than the moving moon did how real Reality really was, if we could listen well, could read properly, could decipher and understand, could meditate and integrate.

Who would not prefer to investigate the world sitting down.

In his essay "The Cult of the Book," Borges reports: "God Omnipotent created the universe by means of the cardinal numbers that go from one to ten and the twenty-two letters of the alphabet." Letters can be written numerically, and numbers can be written as words. These same symbols are the twenty-two letters of the Library and fill the books with their cipher groups—if they are books, if there are groups, if they are in cipher; yet if they are not books, then the universe cannot be a library; however, have no apprehensions, the number of adepts never seems to advance or decline; the librarians make the library: They wander everywhere, in caves, across deserts, into deep seas, among the masses in city squares, on the seats of johns, at the peak of peaks, poking at the snow, turning over leaves, seeing stars, reading the wheel ruts of wagons.

> Then the book [the *Sepher Yetzirah* of the Kabbalists, sometimes spelled Cabbalists, sometimes Cabalists, with what secret changes these imply] reveals which letter has power over the air, which over water, which over fire, which over wisdom, which over peace, which over grace, which over sleep, which over anger, and how (for example) the letter *kaf*, which has power over life, was used to form the sun in the world, the day Wednesday in the year, and the left ear on the body. [*Other Inquisitions, op. cit.*, 119.]

Elsewhere, in his essay on Léon Bloy titled "The Mirror of the Enigmas," Borges lists the characteristics of the beloved "absolute text," a text dictated by the Holy Spirit.

The portentous premise of a book that is impervious to contingency, a book that is a mechanism of infinite purposes, moved them to permute the scriptural words, to sum up the numerical value of the letters, to consider their form, to observe the small letters and the capital letters, to search for acrostics and anagrams; and it led them to other easily ridiculed exegetic rigors. [*Op. cit.*, 128.]

Scribes, unlike scientists, stay in their studies, surrounded by their books, and look for truth in the word—for causation, too, in the word—which after all is alleged to have started the whole thing. There are a few scriveners who aver that any word would have done as well as the word used. If God had said "fright" first, the light would simply have been turned on in a scary way. If God had said "gloom" a dim glow would have appeared that would have made the wide waste of darkness barely perceivable. In any case, it is a fundamental foolishness in librarians: to study the sign instead of the thing signed—"tree" and not a tree, "verb" and not even a verb like "climb," let alone an action like climbing; and to ponder grammar but not geography, to try to learn a vocabulary while ignoring the objects of its inventory.

Words after all are the matter of the mind. It should not be surprising, then, to find in librarians such a preoccupation with reflexivity, for words watch themselves far oftener than they watch the world. They dwell in their spelling, not in ferny forests or grassy meadows, certainly not in town, among chimney pots. They sing homonyms. They cherish their syntactical relations, not the relation between base and plinth, peel and core, star and shoot. They move in place, below an eye that reports directly to the understanding, consequently they have no concern for process: the ripening of fruit, for instance, or the accumulation of fat, or the running of a race between Achilles and the tortoise.

The mirror, the echo, the double, the insidious comparison of business with business, to mention the most depraved of tautologies, have as their unpalatable consequence the idle multiplication of names: Let us give to the word "railroad" the name "scarfy peak," for instance, whereas for "scarfy peak," "triune" will do, and for "triune," "pitchfork."

In "The Circular Ruins," a man dreams a man only to discover, as he enters a fire as calmly as the phoenix, that the flames do not cleanse his bones of their flesh, that he must have been dreamt himself. The dreamer remained untouched because the flames that swirled around him were real. Had they been as unreal as he, he would have smoked and writhed and screamed.

Fate takes swaddled Oedipus from his kingdom, from the unfriendly mountainside where he was cast, the cold homeland and the lowly rescuers he youngstered with, and from the shepherd's arduous daily labors, in order that he should one day rule in his father's place. And beget, through his own mother, another usurpation's kid—the—as if—spitting image of himself. In Borges too, devious lines are straight, choices are relentlessly determined, coincidences are planned, and those straight lines, given sufficient length, circulate. Saul Steinberg has drawn a hand that, after many lines have been laid, can be seen to be depicting itself. If Paul Valéry's M. Teste draws away from the stage into the shelter of his own head, reflecting upon his reflections, deeply, dismally, and if he does so frequently enough, energetically enough, persistently enough, M. Teste will find himself standing on that selfsame stage being stared at by a multitude of indifferent callous-eyed men—for he will have completed a nebulous circle, quite unforeseen, and to everyone's surprise. We replace regress with the recursive, with amiable circularity—bending the endless—and replace circularity with the reflexive, the metronome, the vibrating string—the petitio with echo, corpuscle with wave.

Scientology, anyone? O for a bit of Mormon in the morning.

Open one. At random. Nothing there. A real library would have books in many papers, types, and sizes. Where are the periodicals? the reference works? There would be catalog numbers on the spines, possibly little pasted pockets for withdrawal cards. This is the Universe, so it has to have molecules clinging to one another like clusters of grapes on crawling vines. "Every novel is an ideal depiction of reality." Like Pierre Menard—believe. Read. "In the sixth chapter of Part One the priest and the barber inspect Don Quixote's library; astonishingly enough, one of the books they examine is the *Galatea* by Cervantes." Good choice. "It is also surprising to learn, at the beginning of Chapter IX, that the whole novel has been translated from the Arabic and that Cervantes acquired the manuscript in the marketplace of Toledo." Good spot to shop. Of whom does this tactic remind us? "Of Carlyle, who feigned that the *Sartor Resartus* was a partial version of a work published in Germany by Dr. Diogenes Teufelsdröckh. We are also reminded of the Spanish Rabbi Moisés de León, who wrote the *Zohar* or *Book of the Splendor* and divulged it as the work of a Palestinian rabbi of the third century." ["Partial Enchantments of the *Quixote.*" *Other Inquisitions, op. cit.,* 44.]

Sanson Carrasco, the Knight of the Mirrors, appears. We are in Part Two of *Don Quixote*. Carrasco confesses that he has perused Part One; he reports on the lamentable critiques of other readers, and then boasts in the presence of the don that he has traveled over the whole of Spain compelling every knight he meets to confess that Carrasco's own lady is more lovely than Quixote's Dulcinea. To suffer these words should be humiliation enough, but soon Don Quixote is hearing his own person invoked and defeated, his beloved abjured; for Carrasco claims to have required a certain Don Quixote to submit to him and to praise Carrasco's lady as all others have. Consequently, the mirror man reasons, the don's powers have so far passed over to him that he can now be considered to bear Quixote's name and reflect his glory.

For comments on the curious thing that is going to happen next, Vladimir Nabokov shall be our guide:

> While Cervantes is inventing enchanters who supposedly have written his book and while Don Quixote within the book is clashing with enchanters stemming from romances of chivalry, Cervantes—the real author—is suddenly confronted by an enchanter on the level of so-called real life.

A spurious Part Two of the Don's adventures was published in Tarragona. Its author claimed to be one Alonso Fernández de Avellaneda, and Nabokov tells his students that the problem of the author's identity remains unsolved.

> What Cervantes says of him in the preface to his own second part and elsewhere in it, and also internal evidence, tends to show that the person was a middle-aged Aragonese . . . a professional writer, with a more intimate knowledge of church matters . . . than Cervantes had . . .

Some scholars have searched for Avellaneda's real name submerged in an anagram or "acrostically hidden in the first lines of the spurious Don Quixote," the way Nabokov hides a mysterious message in the last paragraph of "The Vane Sisters."

> Let me drop the dark hint that a great-grandmother of Cervantes was called Juna Avellaneda, and that some have contended that the fake *Don Quixote* was composed by Cervantes himself for the express purpose of having at hand a new device in the second part that he signed. [*Lectures on Don Quixote*. New York: Harcourt Brace, 1983, 79.]

All this is almost too Borgesian to be borne. Who is next, Flann O'Brien?

In "The Town of Lucca," Heinrich Heine recalls his first, naive, reading of *Don Quixote*. He quite completely missed its irony, and thought the don's humiliations necessary. Later, instead of reading the work as if he were its befuddled hero, he reads it as if he were an enlightened but cynical Panza. Who was it better to be?

Lastly, on the subject of the don—in a *Meditation on Quixote* that dwells upon the knight no longer than the fly rests on the bowl's rim on its way to the sugar—José Ortega y Gasset compares the experience of genius to a religious one:

> When a man is absorbed in the contemplation of his inner self, he feels himself to be floating in the universe without any control over himself or anything else; he feels himself depending absolutely on something—let this something be called whatever we wish. So, the healthy mind may be overcome, in the course of reading or of living, by the sensation of an absolute superiority—that is, it finds a book, a character whose limits transcend on all sides the orbit of our comprehensive powers. The symptom of the highest values is their boundlessness.*

It is an observation that perhaps deserves a star, but the star intends us to peer at the foot of the page where we shall not see my bare feet resting upon a plane of hexagons, but where we shall find an admirably expansive note:

> *A short time ago—one afternoon in the Spring, while walking over the plain of Extremadura, with a broad landscape of olive trees, dramatized by the solemn flight of some eagles, with the blue outline of the Gata Mountains as background— my good friend, Pio Baroja, tried to convince me that we admire only what we do not understand, that admiration is an effect of lack of understanding. He did not succeed, it is unlikely that anyone else will. There is, indeed, incomprehension at the root of the act of admiration, but it is a positive incomprehension: the more we understand of genius, the more there is that remains to be understood. [*The Restlessness of Shanti Andia and Other Writings*. Translated by Anthony Kerrigan. Ann Arbor: University of Michigan Press, 1959, 299–300.]

How easy it is to be led away, here in the Library. We cannot locate Sir Thomas Browne, who is a pentagon man, but Pio Baroja will be on a shelf somewhere. Perhaps a lucky hand falls on his *Memoirs* by mistake, taking the last turn in the road as a joke, and thereupon reads a motto of mine, so simply put: "Is a writer supposed to set down that he has just met John Jones? What for?" Yet what else do most of them do? "The Marquis went out at five" is Paul Valéry's example. The Universe is—as if—consecrated to the futile, the trivial, and to boredom. Nothing there.

But there are paths made by authors and their created persons that take us from book to book as though we were following the thread of Ariadne and counting small knots: from Jorge Luis Borges to Saul Steinberg to Paul Valéry to Monsieur Teste to Pierre Menard to Don Quixote and Cervantes, where we took a rest, then on to Carlyle, Diogenes Teufelsdröckh, the Rabbi Moisés de León, Sanson Carrasco, the lovely Dulcinea, to Vladimir Nabokov, Alonso Fernández de Avellaneda, the Vane sisters, and Grandmother Juna Avellaneda, then to sit a spell before continuing with Heinrich Heine, José Ortega y Gasset, Pio Baroja, Sir Thomas Browne, and that O so delicate poet, Johnny Jones.

The Universe may not be the little Carnegie library around the corner, but one must admit it is *like* a library in a lot of ways. Nevertheless I'd like to suggest that, just as there are two sacred texts, Nature and the Gospels, there are two libraries. One is the great book that scientists attempt to read, so far deciphering a secret that tells no story; and second is the Library of Interpretations, of conjectures, wonderments, surmises, our books of belief, written largely to conceal the first bunch of books from view. We are—as if—of two minds. The purpose of the first is to cover matter with meaning as we might bind the sores of a leper with silk; the purpose of the second is to escape meaning in order to get at matter and find out what leprosy is like.

Life is a dream, a palace of pleasure. The universe is a living animal. The universe is a library. All the world's a stage. In these metaphysical tropes something as large as life, as wide as the world, is compared to a sleeping state of mind, an animal, an art, a building—possibly a building for just one book. Presumably the metaphor's predicate is going to explain the subject, and the subject, for its part, shall pick from the predicate only those aspects of it that seem relevant. The master trope will generate a host of other metaphors: that each man in his time plays many parts; that history is a nightmare; that there is (as Danilo Kiš wrote) an encyclopedia of the dead; that stones have feelings. Conclusions will come forth from them like truths released

343

from prison: The world is an organic whole; there is an author of all things; that there is also a script; that human experience is an illusion. Such metaphors will value or devalue objects, aims, and actions; they will suggest best behaviors, outline ideal communities, parcel out power and privilege, hold out promise, dash hopes.

The predicate infiltrates the subject, casts its dubious light wherever it can, insists on conditions for creation that creation cannot meet, and thus causes other metaphors to appear, troops of new tropes: the defenders of the faith, the word police. The function of these submodels is to reinterpret, but more often simply to supply fresh details that will allow the main metaphor to withstand challenges; make corrections that will cancel contradictions, cover up confusions, calm doubts, assail objections. During this life that is a dream, what are we to make of the snore? The metaphors will enlist all the arts. Composers will hymn the central story; painters will illustrate it; architects will build a body where the myth may dwell, where worshippers may soil their knees. For now, out of the major metaphor like a worm from an infected intestine, will crawl the narrative of the world's nativity, the justification of the trope, the selection of its overseers and directors. For Church, Country, and Commerce do we not live, and live to serve? "Does present-day religion consist in God become money," Heine wonders, "or money become God?" Each has its own dogmas, its own heresies, its own armies, its promises, though they be written in postponements, of Kingdoms to come.

Because all of this ingenuity will go for naught if the trope does not eventually amount to a rescue: The graves shall open, souls shall rise, seventh heaven will be laid out in plats like a development in the skies, the powers that be will be protected from the wannabes, their cozy present place assured them, and sense shall be made of everything, justice shall be done, God's will realized. Its devotees will have chosen to live in a poem. Not in one about a rose, but in a romance of the mind.

> The only form of philosophy acceptable in the face of despair would be an attempt to see and present all things as they would present themselves from the point of view of salvation. Knowledge has no light except that which shines upon the world from salvation. . . . [Theodor Adorno, final section of *Minima Moralia*. 4:281.]

The Book of Nature will suffer any other to overlay it. We must assume it doesn't care, even if we human creatures—one of nature's lapses, if not one of God's egregious errors—claim that all that has been made has been made for us, given to us for pillage and as plaything.

It is time for the Mayor of Bordeaux to make his appearance:

> What has made him [man] believe that the wonderful motions of the celestial vault, the eternal light of those luminaries revolving so proudly above his head, and the terrifying motions of the infinite sea were established and continued for many ages for his pleasure and for his service? Is it possible to imagine any thing so ridiculous as this wretched, paltry creature, who, being not even his own master, exposed to the offences of all things, declares himself master and ruler of the universe of which it is not in his power to understand the smallest fragment, far less to govern it? And this prerogative that he attributes to himself, of being the only creature in this great structure who has the ability to recognize its beauty and its parts, the only one who can render thanks to the architect, and keep account of the income and outlay of the world— who has set the seal of this prerogative upon him? [*The Essays of Michel de Montaigne*. In three volumes. Translated by George Ives. New York: The Heritage Press, 1946. From "Apology for Raimond Sebond," Volume 1, 595–6.]

A man loses to fire, to flood, to famine, to earthquake, war, to the bank, everything he has but his own self, which survives the dearth somehow, the smothering smoke, or his eager creditors; and he sinks to his knees to thank God, the God, no doubt, who brought the great wave and made the earth shake and founded banks to encourage usury, and invented cars and guns and tuna fish in cans, but spared the grateful man some loose change. God is good, the man says, and he is as full of gratitude as his head of hot air.

How easy it is to invent falsehoods and how agreeable to love lies: that some part of us is immortal, for instance. Or that the moon shall forever encircle the Earth.

All messiahs must be false, all prophets rogues, their institutions temples of deceit—yet it matters not; the truth stares our stupidity in the face—yet it matters not; we are at the movies; we are loving our living in illusion much as we love living in Boca Raton; perhaps we haven't got it all figured out (though many think so), but we shall continue to hunt for the secret that we know is hidden behind reason's curtain; we shall find our justification in some book; some book will explain the Holocaust and we shall learn how wholesome it ultimately was: how God made AIDS to cleanse man of some mistakes, and set us the task (out of our love of love, of course) to kill those who believe in other books (for all others are in error), while suffering in return their slings and arrows for the always postponed but eventually greater good. God, our Corporation, our Country, will care for us while we live, and afterward, we shall really have fun (they say); when we are as boneless as a filet, in—as if—retirement; when we are a pure ethereal hum (they say), as if in a bird and bugless sky, yet (lest windborne disasters come) under a protective dome as clear and continuous as the ones back once upon a time in natural life that we employed to cover cheese. Then . . . what? . . . then we shall leave life and never know how wrong we were about it, or suffer any further disappointment.

Is it such a disaster to die and stay dead? unknowing and unbeknownst? Every alternative is worse. Our Universe is what it is. We may misinterpret it but it has no talent for deceit or intention to delude. The lies are all in the books. But no . . . the truth too . . . the truth is there, awaiting our recognition . . . as Alfred Percy Sinnett insisted (and who has been immortal since 1921). At death the soul removes itself to the astral plane where it lives in an envelope of consciousness, impervious to heat or cold, incapable of fatigue, requiring no food. The uninstructed may even doubt they've died, life in their capsule will so resemble their life before. Pleasant enough, the astral plane is merely temporary, for soon (as it shall seem) the soul will rise to the Heaven we've been taught exists, where we shall forever be bored by bliss.

It is hard, emotionally hard, to deny the teachings of the family, to refuse the support of friends, the approval of the wider community, to lose the sense of identity that a firm hold on common tenets gives, so one's reason goes forth, like the don, in a climate of credulity, to defend the teachings that can be found in—say—*Oahspe*, the new Bible, whose definition of "abracadabra" is below, and two of whose discovered and interpreted tablets I have reproduced to head this essay's sections; or in the Koran or the New Testament or the Hindu scriptures, and so on. For the billions kept in worse than bestial ignorance there is some excuse. The rest, in their heart of heads, must *know*.

But perhaps not. Dr. John B. Newbrough, with degrees in both medicine and dentistry, and gifted with extrasensory perception, having spent the years between 1871 and 1881 in spiritual purification, purchased, as certain Higher Powers instructed, a brand-new instrument called a typewriter. Perhaps Sam Clemens sold it to him. The doctor discovered that if he sat down to the machine an hour before dawn his hands would begin to type of their own accord (without previous lessons, we have to suppose). Dr. Newbrough had discovered automatic typing. Since this new Bible is full of diagrams and tables, he must have practiced automatic drawing as well as reeling and writhing. He was further instructed by the selfsame Higher Powers not to read a word of what he was writing until the whole of it was completed, which took an entire year. Although *Oahspe* is insufficiently sectarian, and far too generous to its competition to catch the fanatic's fancy, it has nevertheless seen nine American editions from 1882 to 1945, and gone through four English ones from 1910 to '29.

One of its revelations is that God, who ordered *Oahspe's* production, is not the Creator but simply the Earth's chief executive officer, a position similar to that of our American president. One of this religious fiction's most impressive accomplishments is the invention of innumerable unlikely names for countless spheres, countless times, and countless angels. I now list a few found on a single periodic timetable: Gowk, Uklow, Bhiathon, Mentabraw, Wankawank, Wuts, Horatanad, Galeb, Ctaran, Hoesonya, Lunitzzi, Cpenta-armij, Fragapatti. Mouthfuls. Finger food. [*Oahspe*, a New Bible in THE WORDS OF JEHOVAH and his Angel Ambassadors. Los Angles, Sydney, London: Kosmon Press, 1942.]

The song the siren sang has the lyrics of salvation. It tells us that one day we shall be free of life's persistent pain; that rewards will be ours, we shall receive our due; above all that our enemies, the wicked, shall be eternally tortured and denied the pleasures of glory, surviving, as Dante tells us, head over heels in swill and shit, racked and ravaged. Tying ourselves to the mast may be insufficient. Our ears will burn on hearing such a tune and steer our heads toward the singer's reef. Even Heine recanted during his dying days:

> Strange! After spending my whole life whirling about on all the dance-floors of philosophy, abandoning myself to all the orgies of the mind, whoring with all possible philosophical systems and remaining unsatisfied, like Messalina after a night of debauchery—now I find myself adopting the same standpoint as Uncle Tom, that of the Bible, and I kneel down beside my black brother with the same devotion. [Quoted by Ritchie Robertson in *Heine*. New York: Grove Press, 1988, 93.]

William H. Gass

The universe is not a library. On the evidence, the universe must be a madhouse.

Lying on a mattress, in misery, Heine says that Christianity is a perfect religion for the sick. "Where health ends, where money ends, where the human intellect ends, Christianity begins."[*Op. cit.*, 94.]

On sunny days I am inclined to believe him. But disbelief on dismal ones has more allure.

173355 TURIN SHROUD. By L. Picknett & C. Prince. The shocking story behind one of Christianity's holiest relics, reveals that the creator of the shroud and the man whose image appears on it was actually Leonardo da Vinci, and relates the connection of the shroud to a conspiracy by a secret society. Photos. 212 pages. HarperCollins. Pub. at $23.00. **$5.95**

612642 SAINTS: Who They Are and How They Help You. Ed. by Elizabeth Hallam. Groups more than 150 saints by their patronages and specialties, from the patron saint of lawyers to that of stammering children, provides a directory of shrines and pilgrimage sites and a calendar of feast days. 170 illus., most color. 184 pages. S&S. Pub. at $22.00. **$4.95**

OAHSPE

[Dr. John B. Newbrough] was impressed with the thought that he should become pure himself if he would attract the attention of the type of spirit intelligence he sought to commune with. The years between 1871 and 1881 were spent in spiritual purification during which time he became aware of spiritual guidance. Instructed to purchase a typewriter, which had just been invented, he did so. Upon sitting at the instrument an hour before dawn he discovered that his hands typed without his conscious control. In fact he was not aware of what his hands typed unless he read what was being printed. He was told that he was to write a book—but must not read what he was writing until it was completed. At the end of a year when the manuscript was completed he was instructed to read and publish the book titled OAHSPE, a New Bible. [Preface to the Present Edition iv.]

I own a copy of the Ninth American Edition of 1945. While we read, we are admonished not to skip around. O AH SPE was first published in 1882. "The object of OAHSPE is not to supplant the former Bibles, nor Vedas nor other sacred books. . . . It is rather a Bible comprising the causes of all other Bibles, with revelations of the heavens also."

the spirit of the spring   the elves of the glen   the gnomes of the dark
the fairies of the forest   angels of mercy   gods of the mountain
banshees   ghosts   goblins   poltergeists   devils   pixies   imps
palmistry   numerology   astrology   phrenology   physiognomy
witches

At the beginning of this essay I said that most thoughts were wrongheaded. That declaration wasn't true, of course. Many of our ideas are practical, quickly put to the test, and discarded when they don't pay off. We can enjoy kicking them out of the house because we have no more attachment to them than success. Other quaintly attractive notions (for instance, that arroyos, silent and dry, are nonetheless alive) may have seemed eminently reasonable at the time they were made, when on occasion these same peaceful beds bellowed with a rage made from a heavy rain's onset, sudden noise, and peril. However, the more ambitious supposition (that *all* the world's things are alive, for example) is less easily dismissed, because the extent of its rule is so imposing and suited to every surmise, including the river's deceit and dangerous embroiling. Consequently, when our simplest ways of life are satisfactorily explained, and the soul of the arroyo is soothed, we hug the hypothesis to our heart, in love with its fit. Actually, by this time our belief is probably a resolute practice of the tribe, a tenet of the church, an edict of the state, or some cult's customized folly. And we stick to whatever practices these institutions serve like wet crumbs to the cloth. They are not easily brushed off.

NOTES ON CONTRIBUTORS

RAE ARMANTROUT's book *Versed*, published by Wesleyan, won the 2010 Pulitzer Prize in poetry. A new book entitled *Just Saying* is forthcoming from Wesleyan in early 2013.

MATT BELL is the author of the novella *Cataclysm Baby* (Mud Luscious) and the fiction collection *How They Were Found* (Keyhole). His debut novel *In the House upon the Dirt between the Lake and the Woods* is forthcoming from Soho Press. He is the senior editor at Dzanc Books.

JEDEDIAH BERRY is the author of the novel *The Manual of Detection* (Penguin Press). The stories appearing here are from a series titled "The Watchers."

MEI-MEI BERSSENBRUGGE's most recent books are *I Love Artists, New and Selected Poems* (University of California Press), and *A Lit Cloud*, in collaboration with Kiki Smith (Galerie Lelong). *Hello, the Roses* is forthcoming from New Directions.

MICHAEL REID BUSK's work appears or is forthcoming in *Gettysburg Review, Michigan Quarterly Review, Fiction International, Florida Review*, and other journals.

ARNALDO CALVEYRA is an Argentine poet, novelist, and playwright, living in Paris. In 1999, Calveyra was made a Commander of the French Order of Arts and Letters. His works include *Cartas para que la alegría, Iguana iguana, Diario del fumigador de guardia, El hombre del Luxemburgo, El libro del espejo, Maizal del gregoriano, Diario de Eleusis, Cuaderno griego, La cama de Aurelia, El origen de la luz*, and the book-length essay *La novela nacional*.

ROBERT COOVER is the author of three story collections, including *Pricksongs and Descants*; and ten novels, among them *The Origin of the Brunists, The Public Burning*, and *The Adventures of Lucky Pierre* (all Grove Press). His most recent books are *Noir* (Overlook) and *A Child Again* (McSweeney's).

JOHN CROWLEY is a three-time winner of the World Fantasy Award and the author of eleven novels, including *Little, Big* (Harper Perennial) and the *Ægypt* cycle (Overlook).

LYDIA DAVIS's recent books are *The Collected Stories of Lydia Davis* (Farrar, Straus and Giroux), a new translation of Flaubert's *Madame Bovary* (Viking Penguin), and a chapbook entitled *The Cows* (Sarabande).

NGOC DOAN's poems appear or are forthcoming in *Web Conjuctions, Everyday Genius, Sink Review, Death and Life of American Cities*, and elsewhere.

BRIAN EVENSON is the author of twelve books of fiction, most recently *Windeye* (Coffee House Press) and *Immobility* (Tor).

THALIA FIELD's books include *A Prank of Georges* (with Abigail Lang, Essay Press); *Bird Lovers, Backyard*; *Incarnate: Story Material*; *Point and Line* (all New Directions); and *ULULU (Clown Shrapnel)* (Coffee House Press). The collaboration with Abigail Lang that appears in this issue is an excerpt from a work in progress.

WILLIAM GADDIS (1922–1998) is one of America's most highly regarded writers, described by *The New York Times Book Review* as "a presiding genius . . . of postwar American fiction." He is the author of the novels *The Recognitions, J R* (both Dalkey Archive Press), *Carpenter's Gothic* (Penguin), *A Frolic of His Own* (Scribner), and the posthumously published *Agapē Agape* (Penguin), as well as the 2002 essay collection *The Rush for Second Place* (Penguin). Both *J R* and *A Frolic of His Own* won the National Book Award; the latter was also a finalist for the National Book Critics Circle Award. Gaddis received a MacArthur Award in 1982, and his work has been the subject of numerous critical studies.

WILLIAM H. GASS is the author, most recently, of *Life Sentences* (Knopf), a collection of essays. His novel *Middle C.* will be published by Knopf in April 2013.

PETER GIZZI's recent books include *Threshold Songs* and *The Outernationale* (both Wesleyan).

World Fantasy Award winner THEODORA GOSS's publications include *In the Forest of Forgetting* (Prime Books); *Interfictions* (Small Beer Press), co-edited with Delia Sherman; *Voices from Fairyland* (Aqueduct Press); and *The Thorn and the Blossom* (Quirk Books).

EVELYN HAMPTON (Lispservice.com) is the author of *We Were Eternal and Gigantic* (Magic Helicopter Press).

SHELLEY JACKSON is the author of *The Melancholy of Anatomy* (Anchor), *Half Life* (Harper Perennial), hypertexts including *Patchwork Girl* (Eastgate Systems), children's books including *Mimi's Dada Catifesto* (Clarion Books), and "SKIN," a story published in tattoos on 2,095 volunteers. All vocabulary used in "The Pearls That Were His Eyes" was taken from the front page and its verso of the May 13, 2010, *New York Times*.

Recent publications by ROBERT KELLY include the novel *The Book from the Sky* (North Atlantic/Random), the story collection *The Logic of the World* (McPherson), and the long poems *Fire Exit* (Black Widow) and *Uncertainties* (Station Hill).

ALEXANDRA KLEEMAN's fiction has appeared previously in *Conjunctions*, as well as in *Zoetrope: All-Story*, *DIAGRAM*, and *The Paris Review*.

ABIGAIL LANG is the author, with Thalia Field, of *A Prank of Georges* (Essay Press). She translates American poetry into French, teaches at Université Paris-Diderot, and is a member of the Double Change collective.

351

JONATHAN LETHEM is the author of eight novels, among them *Motherless Brooklyn* and *Chronic City* (both Doubleday). He lives in Maine and Los Angeles.

NATHANIEL MACKEY's *From a Broken Bottle Traces of Perfume Still Emanate, Volumes 1–3*, and Volume 4, *Bass Cathedral*, are available from New Directions, as is his National Book Award–winning poetry collection, *Splay House*. His most recent book is *Nod House* (also New Directions).

TED MATHYS is the author of two books of poetry, *The Spoils* and *Forge* (both Coffee House Press).

EDIE MEIDAV (www.ediemeidav.com) is the author of *Lola, California* (FSG/Picador), *Crawl Space* (FSG), and *The Far Field: A Novel of Ceylon* (Houghton Mifflin Harcourt). A companion nonfiction piece about living in Cuba appears in the Fall 2012 issue of *Zyzzyva*.

CHINA MIÉVILLE is the award-winning author of several novels, including *Perdido Street Station* and *The City and the City*; one story collection; and various works of nonfiction. His latest novel, for readers of all ages, is *Railsea* (all Del Rey).

JAMES MORROW is the author of nine novels, including *The Last Witchfinder*, *The Philosopher's Apprentice* (both Morrow), and the Godhead Trilogy (Harcourt). He has received the World Fantasy Award, the Nebula Award, the Grand Prix de l'Imaginaire, and the Prix Utopia. His recent novella, *Shambling Towards Hiroshima* (Tachyon), won the Theodore Sturgeon Memorial Award.

LANCE OLSEN is the author of more than twenty works of and about innovative fiction, including, most recently, the anti-textbook *Architectures of Possibility* (Raw Dog Screaming) and the novel *Calendar of Regrets* (FC2).

AURELIE SHEEHAN is the author of a story collection, *Jack Kerouac Is Pregnant* (Dalkey Archive Press), and two novels, *History Lesson for Girls* (Viking) and *The Anxiety of Everyday Objects* (Penguin).

PETER STRAUB is the author of seventeen novels, most recently *A Dark Matter* (Doubleday), as well as two collections of shorter fiction. His work has won many Stoker and World Fantasy Awards.

COLE SWENSEN is the author of fourteen books of poetry, most recently *Gravesend* (University of California Press) and *Stele* (Post-Apollo Press). She is also a translator and the founding editor of La Presse Books.

ARTHUR SZE's latest book of poetry is *The Ginkgo Light* (Copper Canyon Press). He also edited *Chinese Writers on Writing* (Trinity University Press).

SARAH TOURJEE's fiction has appeared in *PANK*, *The Collagist*, *Anomalous Press*, *Lady Churchill's Rosebud Wristlet*, and elsewhere, and is forthcoming in *The &NOW Awards: Best Innovative Writing II* (&NOW Books).

KEITH WALDROP's recent poetry books are *Transcendental Studies* (University of California Press), winner of the 2009 National Book Award; *The Real Subject* (Omnidawn); and a trilogy: *The Locality Principle, The Silhouette of the Bridge,* and *Semiramis If I Remember* (Avec Books).

ROSMARIE WALDROP's recent books are *Driven to Abstraction, Curves to the Apple, Blindsight* (all New Directions), and *Love, Like Pronouns* (Omnidawn).

ELIZABETH ZUBA is a poet, translator, and the co-editor of *La familia americana* (Antonio Machado Libros). She is currently translating and editing Belgian artist Marcel Broodthaers's first four books of poetry.

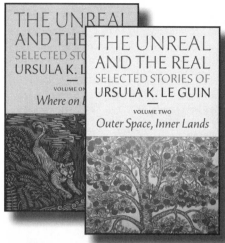

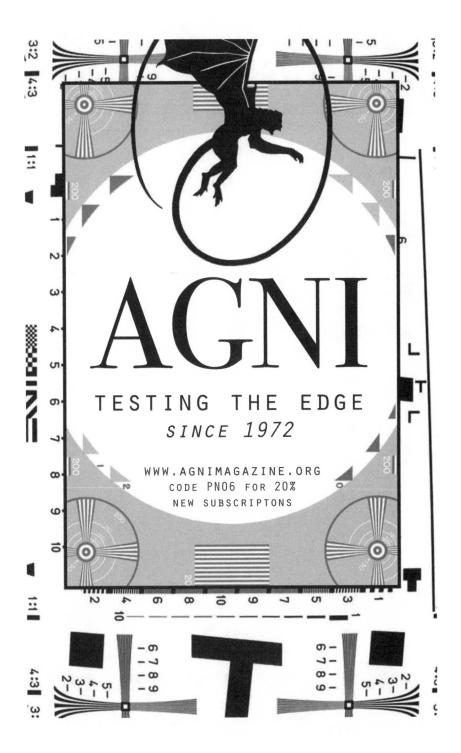

BROWN UNIVERSITY LITERARY ARTS

Program faculty

John Cayley
Brian Evenson
Thalia Field
Forrest Gander
Renee Gladman
Michael S. Harper
Carole Maso
Meredith Steinbach
Cole Swensen
CD Wright

Joint-appointment, visiting & other faculty

Joanna Howard
Ian McDonald
Shahriar Mandanipour
Gale Nelson
John Edgar Wideman

For over 40 years, Literary Arts at Brown University has been a home for innovative writing. To learn about the two-year MFA program and the undergraduate concentration or to have access to Writers Online, an archive of literary recordings, visit http://www.brown.edu/cw

THE ONLINE MFA APPLICATION DEADLINE IS 15 DECEMBER

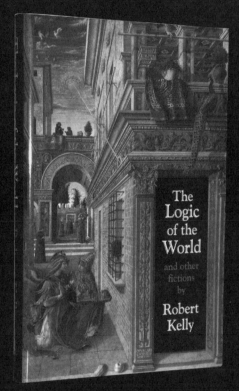

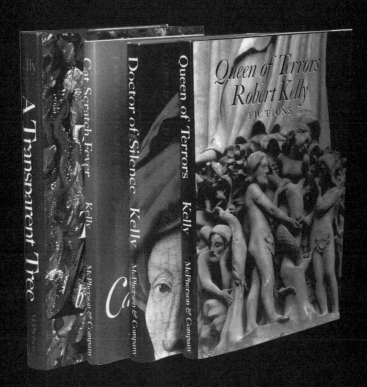

P. Inman: *per se*

P. Inman fractures the conventions of language in order to build everything up again from a more elemental level. In *per se*, the composers Luigi Nono, Hans Lachenmann, and Morton Feldman provide musical structure for his jazz-inflected words in motion. The book lives in the tension between the free, multidirectional movement of words and the highly orgazined macro-structures. "In Inman's work 'the dialectic of sound and silence has moved several logical steps beyond Beckett.'"
—Joan Retallack, "Post-scriptum-high-modern"
Poetry, 88 pages, offset, smyth-sewn, original paperback $14

Elfriede Czurda:
Almost 1 Book/ Almost 1 Life

[translated from the German by Rosmarie Waldrop]
This volume contains almost all of Elfriede Czurda's first book and all of her second, *Fast 1 Leben*.
Czurda comes out of the experimental *Wiener Gruppe*, but is not averse to thumbing her nose at the experimental imperative. In *Almost 1 Life* (novella? politco-cultural satire?), the ruling avantgarde has licenced "monomania" as official language and punishes misuse by expelling the offender: into reality. Which is where Czurda positions herself. She explores language, but also the social power structures embedded in it — all with lots of fun and humor.
Poetry, 96 pages, offset, smyth-sewn, orig. paperback $14

Sébastien Smirou: *My Lorenzo*

[translated from the French by Andrew Zawacki]
An elegant, funny, often sad meditation on the 15th-century Italian statesman, art patron, and poet Lorenzo de Medici. Obliquely narrated, it telescopes historic depth into intimacy.
Poetry, 96 pages, offset. smyth-sewn, original pbk. $14

 This work, published as part of a program providing publication assistance, received financial support from the French Ministry of Foreign Affairs, the Cultural Services of the French Embassy in the United States and FACE (French American Cultural Exchange).

Sarah Riggs:
Autobiography of Envelopes

"In these brief, crisp and thought-provoking stanzas, Riggs investigates notions of address and possibilities of correspondences.... They are finely tuned time pieces with poetry's insistent concerns of number, counting, what counts and what it may mean to count.... Here, instant after instant, at once stunning and muted, mutably, 'The poem addresses itself. We open, listen, magnify.'"—Stacy Doris
Poetry, 160 pages, offset, smyth-sewn, original pbk. $14

Orders: www.spdbooks.org, www.burningdeck.com

OCTOBER 2012
SOPHIE CALLE: THE ADDRESS BOOK

NOVEMBER 2012
JESS: O! TRICKY CAD & OTHER JESSOTERICA

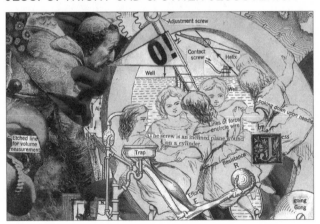

siglio

www.sigliopress.com

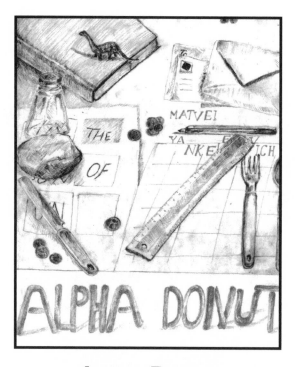

ALPHA DONUT
MATVEI YANKELEVICH
100 pages, paperback   ISBN 0-935992-29-8
$16.00   Cover art by Nora Griffin

Reading Yankelevich's poems, we get to know where and how he lives, and how the library of all the poetry that truly matters in this world...affects those facts of existence.   Anselm Hollo

ALPHA DONUT makes me happy to be alive. Every poem is a surprise--the kind of poignancy that hits close to home, and the kind of sarcasm that heals.
Kristin Prevallet

united artists books

These and other UAB titles available from
Small Press Distribution
spdbooks.org

UNITEDARTISTSBOOKS.COM

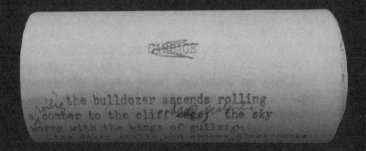

NOON

A LITERARY ANNUAL

1324 LEXINGTON AVENUE   PMB 298   NEW YORK NY 10128

EDITION PRICE $12 DOMESTIC $17 FOREIGN

THE NEW SCHOOL

Discover the Writer's Life in New York City

CREATIVE WRITING AT THE NEW SCHOOL

Master of Fine Arts in Creative Writing

Concentrations in fiction, poetry, nonfiction, and writing for children.
Fellowships and financial aid available.

2012–2013
Director: Robert Polito
Associate Director: Jackson Taylor

FACULTY
Jeffery Renard Allen, Jonathan Ames, Robert Antoni, Susan Bell, Mark Bibbins, Susan Cheever, Jonathan Dee, Elaine Equi, David Gates, Jennifer Michael Hecht, Ann Hood, Shelley Jackson, Zia Jaffrey, Hettie Jones, James Lasdun, David Lehman, Suzannah Lessard, David Levithan, Phillip Lopate, Patrick McGrath, Honor Moore, Sigrid Nunez, Meghan O'Rourke, Dale Peck, Darryl Pinckney, Helen Schulman, Tor Seidler, Laurie Sheck, Darcey Steinke, Benjamin Taylor, Sarah Weeks, Brenda Wineapple, Stephen Wright

VISITING FACULTY
Max Blagg, Deborah Brodie, Patricia Carlin, Marilyn Goldin, Vivian Gornick, Fannie Howe, Gary Indiana, Dave Johnson, Joyce Johnson, Mary Lee Kortez, Wendy Lesser, Sharon Mesmer, Marie Ponsot, David Prete, Lloyd Schwartz, Susan Shapiro, Frederic Tuten, Susan Van Metre, Victoria Wilson

Both in the classroom and through our public programs and readings, we seek to animate and intensify the writer's life. Learn more today.

www.newschool.edu/writing16
THE NEW SCHOOL FOR PUBLIC ENGAGEMENT

Bard MFA offers a non-traditional approach to the creative arts. Intensive eight-week summer sessions emphasize individual conferencing with faculty and school-wide interdisciplinary group conversation and critique. Forms such as innovative poetry, short fiction, sound, and mixed-media writing are particularly well-suited to the structure and nature of the Writing program.

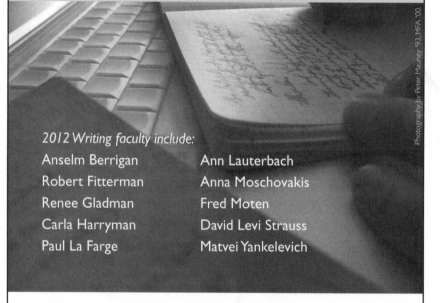

2012 Writing faculty include:

Anselm Berrigan

Robert Fitterman

Renee Gladman

Carla Harryman

Paul La Farge

Ann Lauterbach

Anna Moschovakis

Fred Moten

David Levi Strauss

Matvei Yankelevich

mfa@bard.edu

845.758.7481

bard.edu/mfa

Bard**MFA**

MILTON AVERY GRADUATE SCHOOL OF THE ARTS